T0302161

# Service Leadership

*Service Leadership* offers students, researchers, and leaders a leadership model originating in the service economy – but which is gaining ground in all sectors and industries – explained by experts that were key actors in that origination at DHL International.

Designed for undergraduates and graduates but also useful for professionals in leadership positions, Hoshmand and Chung structure the book around the 3Cs of leadership in the service economy: Competence, Character, and Care. It shows how the integration of the 3Cs when applied in combination with each other creates an environment of trust within and outside the organization. Most importantly, it allows the reader to understand how a move from the manufacturing mindset (hierarchical decision making) to a service mindset (collective, qualitative, culturally sensitive) creates an ethical habitat and ecosystem that contributes to a firm's competitiveness and adds value to its brand image.

Incorporating elements of leadership literature, philosophy, psychology, sociology, economics, and political science, including cases, and supported by a teaching manual and a full set of slides, this book is ideal core reading for students of service leadership and leadership in the service economy, and valuable to those learning about leadership more broadly.

**A. Reza Hoshmand**, PhD, is Senior Special Advisor for the Global Institute of Service Leadership. He has taught at various public and private universities including Harvard.

**Po Chung** is Chairman of the Global Institute of Service Leadership. He was the chairman and co-founder of DHL International.

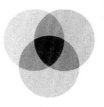

# Service Leadership

Leading with Competence, Character and
Care in the Service Economy

# A. REZA HOSHMAND and
PO CHUNG

Routledge
Taylor & Francis Group

LONDON AND NEW YORK

First published 2022
by Routledge
2 Park Square, Milton Park, Abingdon, Oxon OX14 4RN

and by Routledge
605 Third Avenue, New York, NY 10158

*Routledge is an imprint of the Taylor & Francis Group, an informa business*

*British Library Cataloguing-in-Publication Data*
A catalogue record for this book is available from the British Library

*Library of Congress Cataloging-in-Publication Data*
Names: Hoshmand, A. Reza, author. | Chung, Po, author.
Title: Service leadership : leading with competence, character and care in the service economy / A. Reza Hoshmand and Po Chung.
Description: 1 Edition. | New York : Routledge, 2022. | Includes bibliographical references and index.
Identifiers: LCCN 2021004413 (print) | LCCN 2021004414 (ebook) | ISBN 9781032009629 (hardback) | ISBN 9781032009575 (paperback) | ISBN 9781003176565 (ebook)
Subjects: LCSH: Service industries—Management. | Leadership—Social aspects. | Organizational effectiveness.
Classification: LCC HD9980.5 .H667 2021 (print) | LCC HD9980.5 (ebook) | DDC 658.4/092—dc23
LC record available at https://lccn.loc.gov/2021004413
LC ebook record available at https://lccn.loc.gov/2021004414

ISBN: 978-1-032-00962-9 (hbk)
ISBN: 978-1-032-00957-5 (pbk)
ISBN: 978-1-003-17656-5 (ebk)

Typeset in Minion
by Apex CoVantage, LLC

Access the Support Material: www.routledge.com/9781032009575

This book is dedicated to our families.

# Contents

# About the authors

**A. Reza Hoshmand**, PhD, is Special Senior Advisor to the Global Institute of Service Leadership Education. He served as the founding director of General Education at Baptist University of Hong Kong from 2011 to 2019. He has taught at public and private universities including Harvard. As a Fulbright Scholar in 2008 at the City University of Hong Kong, his research involved foreign direct investment in China. He also completed a book titled *Business Forecasting* that was published by Routledge.

**Po Chung** is a co-founder of DHL International and Chairman of the Global Institute of Service Leadership Education. He obtained a degree in fisheries management from California State University at Humboldt and later attended an Executive Program at Stanford University. He also served on the Board of Trustees of the Hoover Institution at Stanford. He has been awarded an honorary doctorate from the Royal Melbourne Institute of Technology and has written numerous publications on entrepreneurship and service leadership.

# Acknowledgments

'When a good idea comes, you can never stop it.'

First, I would like to thank Professor A. Reza Hoshmand, the coauthor of this textbook. Reza and I are good friends. We always meet to discuss various matters, and leadership for the 21st century is the topic dearest to our hearts. When I told Reza of my intention to write a textbook on service leadership, he was very supportive of the idea. So, my heartfelt thanks to Reza for his encouragement and, of course, for his close involvement and dedicated efforts in all aspects of the book's publication and for making it real.

I am also thankful to Ran Elfassy who has helped in writing and editing all my book publications. My special thanks to my assistant, Fanny Sze, for her enthusiastic support.

I feel particularly grateful to Remar Sutton, my dear old friend who has given me many insightful ideas and invaluable suggestions, and also to his FoolProof team for helping me convert my Service Leadership Excellence materials into an online teaching course.

I also extend my gratitude to my Service Leadership Education team consisting of Peter Chan, Dexter Cheng, Saimond Ip, and Francis Lo for their generous advice and inspirations throughout my Service Leadership Education journey.

My heartfelt thanks to Professor Daniel Shek for his huge support and contribution to the success of Service Leadership Education.

Lastly, I am also indebted to the DHL Family. Special thanks to Ken Allen, Roger Bowie, and Andy Tseng.

Finally, this book is dedicated to my dearest wife, Helen, and my three lovely daughters, Yana, Anca, and Yangie, for their endless good cheer.

Po Chung

# Figures

# Tables

# Preface

This book is intended as an undergraduate and graduate text but can also be used by other professionals in leadership positions. The book's aim is to introduce the concept of 3Cs of leadership (competence, character, and care) in the service economy. It shows how the integration of the 3Cs when applied in combination with each other creates an environment of trust within and outside the organization. Most importantly, it allows the reader to understand how a move from the manufacturing mindset (hierarchical decision making) to a service mindset (collective, qualitative, culturally sensitive, and transformative leadership) creates an ethical habitat and ecosystem that contributes to a firm's competitiveness and adds value to its brand image. This book is an interdisciplinary text that combines theoretical elements from leadership literature, philosophy, psychology, sociology, economics, and political science into a framework that is more relevant to the 21st century service economy. Case studies along with 'key points to remember' at the end of each chapter give the reader a firm grasp of ideas discussed.

Chapter 1 introduces the concept of service leadership by describing the components of the 3Cs of service leadership and how this conceptualization is related to the changing economic environment around the world. Service leadership goes beyond what is stated in the leadership literature. It emphasizes that to be a service leader, one must improve one's competencies, abilities, and willingness to help satisfy the needs of self and others ethically. Furthermore, the reader will understand how Maslow's self-actualization fits in the framework of service leadership.

Chapter 2 discusses the realities of the 21st century and sets the stage for the need for service leadership. Economic data on services around the world all suggest a dramatic shift from manufacturing to a service economy. This chapter provides a perspective on economic development and on how service leadership contributes to economic growth. Today's world is characterized by virtual communication, capital and labor movement, and dispersion of information at a pace that has not been seen before. The dramatic shifts in technological development have had a significant impact on all aspects of humanity, be it in economics, politics, social issues, environment, or any other area. In this context, the concept of service leadership as a tool to effectively deal with these changes has become a necessity.

Chapter 3 provides a view of leadership models of the past and juxtaposes them with the realities of the service era. Since the work environment has changed tremendously from the decades before, it demands leadership tools to cope with organizational structure, cultural, and gender diversity along with the nature of work. Today's organizations have recognized the benefits of restructuring the work environment to increase productivity and creating environments for collaboration, cost management, innovations and sharing, and better employee experience. Service leadership suggests mechanisms to appropriately engage all members of an organization in dealing with the changes.

Chapter 4 highlights the method of service leadership. Specifically, it deals with the dynamics of why, who, and what of service leadership. The previous chapters discuss different models of leadership and their application in organizations that mostly emphasize products rather than service. This is not to say that those principles do not apply to the service sector; they do, but in a limited sense. Since the manufacturing mindset is rigid in nature and requires a commitment from the followers to adhere to a set of rules for the sake of consistency and efficiency, it is not consistent with the dynamic nature of service. Hence, a shift in paradigm is needed to move away from a command and control toward a more humanistic approach of service mindset.

Chapter 5 discusses the role of service leadership in the economic growth and sustainability of the firm. Several factors are critical in achieving this. Specifically, the chapter discusses the role of return on investment (ROI), building trust within and the outside community, as well as the decision-making processes in the organization.

Joyful leadership is discussed in Chapter 6. Today's leaders have to contend with changes such as economic uncertainty in the marketplace, increasing internationalization of the workforce, demographic shifts, and a growing disparity of income between the rich and poor. In the face of such challenges, the call for leadership has never been greater. Yet the very concept of leadership is contested – with different scholars or practitioners placing greater or lesser emphasis on the person, the position, the process, or the outcome. This gives rise to the question of what kind of leadership is needed today. As stated, the world of work can be rigid, demanding, stressful, and tiring, or it can be a happier experience with a joyful disposition. How one turns all of those negative elements of work into a positive experience is at the core of this chapter.

Chapter 7 deals with the ethical dilemmas that service leaders face in delivering their service. Dealing with such situations requires an ethical judgment. Such judgment calls for the application of ethical principles. What are these ethical principles and how do they affect the service industry? Ethical principles from the Western and Eastern perspective are highlighted to show the basic premises of these philosophies of life. Humans have the capacity for being virtuous, moral, and just. How philosophers, through time, view the notion of virtue and morality depends on the school of thought. The chapter highlights recent ethical dilemmas and the consequences of unethical decisions in the service sector that have caused major financial losses and lack of trust in these organizations.

As services have become the major economic activity around the world, it has become the crucible for the development of new ideas (innovations) for entrepreneurs. Chapter 8 highlights the approach taken in service leadership by offering a holistic view of the role that leadership plays in what is called the entrepreneurial cycle. The ways and means of entrepreneurial cycle in the service sector are discussed in this chapter. The basic premise of the entrepreneurial cycle is to identify the needs of the customer, deconstruct the process of meeting the needs, and recognize the elements that will contribute to the entrepreneurial endeavor. Furthermore, the entrepreneur has to articulate the idea, design a solution, create a prototype, implement or operate the idea, and finally upgrade the process to make sure the needs of the customer are met.

Chapter 9 offers a view on organic versus mechanistic leadership. The manufacturing era brought with it strategies in leadership that aimed at the notion of efficiency over other factors that contribute to the success of a firm. Now that the service era is here, it is important to understand the relevance of organic leadership in the 21st century and to look at other leadership strategies such as service leadership, being organic in nature, to respond to the needs of customers. Organic leadership is defined as a series of dynamic, open, complex relational and dialogic processes focused on facilitating the emergence of high-performance environments that organize human experience around social change agendas.

Chapter 10 discusses the role of service leadership in microenterprises. Microenterprises serve as the economic backbone of many countries around the world. Small and medium enterprises (SMEs) account for the majority of businesses worldwide and are important contributors to global economic development. They represent about 90% of businesses and more than 50% of employment worldwide. Formal SMEs contribute up to 40% of national income (GDP) in emerging economies. The growth and vibrancy of these firms are also important for broader economic growth and diversification of economic base and are a source of innovation that is exhibited by some of the start-ups. The tools of service leadership, namely, competence, character, and care play a critical role in the survival of these businesses.

The concluding chapter deals with the role of service leadership in times of crisis. The nature of the crisis may be organizational, political, or economic. They could also be national, regional, or international in nature. One of the critical aspects of service leadership is how leaders and followers work together to attend to the needs of those who are affected by the changes in their communities, organizations, or nation. Those leaders who have high *competence*, *character*, and *care* – the *3Cs* – are able to engage everyone in their service ecosystem to respond and deliver service in an effective and a caring manner. The framework to be used in times of crisis has its roots in the work of other scholars that is relevant to service leadership. Such framework has the following dimensions: Early recognition of a crisis, making sense of a crisis, making decisions, communicating, implementing, being accountable, learning from a crisis, and enhancing resilience.

A. Reza Hoshmand
Po Chung
Hong Kong, SAR

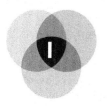

# Introduction to service leadership

## 1.1 What is service leadership?

The concept of service leadership is an outgrowth of the changing economic environment around the world. It is important to note that service leadership is more than leadership offered in services. It refers to a changing mindset that redefines leadership in the context of change from manufacturing to services. There are several definitions of service leadership that others have offered that should be highlighted before any expansion on the definition that is at the core of this text. Gronfeldt and Strother (2006) defined service leadership as the 'culture that empowers the organization to strategize its promises, design its processes, and engage its people in a proactive quest for competitive advantage' (p. 5). Others such as Edvinsson (1992) defined service leadership as a 'collective leadership mindset' (p. 34) that includes thought leaders, process leaders, and commercial leaders. Individuals who acquire these skills meet the basic requirements for service leadership as envisioned by us. The conceptualization of service leadership goes beyond what is stated earlier. To be a service leader, one must improve one's competencies, abilities, and willingness to help satisfy the needs of self and others ethically. This implies both an active and proactive attitude to meet the needs of a modern society. Hence, service leadership's unique characteristic is to provide service with *competence*, *character*, and *care* to everyone that the server encounters.

The model of service leadership has several attributes that must be considered for its effective application. The basic framework as stated by Chung (2012) is that service leadership is based on *competence*, *character*, and *care* (*3Cs*). In the following section, the elements that contribute to each of the *3Cs* will be discussed.

### 1.1.1 *Competence*

When discussing competence in leadership, the interest is not only in the ability of a leader to inspire competitive advantage, but also to be aware of one's and others' emotions to overcome adversity and transcend materialistic pursuits (Shek & Lin, 2015). What this means is that an effective service leader has internalized cognitive and emotional competence, resilience, and spirituality. Literature points out that effective leaders are differentiated from other leaders through the exercise of a limited range of skills or competence areas (Higgs & Roland, 2001; Hogan & Hogan, 2001; Goffee & Jones, 2000). These competencies include interpersonal and intrapersonal leadership, moral character, caring disposition, self-improvement in leadership, and self-reflection.

Psychologists have extensively elaborated on the role of cognitive competence and how it affects leadership (Mumford, Todd, Higgs, & McIntosh, 2017; Marcy, 2015; Marcy & Mumford, 2010). There are many factors that influence decision making; however, it would be important to highlight those elements of cognition that researchers have found to contribute more effectively to the concept of service leadership. A look at the competency model, shown in Figure 1.1, suggests that there are stages in developing competency in whatever task one does, including leadership. Specific competencies of service leadership will be discussed later, but for the moment, let's discuss the stages of development of the competency model.

Aptitude is the natural ability an individual has in accomplishing a task. As individuals, all of us have certain personal characteristics that have been acquired as we go through life. These characteristics play a critical role in the ability of a leader. Some of the innate qualities such as humility, the ability to put the needs of others ahead of one's own; empathy, the ability to understand and share the feelings of another; and vision, an essential means for focusing attention on what matters most, what an individual wants to accomplish in life, and what kind of leader that individual wants to be are the cornerstones of a service leader.

In addition to those innate qualities, there are certain skills that can be learned through exposure to knowledge in a field of study including leadership.

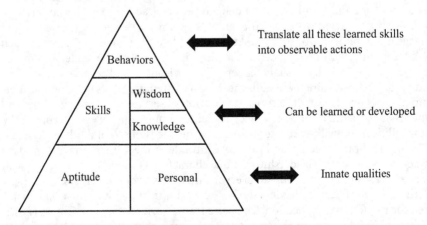

*Figure 1.1* Competency pyramid model

*Source:* Adapted from Lucia, A. and Lepsinger, R. (1999). *The Art and Science of Competency Model: Pinpointing Critical Success Factors in Organizations.* Jossey-Bass: San Francisco.

Knowledge can be gained through facts, information, experience, or education, be it theoretical or practical. A contemporary philosopher advocates that academic institutions ought to alter their focus from the acquisition of knowledge to seeking and promoting wisdom (Maxwell, 2007). In the context of service leadership, such wisdom is an outgrowth of innate qualities and skills gained through information. Wisdom is the capacity to realize what is of value in life, for oneself and others. Theories about wisdom have also been elaborated by psychologists who suggest that 'there is an overlap of the implicit theory of wisdom with intelligence, perceptiveness, spirituality and shrewdness. It is evident that wisdom is an expertise in dealing with difficult questions of life and adaptation to the complex requirements' (Brown & Greene, 2006; Sternberg, 1985).

Ultimately, the interplay of innate qualities, skills, knowledge, and wisdom defines how a leader behaves in his or her role as a service leader. When the basic competencies of service leadership are contrasted with Maslow's stages of need, there is a parallel between the two. For a better understanding of the connection between Maslow's motivation theory and service leadership, Maslow's revised model will be briefly highlighted here. In his original conceptualization, Maslow suggested only five stages of need and posited that an individual would have to go through them in sequence to achieve the ultimate goal of self-actualization. Later, he revised his framework to eight stages and offered that one does not have to follow the successive stages of needs in order to achieve the ultimate goal of transcendence. For service leadership in which there is an interplay of the 3Cs (*competence*, *character*, and *care*), competence falls in the area of 'deficiency needs' and character and care fall in the 'growth needs' of an individual.

Figure 1.2 shows the essential elements of the hierarchy of needs as conceptualized by Maslow.

For further elaboration of the essential elements of the frameworks, a comparison of Maslow's 'stages of needs' with those of 'service leadership' are presented in Table 1.1.

The conceptual framework of service leadership includes *character* and *care*. Hence, by adding *character* and *care* to the basic needs, a service leader can move to the higher stage of hierarchy of needs as proposed by Maslow. This way a service leader can achieve the higher-order needs of self-esteem, cognition, and aesthetic by internalizing cognitive and emotional competence, resilience, spirituality, and reflexivity. Maslow (1970b) suggested that self-actualization can be achieved by the following behaviors:

1   Experiencing life like a child, with full absorption and concentration.
2   Trying new things instead of sticking to safe paths.
3   Listening to your own feelings in evaluating experiences instead of the voice of tradition, authority, or the majority.
4   Avoiding pretense ('game playing') and being honest.
5   Being prepared to be unpopular if your views do not coincide with those of the majority.
6   Taking responsibility and working hard.
7   Trying to identify your defenses and having the courage to give them up.

Other research also has shown that outstanding leaders (particularly service leaders), managers, advanced professionals, and people in key jobs, from sales to

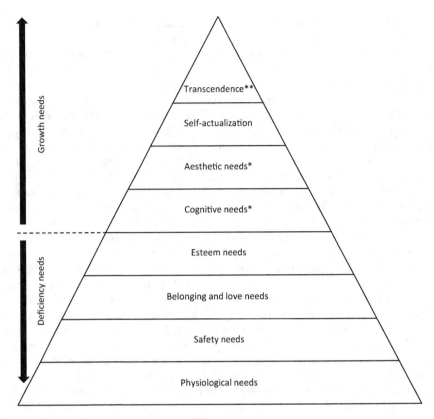

*Figure 1.2* Maslow's motivation theory model

*Source:* A Theory of Human Motivation by Maslow (1943), *Psychological Review*, 50(4), 370–396. *Maslow (1970a). **Maslow (1970b).

bank tellers, generally require the basic competencies for a job that are referred to as threshold competencies. They include basic knowledge, whether it is declarative, procedural, functional, or competencies in memory, and deductive reasoning. In the context of service leadership, there are differentiating competencies that defines outstanding performance from average (Kotter, 1982; Goleman, Boyatzis, & McKee, 2002). These are (1) cognitive competencies, such as systems thinking and pattern recognition; (2) emotional intelligence (or emotional quotient) competencies, including self-awareness and self-management competencies, such as emotional self-awareness and emotional self-control; and (3) social intelligence competencies, including social awareness and relationship management competencies, such as empathy and teamwork (Boyatzis, 2007).

## 1.1.2 Character

Academic research has shown that there is no consensus on the definition of character (Conger & Hollenbeck, 2010). However, one may look at character as the collection of core values possessed by an individual. Character is the driving force behind how one engages the world in conversations and in expressing values, and how to act on certain decisions. A study of world leaders over the past

Table 1.1 A comparison between Maslow's needs theory and service leadership's competence, character, and care

| Maslow's needs stages | Service leadership (competence, care, character |
|---|---|
| 1 Biological and physiological needs – air, food, drink, shelter, warmth, sex, sleep, etc. | Care |
| 2 Safety needs – protection from elements, security, order, law, stability, etc. | Care |
| 3 Love and belongingness needs – friendship, intimacy, trust, and acceptance, receiving and giving affection and love. Affiliating, being part of a group (family, friends, work). | Care |
| 4 Esteem needs – which Maslow classified into two categories: (1) Esteem for oneself (dignity, achievement, mastery, independence) and (2) the desire for reputation or respect from others (e.g., status, prestige). | Competence  and character |
| 5 Cognitive needs – knowledge and understanding, curiosity, exploration, need for meaning, and predictability. | Competence |
| 6 Aesthetic needs – appreciation and search for beauty, balance, form, etc. | Care |
| 7 Self-actualization needs – realizing personal potential, self-fulfillment, seeking personal growth and peak experiences. | Character |
| 8 Transcendence needs – a person is motivated by values that transcend beyond the personal self (e.g., mystical experiences and certain experiences with nature, aesthetic experiences, sexual experiences, service to others, the pursuit of science, religious faith, etc.). | Character |

Source: www.simplypsychology.org/maslow.html, retrieved July 9, 2019.

150 years points out that leaders who possess strong character will create a better world for everyone (Cooper, Sarros, & Santora, 2007).

It is generally agreed that good leaders also possess strong character, that is, they have a moral imperative that underwrites their actions. Hence, a person's observable behavior is a good indicator of that individual's character. Such behavior can be strong or weak, good or bad. Strong character implies that the leaders show consistency in their values, ethical reasoning, actions, and integrity. These behavioral attitudes develop positive psychological state such as confidence, optimism, hope, and resilience in themselves as well as those around them.

From the perspective of service leadership, the key attributes or dimensions of a leader's character are respect for others, fairness, cooperation, and compassion. Additionally, the attributes of courage, passion, and benevolence play a central role in service leaders. Further elaboration on each of these dimensions will be done later. The importance of character in a leader cannot be ignored even when the leader has achieved the goals of an organization. More often than not, the culture of an organization is largely a reflection of the character of the leader.

Research has shown that weakness of character and moral values would lead to failures of unimaginable proportions. The global financial crises of 2008–09 where boldness and instant gratification triumphed over temperance (Crossan et al., 2017) is an example of failure of character that brought the world to the brinks of economic collapse. In a world where digital technology has created networks that can be disrupted immediately, and felt globally, the strength of character underpins the disposition to lead not only for those in a position to lead but also for all members of an organization. As was pointed out earlier, to be a great service leader requires *competence*, *character*, and *care*. Deficiency in any of these three pillars will create problems for a service organization. It is important to keep in mind that developing character is a continuing process in which an individual learns to adapt to changing circumstance and acquires knowledge and experience. As Aristotle states, 'it is practical wisdom' that makes up the character of a leader. Similarly, as Henry David Thoreau noted, 'You cannot dream yourself into a character; you must hammer and forge yourself one.' Hence, a person's character is an outgrowth of the seed planted within us for reconciling who we are, why we behave the way we do, and what we want to become. A great service leader will facilitate sound judgments to serve the interest of all stakeholders. The capacity of the leader to further strengthen the following dimensions of character is essential to any service organization. These dimensions have been explored in an earlier text by Chung and Elfassy (2016) and will be elaborated later.

*Respect*: In today's world where cultural differences are permeating organizational environments, clashes of ideas are bound to happen. A service leader has to establish and nurture respectful relationships between and among different groups so as to minimize disagreement and conflicts. Respect for others is shown in a variety of ways. Listening is a critical element of showing respect. People feel respected when they have been heard and understood. This does not mean that the leader must agree with the point of view of others to show respect, but listening carefully to others' experiences, ideas, and perspective is being respectful. Another way of showing respect is to act respectfully. Rude behavior and language do not show respect. Keep in mind that perception of respect by individuals is influenced by their culture, family, peer, and social relationships.

*Fairness*: As a leader, one must always remember that unequal treatment of individuals and actions that are not consistent with the organization's rules, policies, and practices would leave the perception of unfairness of the leader. Both fairness and consistency are important for leadership. Fairness implies that the leader treats each member of the organization uniquely, and with equity based on their contributions. Consistency suggests that the leader treats all members of his or her constituency, equitably at all times and situations.

Rawls (1971) argues that fairness is the essence of morality. He points out that fairness leads to creating an ethical culture within an organization. A service leader must be vigilant and monitor whether the organizations' policies are fair to all. This translates to asking the following: Does every employee receive equal respect, and is every employee appreciated? Is there a fair process to address complaints and appeals? Is there transparency in the decisions made? Do the qualified employees have equal opportunity for advancement and promotion, and is there a fair compensation for different ranks of employees? The attribute of fairness that is modeled by a leader inspires positive change in an organization.

*Cooperation*: A leader being cooperative with employees when decisions are made generally results in a meaningful relationship between the organization and the employees. This ability has strategic advantages that must be remembered. Cooperative leadership implies a leader who engages in the same activities as everyone else and claims no special privileges. In the manufacturing mindset where hierarchy prevails, the ability to use teamwork as a cooperative model does not necessarily bring about changes in the organization as desired. Hence, in the service mindset, cooperation by the leader creates a sense of identity between the individuals and the organization's destiny. When a leader collaboratively defines work identity for the employees of the organization, it encourages worker commitment and building a cooperative work environment. It is important to keep in mind that cooperative leadership style is appreciative, positive, confident, and flexible.

To achieve the goals of an organization, a leader may downplay his or her leadership position and emphasize similarities in action with the employees. This works effectively if the leader can control the progression of events. Having recognized the strategic role of cooperative leadership or teamwork, some organizations, such as Merck, a well-known pharmaceutical company in the United States, has incorporated it into its core values.

*Empathy*: Empathy has been defined differently in the literature. However, there is a commonality in all the definitions. The best way to capture the concept of empathy is given by Plutchik (1987), who states that empathy is 'the ability to comprehend another's feelings and re-experience them oneself.' As an outcome, empathy bonds people together. From a service leadership point of view, it is a potent factor that contributes to change and learning. Yukl (2001) emphasizes that displaying empathy by a leader is an important factor in managing relations. Some have noted that outstanding leaders differ from less effective leaders by how sensitive they are to the needs of their followers (House & Podsakoff, 1994). It has been suggested that 'empathy is particularly important today as a component of leadership for at least three reasons: the increasing use of teams, the rapid pace of globalization, and the growing need to retain talent.' It means 'thoughtfully considering employees' feelings – along with other factors – in the process of making intelligent decisions' Goleman (1998, p. 100).

*Sincerity*: A leader who can show personal commitment and consistency between what is professed and what is done is recognized as being sincere. As a provider of service to customers, the attribute of sincerity is just as important as any other elements of character. The sincerity shown by a service leader influences the frontline employees' motivation that ultimately affects the quality of service offered by the organization. In this context, sincerity is one of those attributes that can determine job satisfaction of employees and make the customers happy. Hence, sincerity is vital to customers, to the company, and most importantly, to one's self and one's values.

*Integrity*: An essential element of character is integrity. Depending on the nature of the subject, the meaning changes. In this text, integrity is defined as a virtue that refers to a quality of a person's character. This attribute shows up in the professional, intellectual, or artistic work of an individual. It has been argued that ordinary discourse about integrity involves two aspects – one dealing with the relation one has with oneself and the other is the integrity connected with acting morally with others (Cox, La Case, & Levine, 2017). Integrity can be looked upon as the integration of self or maintaining one's identity. It could also be the compass, as one stands for something or serving as the moral purpose in an individual's life, not to mention as a virtue. As Chung and Elfassy (2016) put it, integrity is a commitment to being moral in dealings with others, personal straightforwardness, honesty, and coherence. Individuals or groups who show integrity in their actions have the capability for a process that repeatedly aligns moral awareness, deliberation, and conduct that shows a balanced judgment, and supports a system of moral decision making (Quinn, 2010). In service leadership, the emphasis is placed on the vital elements that encompass integrity, which are process, judgment, development, and system.

*Resilience*: This ability to look at temporary setbacks or failures as a learning moment and recover from them quickly shows how resilient individuals or groups are. A service leader maintains a positive attitude and looks at the failure or setback as an opportunity for his or her organization. Studies have shown the importance of resilience as both an individual and leadership trait. A study done by Zenger Folkman of 1,300 business leaders globally found that people with a strong preference for resilience

> were quick to take action and act independently. The most resilient people were more reactive than thoughtful and more focused on action than relationships. They were also more willing to take risks and make decisions quickly. Being resilient as an individual, and being viewed as a resilient leader, requires that you bring others along with you.
>
> (Folkman, 2017)

Kobasa (1979) points out that there are three elements that contribute to becoming a resilient service leader. These are challenge, commitment, and personal control. Individuals who face difficult situations in life and look upon these difficulties as challenges are resilient people. They look at these challenges as opportunities for personal growth. Similarly, resilient people show a commitment to work and social relations and care for others. Such commitment becomes a mechanism to fight and deal with any adversity they face. Resilient individuals also focus their energy on those events that they can control. This behavior of self-empowerment allows them to spend their efforts that can have most impact.

*Humility*: This element of character refers to the ability of individuals who approach life with humbleness and an attitude of self-restraint from showing vanity or pride. Individuals with humility show generosity to others. Leaders who are humble will use their skills, experience, and knowledge to inspire followers. They bring people together and contribute to the well-being of their organization and community. From a service leadership point of view, humility inspires trust, loyalty, and enthusiasm among the employees and customers. A humble leader has the courage to set aside personal gains for the benefit of others. Such courage drives a self-regulatory capacity in a leader to guard against excess and promotes pro-social tendencies (Owens, Johnson, & Mitchell, 2013). Theories of positive leadership, such as authentic and servant leadership, suggest that leaders described as humble (Nielson & Marrone, 2018) are those who value humility over recognition for tasks accomplished.

*Wisdom*: As Aristotle has put it, 'The wise man has the knowledge of all things, insofar as possible.' Psychologists have defined it as an integration of knowledge, experience, and deep understanding that incorporates tolerance for the uncertainties of life. Similarly, Staudinger (2008) views it as the ideal of human knowledge and character. From the view of psychologists, wisdom is the search for the moderate course between extreme actions. It is also looked upon as a dynamic force between knowledge and doubt. Service leadership looks upon wisdom as a well-balanced coordination of emotion, motivation, and thought when a service is provided. In sum, it is the possession of sound judgment that informs practice (Chung & Elfassy, 2016).

*Courage*: This is the capacity to act despite known fears, risks, and uncertainty. As Nelson Mandela has learned and stated, 'courage was not the absence of fear, but the triumph over it. The brave man is not he who does not feel afraid, but he who conquers that fear' (Daum, 2019). The defining characteristic of the best leaders in the world of business is courage. These individuals make bold moves that transform their businesses. The poet Maya Angelou states that 'Courage is the most important of all the virtues, because without courage you can't practice any other virtue consistently' (Persio, 2018).

Many a time, leaders who are lacking in courage also create environments that are filled with fear. Fear of failure compels these leaders to create defensive barriers that might have protected their ability to succeed. In the fear-ridden organizations, employees are mostly driven to survive and follow directions given by the leadership team. It is imperative for the leaders to be courageous and give employees the encouragement, energy, and support to try new things and new challenges to focus on the greater good of the overall organization, community, and human advancement. Here are a few suggestions on how leaders could change the culture of fear into a culture of drive and motivation. First, reevaluate the responsibilities of the employees and match their strength with the responsibility. Second, engage the employees in all levels of service in the decision making. This gives employees the courage to offer suggestions and improve the quality of service. Third, reward courageous behavior of the employees. Fourth, be a moral leader whose actions exhibit courageous behavior.

### 1.1.3 Care

As the third pillar of service leadership, *care* is an important element that service organizations must recognize and apply to be successful in a highly competitive world. Chung and Bell (2015) posited that 'caring' comes from the Old English 'caru,' with the interesting and unexpected meaning of 'sorrow, anxiety, grief.' In service leadership, *care* implies a slightly different attitude, that is, 'concern, consideration, or special attention.' As Chung and Bell point out, one should take seriously the old and important roots of the word 'care': The Anglo-Saxons meant by that word that you felt deep and often painful emotions if things weren't going right in a relationship or situation. In today's service context, *care* suggests to the recipients that attention is being given to them sincerely with an outcome that satisfies their needs.

Business organizations compete in many realms. What literature shows is that a caring attitude on the part of service leaders toward their employees or customers does have a significant impact on the organization in many ways. A service organization's success depends on the ability of its frontline service employees. When a service organization adopts a 'caring' attitude among all its employees and leaders teach its employees a caring posture, they will reap many benefits. Since service employees are the first line of connection with customers, they significantly shape the customers' service experience (Hausknecht & Langevin, 2010; Berry, 2009) and determine customer value and the brand promise (Sirianni, Bitner, Brown, & Mandel, 2013; Zhang, Liu, Wang, & Shen, 2011). Frontline employees tend to have a good understanding of customer needs and wants, can adapt the service delivery accordingly, and thereby frequently help to establish personalized relationships with customers and build loyalty toward the organization (Rafaeli, Ziklik, & Doucet, 2008). Service personnel with a 'caring' attitude draw more customers to the service organization and hence help in generating the firm's revenue (Jasmand, Blazevic, & de Ruyter, 2012; Yu, Patterson, & de Ruyter, 2012). Finally, highly motivated employees with a caring attitude showing discretionary effort are at the core of service excellence (Heracleous &Wirtz, 2010).

As was pointed out earlier, to achieve self-actualization, nurturing a caring disposition is a must in service leadership, as it allows one to develop capabilities for patience, kindness, and compassion and to gain a sense of satisfaction (Bevis, 1981).

## 1.2  Why service leadership?

In the globalized world of the 21st century, a significant shift from the industrial age into a service age has taken place. This shift requires competencies in leadership that go beyond the command and control of the earlier times. Service leadership emphasizes that in addition to the hard skills or competencies needed to lead, the leader must acquire and enhance soft skills or competencies that are essential in today's world. In Sections 1.1.2 and 1.1.3, elaboration was made on those soft skills that constitute the elements of *character* and *care* that distinguishes successful organizations from the less successful ones.

As was mentioned in the introduction of this chapter, service leadership is changing one's frame of reference or mindset that redefines leadership in the context of change from manufacturing to services. In the manufacturing era in which command and control led to significant changes in the production systems, decisions were being made by a few and followed by those who were given the task of assembly-line production. Efficiencies in production were the outcome of such strategies. In the service era, in which frontline employees are self-directed as they operate frequently on their own and face-to-face with their customers, it is difficult for supervisors to closely monitor (Yagil, 2002) and guide them in their tasks. Hence, decisions would be made by the service employee on the spot. This shift of distributive leadership requires the service leaders to be flexible in attitude and empower employees to make appropriate decisions about customizing service delivery and finding solutions to service problems (Lashley, 2001).

Given the distinctive features of service activities as being intangible, perishable, inseparable, and variable, the discussion of service leadership has to be contextualized with economic activities such as wholesale and retail trade, restaurant and hotels, transport and storage, supply chain, communication, finance, insurance, real estate, business services as well as community and social and personal services that share these characteristics.

The service sector produces 'intangible' goods, some well-known – government, health, education – and some quite new – modern communications, information, and business services. These services tend to require relatively less natural capital and more human capital than producing industrial goods. As a result, demand has grown for more educated workers, prompting countries to invest more in education – an overall benefit to their people. Another benefit of the growing service sector is that by using fewer natural resources than agriculture or industry, it puts less pressure on the local, regional, and global environment.

The development of Internet-based self-service delivery in categories such as banking, insurance, news, research, weather forecasting, and software provides a whole new set of highly intangible services (Lovelock & Gummesson, 2004).

Perishability is the concept that services cannot be saved or stored for use at a later date (Zeithaml & Bitner, 2003). For service firms, the concept of perishable capacity for products that cannot be stored is one in which demand in an industry is subject to wide fluctuations (Lovelock & Gummesson, 2004).

The element of inseparability of production and consumption in services is linked to the idea of interaction between the server and the receiver. A simultaneous customer-to-employee interaction is readily observable in many service environments and can form a critical distinguishing property between manufactured goods and many types of services.

Lastly, heterogeneity or variability is also a characteristic of service industry in that achieving uniform output, especially in labor-intensive services, is difficult. Controlling service quality when customers are actively involved in the production process creates variability in how a service is performed and received. How service providers attend to these issues as they perform their duties is of essence in service leadership.

Economists will look at the growth of a sector based on its contribution to the gross domestic product (GDP) and employment generated by the sector. With increasing emphasis throughout the world on services, a topic that will be discussed in Chapter 2, it is apparent that post-industrialization has taken root, and the service era has begun (Economist, 2011). As such, service leadership is needed to drive the economic growth and development of the service sector as well as the economy. How competitive one is in the new market depends on shifting the mindset in which attitude and care are the drivers.

Aside from the significant contribution of the service sector to the GDP of countries, the most crucial aspect of the service sector's ascendance is thorough integration of services with virtually every other aspect of the present-day world economy (Hoshmand, 2018). Contribution of the service sector in creating new local jobs, as well as creating a commercial environment that is conducive to entrepreneurship is an important link to the wider world economies (Economy Watch Content, 2016). On a global scale, the service sector is growing rapidly. It does not matter whether it is Hong Kong or New York; the employment generated by the service sector as compared with the manufacturing sector is unprecedented.

Given these developments, the question should be how to respond, in leadership terms, to accommodate these drastic changes in the structure of economies. The role that service leadership plays in the economy will have a significant impact on the future direction that economies in the developed and developing world would follow.

With the technological developments and the speed with which information travels, societies and communities will have to prepare themselves to take advantage of their comparative advantage in delivering services not only locally but globally.

## 1.3 Who is a service leader?

Having discussed what is meant by service leadership and why there is a need service leadership, the discussion should be turned to who is a service leader. In this context, the aim is not to talk about organizations that are the leading service providers, but rather about the characteristics of a service leader. In the earlier section, various elements of *character* and *care* were defined that encapsulate service leadership, and why possessing them separates leaders who have a service leadership mindset from those who served as leaders in the manufacturing era.

A service leader is one who has the moral character to lead his or her organization with authenticity, integrity, and care. Since specifics of each of the 3Cs were discussed earlier, the intention is to turn your attention to what is found in the literature on management and leadership that supports the concepts of a service leader. Service leaders are responsible for creating a supportive culture and climate for service (Wirtz & Jerger, 2016). This is accomplished in several ways. Leaders who aspire to take a company to greatness need to have personal humility blended with intensive professional will, ferocious resolve, and a willingness to give credit to others while taking the blame themselves (Collins, 2001). These characteristics were discussed earlier. Furthermore, leaders who create a strong climate for service generally demonstrate a commitment to service quality by setting a strategy that drives change (Bowen & Schneider, 2014), set high standards, recognize and remove obstacles, and ensure the availability of resources required to do it. Successful leadership often is aligned with the ability to model behavior and thereby focus the organization on the basics. Modeling such behaviors as meeting regularly with employees and customers to have a first-hand knowledge of the operational issues is important. This can be motivating for employees when encountering senior leaders on such visits and it provides leaders with an opportunity to model service excellence. Empirical research has shown why it is so important for management to model such behavior. Simons (2002) showed that behavioral integrity of a hotel's manager was highly correlated to employees' trust, commitment, and willingness to go the extra mile. In fact, of all manager behaviors measured, it was the single most important factor driving profitability. Empirical studies have also demonstrated the negative outcomes of the dark side of leadership in terms of a lack of essential qualities. Incompetence of leaders often causes organizational ineffectiveness (Schilling, 2009). Incompetence here does not refer only to technical incompetence, but rather social and cultural incompetence as well. Others have argued that immoral and uncaring leadership behavior is more destructive, and often negatively related to individual outcomes, such as employees' working attitudes, task performance, and psychological well-being (Shek, Chung, & Dou, 2019; Tepper, 2000), as well as organizational outcomes, such as commitment, relationship, and performance (Ashforth & Anand, 2003).

The service leaders focus on the needs of employees and customers, rather than on their position as a leader of an organization. Most notably, they are driven by integrity, trust, respect, delegation, vision, and influence on followers. Furthermore, they serve as a role model in appreciation, mentoring, recognition, listening skills, and empowering employees in decision making.

In sum, what distinguishes service leaders from leaders of the manufacturing era is how they have combined *competence*, *character*, and *care* in their approach to leading. This is what distinguishes service leadership from other forms of leadership in organizations. In subsequent chapters, the various styles of leadership that have been adopted by leaders given the circumstances of their organizations will be discussed.

## Key points to remember

The discussion of this chapter begun with 'What,' 'Why,' and 'Who' of service leadership.

- Service leadership is simply more than leadership offered in services. It refers to a changing mindset from manufacturing to services. This means moving beyond the command-and-control approach to leadership that was prevalent in the manufacturing era.
- Conceptualization of service leadership is based on the *3Cs*: *Competence*, *character*, and *care*.
- It is believed that in addition to competence, service leaders must have elements of character and care in their daily activities to achieve the self-actualization that Maslow has put forward.
- The notion of perishability, inseparability, and homogeneity of service requires that leaders of service organization be adaptable in delivering a quality service.
- Perishability is the concept that services cannot be saved or stored for use at a later date.
- The element of inseparability of production and consumption in services is linked to the idea of interaction between the server and the receiver. A simultaneous customer-to-employee interaction exists.
- Heterogeneity or variability is also a characteristic of service industry in that achieving uniform output, especially in labor-intensive services, is difficult.

## Case study

### The Peninsula Hotel in Hong Kong

The Peninsula Hotels group operates prestigious properties in major cities around the world and is known for setting the highest standards of comfort and impeccable service. Established in 1928, they operate prestigious luxury properties in ten major cities. These include their flagship in Hong Kong, plus Shanghai, Tokyo, Beijing, New York, Chicago, Beverly Hills, Bangkok, Manila, and Paris. Each of these establishments has maintained the reputation that makes Peninsula Hotels what they are today.

This case looks at one area of service to show how Hong Kong Peninsula has achieved its goal and reputation. After reading this case, the reader is asked to answer a few questions that relates to service leadership.

Among many of elements of service, this case highlights how the staff of the food and beverage (F&B) section of the hotel are driven to provide exceptional service. The staff canteen, where all the staff have their breakfast before they start meeting hotel guests, is in a league of its own. It is much more spacious than a typical fast-food restaurant. It has an abundance of big windows facing the street. There is excellent lighting throughout. This is a place that will allow anyone to relax and enjoy a hearty breakfast. There is a resting room next to the canteen, giving off-duty F&B staff a chance to relax or even take a nap.

Visiting the uniform room of the Peninsula is an experience. Every staff member gets a fresh shift uniform each day. In fact, 'freshness' is the word that comes to mind. Peter Borer had mentioned that once a staff member walked through the staff entrance, he wanted them to get a feeling of freshness.

Peter, who studied in Switzerland and worked in many hotels in Europe and the US, remembers, 'In those days, junior hotel staff did not always get the respect they deserve.' The Peninsula Hotels invests in staff facilities to make sure staff start the day with the right frame of mind. As Peter put it,

> The customer experience is dependent on each member of staff. I want the staff to feel the organization's respect and the pride for them. I want them to feel safe, hygienic and fresh. I am quite happy if 80 percent of the staff start with the right frame of mind.

Peter explained what they did when they opened a brand-new Peninsula hotel. They typically spent three months to 'mobilize' a new hotel. And where did they start? The staff facilities, of course.

They wanted every staff member to feel respect so that they would show the same respect to hotel guests. Respect is not just about the work environment. It is also about how you engage your staff.

Peter will always make an extended site visit during the two- to three-month mobilization period before a new hotel opens. A task force composed of staff from all the other Peninsula hotels will also be there. Peter typically stays for ten days. 'There are a thousand problems when a hotel opens. I just walk around a lot,' Peter recalls. 'I put on my jeans and t-shirt. I will often sweep the floor to show the new staff how this is done in the Peninsula Hotels. This action on my part will break down any barriers and the staff will share with me the real problems they experience. I make it a habit just sit "over there," listening to all their problems.'

*Source*: Adapted from Chung, P. and Ip, S. (2018). *Pillars of a service hub* (pp. 101–3). New York: Lexingford Publisher.

## Questions related to the case

1 Which elements of *character* or *care* show up in this case study?
2 Give reasons why you have selected the element that best exemplifies this case.

## End of chapter questions

1 What is meant by service leadership, and how does it differ from other organizational leadership?
2 How does a service leader accomplish the goals of service leadership?
3 What is meant by character?
4 What are the elements or distinguishing features of character?
5 How is the concept of *care* defined in service leadership?
6 What would it take for a leader to become a service leader?
7 What does intangibility in service imply? Why is this relevant to service leaders?
8 Why do perishability, inseparability, and heterogeneity define the context of service?

## References

Ashforth, B., & Anand, V. (2003). The normalization of corruption in organizations. *Research in Organizational Behavior, 25*(3), 1–52.
Berry, L. L. (2009). Competing with quality service in good times and bad. *Business Horizons, 52*, 309–317.
Bevis, E. (1981). Caring: A life force. In M. Leininger (Ed.), *Caring: An essential human need. Proceedings of the three national caring conferences* (pp. 49–59). Detroit: Wayne State University Press.
Bowen, D., & Schneider, B. (2014). A service climate synthesis and future research agenda. *Journal of Service Research, 17*(1), 5–22.
Boyatzis, R. (2007). Competencies in the 21st century. *Journal of Management Development, 27*(1), 5–12.
Brown, S. C., & Greene, J. (2006). The wisdom development scale: Translating the conceptual to the concrete. *Journal of College Student Development, 47*, 1–19.
Chung, P. (2012). *Service reborn: The knowledge, skills, and attitude of service companies.* Hong Kong: Lexingford Publishing.
Chung, P., & Bell, A. (2015). *25 principles of service leadership.* Hong Kong: Lexingford Publishing.
Chung, P., & Elfassy, R. (2016). *The 12 dimensions of a service leader: Manage your personal brand for the service age.* Hong Kong: Lexingford Publishing.
Collins, J. (2001). Level 5 leadership: The triumph of humility and fierce resolve. *Harvard Business Review, 79*, 66–76.
Conger, J., & Hollenbeck, G. (2010). On defining and measuring character in leadership. *Consulting Psychology Journal Practice and Research, 62*(4), 311–316.
Cooper, B., Sarros, J., & Santora, J. (2007). The character of leadership. *Ivey Business Journal, 71*(5), 1–99.

Cox, D., La Case, M., & Levine, M. (2017). Integrity. In E. N. Zalt (Ed.), *The Stanford encyclopedia of philosophy*. The Metaphysics Research Lab, Center for the Study of Language and Information, Stanford University.

Crossan, M., Byrne, A., Seijts, G., Reno, M., Monzani, L., & Gandz, J. (2017). Toward a framework of leader character in organizations. *Journal of Management Studies, 54*(7), 986–1018.

Daum, K. (2019). *30 quotes on how to be a great leader from Nelson Mandela*. Retrieved September 20, 2019, from www.inc.com/kevin-daum/31-quotes-on-how-to-be-a-great-leader-from-nelson-.html

Economist. (2011, May 19). The service elevator. *Economic Focus*.

Economy Watch Content. (2016). *Hong Kong economic structure*. Retrieved April 7, 2016, from www.economywatch.com/world_economy/hong-kong/structure-of-economy.html

Edvinsson, L. (1992). Service leadership: Some critical roles. *International Journal of Service Industry Management, 3*(2), 33–36.

Folkman, J. (2017, April 6). 7 ways to become a more resilient leader. *Forbes*.

Goffee, R., & Jones, G. (2000, September–October). Why should anyone be led by you? *Harvard Business Review*, 63–70.

Goleman, D. (1998, November–December). What makes a leader? *Harvard Business Review*, 93–102.

Goleman, D., Boyatzis, R., & McKee, A. (2002). *Primal leadership: Realizing the power of emotional intelligence*. Boston, MA: Harvard Business School Press.

Gronfeldt, S., & Strother, J. (2006). Introduction. In S. Gronfeldt & J. Strother (Eds.), *Service leadership: The quest for competitive advantage*. Thousand Oaks, CA: Sage.

Hausknecht, J., & Langevin, A. (2010). Selection in sales and service jobs. In J. L. Farr & N. T. Tippins (Eds.), *Handbook of employee selection* (pp. 765–780). New York, NY: Routledge.

Hedlund, J., Forsyth, G., Horvath, J., Williams, W., Snook, S., & Sternberg, R. (2003). Identifying and assessing tacit knowledge: Understanding the practical intelligence of military leaders. *The Leadership Quarterly, 14*(2), 117–140.

Heracleous, L., & Wirtz, J. (2010). Singapore airlines' balancing act – Asia's premier carrier successfully executes a dual strategy: It offers world-class service and is a cost leader. *Harvard Business Review, 88*(7–8), 145–149.

Higgs, M., & Roland, D. (2001). Developing change leaders: Assessing the impact of a development programme. *Change Management Journal, 2*(1), 47–64.

Hogan, R., & Hogan, J. (2001). Assessing leadership: A view from the dark side. *International Journal of Development and Selection, 9*(1–2), 40–51.

Hoshmand, A. (2018). Service leadership at Hong Kong Baptist University: A new concept in general education. *International Journal on Disability and Human Development, 17*(1), 45–52.

House, R., & Podsakoff, P. (1994). Leadership effectiveness: Past perspectives and future directions for research. In J. Greenberg (Ed.), *Organizational behavior: The state of the science* (pp. 45–82). Hillsdale, NJ: Lawrence Erlbaum Associates.

Jasmand, C., Blazevic, V., & de Ruyter, K. (2012). Generating sales while providing service: A study of customer service representatives' ambidextrous behavior. *Journal of Marketing, 76*(1), 20–37.

Kobasa, S. (1979). Personality and resistance to illness. *American Journal of Community Psychology, 7*(4), 413–423.

Kotter, J. P. (1982). *The general managers.* New York, NY: The Free Press.

Lashley, C. (2001). *Empowerment HR strategies for service excellence.* Oxford: Butterworth Heinemann.

Lovelock, C., & Gummesson, E. (2004). Whither services marketing? In search of a new paradigm and fresh perspectives. *Journal of Service Research, 7*(1), 20–41.

Lucia, A., & Lepsinger, R. (1999). *The art and science of competency model: Pinpointing critical success factors in organizations.* San Francisco, CA: Jossey-Bass.

Marcy, R. (2015). Breaking mental models as a form of creative destruction: The role of leader cognition in radical social innovation. *The Leadership Quarterly, 26,* 370–385.

Marcy, R., & Mumford, M. (2010). Leader cognition: Improving leader performance through causal analysis. *The Leadership Quarterly, 21,* 1–19.

Marta, S., Lertize, L., & Mumford, M. (2005). Leadership skills and the group performance: Situational demands, behavioral requirements, and planning. *The Leadership Quarterly, 16,* 97–120.

Maslow, A. (1943). A theory of human motivation. *Psychological Review, 50*(4), 370–396.

Maslow, A. (1970a). *Motivation and personality.* New York, NY: Harper & Row.

Maslow, A. (1970b). *Religions, values, and peak experiences.* New York, NY: Penguin (Original work published 1966).

Maslow, A. (1987). *Motivation and personality* (3rd ed.). New Delhi: Pearson Education.

Maxwell, N. (2007). *From knowledge to wisdom: A revolution for science and the humanities* (2nd ed.). London: Pentire Press.

McKenna, B., Rooney, D., & Boal, K. (2009). Wisdom principles as a metatheoretical basis for evaluating leadership. *The Leadership Quarterly, 20*(2), 177–190.

Mumford, M., Connelly, S., & Gaddis, B. (2003). How creative leaders think: Experimental findings and cases. *The Leadership Quarterly, 14*(4), 411–432.

Mumford, M., Todd, E., Higgs, C., & McIntosh, T. (2017). Cognitive skills and leadership: The nine critical skills. *The Leadership Quarterly, 28,* 24–39.

Nielson, R., & Marrone, J. (2018). Humility: Our current understanding of the construct and its role in organizations. *International Journal of Management Review, 20,* 805–824.

Owens, B., Johnson, M., & Mitchell, T. (2013). Expressed humility in organizations: Implications for performance, teams, and leadership. *Organization Science, 24,* 1517–1538.

Persio, S. (2018). Maya Angelou Google Doodle: Quotes from the American poet and activist. *Newsweek.* Retrieved September 20, 2019, from www.newsweek.com/maya-angelou-google-doodle-quotes-american-poet-and-activist-871229

Plutchik, R. (1987). Evolutionary bases of empathy. In N. Eisenberg & J. Strayer (Eds.), *Empathy and its development* (pp. 38–46). New York, NY: Cambridge University Press.

Quinn, C. (2010). On integrity. *International Journal of Applied Philosophy*, *23*, 189–197.

Rafaeli, A., Ziklik, L., & Doucet, L. (2008). The impact of call center employees' customer orientation behaviors and service quality. *Journal of Service Research*, *10*, 239–255.

Rawls, J. (1971). *The theory of justice*. Boston, MA: Harvard University Press.

Schilling, J. (2009). From ineffectiveness to destruction: A qualitative study on the meaning of negative leadership. *Leadership*, *25*(1), 102–128.

Schwartz, B., & Sharpe, K. (2006). Practical wisdom: Aristotle meets positive psychology. *Journal of Happiness Studies*, *7*, 377–395.

Shek, D., Chung, P., & Dou. (2019). The dark side of service leaders. In M. Brandebo (Ed.), *The dark sides of organizational behavior and leadership* (pp. 125–145). London: InTechOpen.

Shek, D., & Lin, L. (2015). Character strength and service leadership. *International Journal on Disability and Human Development*, *14*(3), 255–263.

Simons, T. (2002). The high cost of lost trust. *Harvard Business Review*, *80*, 18–19.

Sirianni, N., Bitner, M., Brown, S., & Mandel, N. (2013). Branded service encounters: Strategically aligning employee behavior with the brand positioning. *Journal of Marketing*, *77*(4), 108–123.

Staudinger, U. (2008). A psychology of wisdom: History and recent development. *Research in Human Development*, *5*(2), 107–120.

Sternberg, R. J. (1985). Implicit theories of intelligence, creativity, and wisdom. *Journal of Personality and Social Psychology*, *49*, 607–662.

Tepper, B. (2000). Consequences of abusive supervision. *The Academy of Management Journal*, *43*(2), 178–190.

Wirtz, J., & Jerger, C. (2016). Managing service employees: Literature review, expert opinions, and research directions. *Service Industries Journal*, *36*(15–16), 757–788.

Yagil, D. (2002). The relationship of customer satisfaction and service workers' perceived control – examination of three models. *International Journal of Service Industry Management*, *13*, 382–398.

Yu, T., Patterson, P., & de Ruyter, K. (2012). Achieving service-sales ambidexterity. *Journal of Service Research*, *16*, 52–66.

Yukl, G. (2001). *Leadership in organizations*. Upper Saddle River, NJ: Prentice-Hall.

Zeithaml, V., & Bitner, M. (2003). *Services marketing: Integrating customer focus across the firm* (3rd ed.). New York, NY: McGraw-Hill.

Zhang, R., Liu, X., Wang, H., & Shen, L. (2011). Service climate and employee service performance: Exploring the moderating role of job stress and organizational identification. *The Service Industries Journal*, *31*, 2355–2372.

# 21st century realities

## 2.1 Globalization

Over the centuries, the world community has gone through many stages of globalization, although not at the same speed or magnitude. Social science disciplines have identified elements that constitute globalization from their perspectives. We are interested in globalization as it relates to economic development and managerial leadership. In our view, the world is characterized by virtual communication, capital and labor movement, dispersion of information at a pace that has not been seen before, and institutional deregulation, which constitute 'globalization.'

Some have argued that globalization began to expand in the 1980s in response to new forms of capitalist hegemony (Robertson, 1992). Beynon and Dunkerley (2000, p. 3) state that 'globalization, in one form or another, is impacting on the lives of everyone on the planet . . . globalization might justifiably be claimed to be the defining feature of human society at the start of the twenty-first century.'

No matter how the term is defined, its inescapable impact is undeniable. Throughout history, humans have attempted to improve the quality of life by looking at science, which led to modernity, as a tool. Science has been at the forefront of modernization and hence some have argued that globalization is coterminous with the modern era. That is, it had to happen in step with the process of modernization (Schirato & Webb, 2003, p. 2).

In short, the dramatic shifts in technological development have had a significant impact on all aspects of life, be it in economics, politics, social issues, environment, or any other area.

Economic globalization, simply stated, is the integration of national economies into the international economy through trade, direct foreign investment, short-term capital flows, labor movement across boundaries, and the flow of technology. The relationship between economic globalization and services is direct and clear. Taken as a whole, economic globalization depends on how the service sector facilitates activities between people as clients, customers, workers and more broadly and those they serve. Section 2.2 will discuss the role that services have in the world's economies.

As one can expect, there are advantages and disadvantages to globalization (Moudoukoutas, 2011). These will be discussed briefly to determine where improvements in policy could be made to better facilitate the provision of services.

Among the many advantages associated with globalization, those that directly link with the service sector will be discussed. Globalization enhances free trade and communication between nations, along with increased access to technology, media, education, health care, consumer goods, and other resources.

Economic theory has always highlighted the benefits of free trade. Adam Smith (1776) stated that 'a nation's wealth is really the stream of goods and services that it creates. And the way to maximize it, he argued, was not to restrict the nation's productive capacity, but to set it free.' David Ricardo further encouraged free trade by introducing his theory of comparative advantage (Ricardo, 1817). Nations have long recognized the importance of trade and its contribution to economic development. The basic premise of freed trade is to reduce barriers such as tariffs, value added taxes, subsidies provided to the domestic industries, and other obstacles between nations.

As an approach to promote international trade by reducing or eliminating trade barriers such as tariffs and quotas, in 1947 the United Nations put forth the General Agreement on Tariffs and Trade (GATT) that was signed by 23 nations. It remained in effect until 1994 when the 123 nations that were signatories to the agreement agreed to establish the World Trade Organization (WTO), which launched its operations on January 1, 1995. Both the GATT and WTO have successfully reduced tariffs (Goldstein, Rivers, & Tomz, 2007). Average tariff levels for the major GATT participants were about 22% in 1947 but were 5% after the Uruguay Round in 1999 (Irwin, 2007). Ever since its establishment, the GATT has had many rounds of negotiation to reduce tariffs and facilitate international trade. This reduction in the tariff has contributed to the flow of goods among nations and in the process has created employment and economic growth throughout the world.

Succeeding GATT's various rounds of negotiation, WTO started its operation in 1995 and now has 164 members (World Trade Organization, 2019). The aim is to help producers of goods and services, exporters, and importers conduct their business in an environment that promotes free trade. As a global international organization, it deals with the rules and regulation of trade among member states. WTO works with member states to strengthen the trading system so that nations will be able to better respond to the challenges of today's economy. This includes rapid technological change that is creating huge shifts in patterns of employment. Among the many approaches to improve the functioning of WTO, the member states have recognized the need to address trade-distorting practices, such as subsidies, and to remedy issues related to the dispute settlement system. Furthermore, WTO is working to improve negotiation and trade facilitations such as the abolishment of agricultural subsidies, the expansion of the Information Technology Agreement, and assistance to the least developed countries (LDCs) to build their trade capacity and practices (WTO Annual Report, 2019). Parallel with the multilateral agencies, world trade is also driven by bilateral agreements.

Globalization also has the advantage of creating competition among countries where comparative advantage leads to lower prices for goods and services. It has to be kept in mind that the true impact of lower prices is felt when the manipulation of currency is kept at bay. The worldwide market for companies and consumers offers unprecedented choices for all the market players. Another benefit of globalization is the infusion of foreign capital and technology, which can boost the economic conditions of a country and reduce poverty. Additionally, employment conditions may improve depending on the nature of the investment. With the influx of information between countries, one would expect cultural intermingling. Such interactions allow people to have a better understanding of one another. This could create more open and tolerant communities around the world. A basic premise of service leadership is to have empathy for others so that the environment or habitat for toleration is expanded. Furthermore, mass communications and quick dissemination of information through the Internet allow for the exchange of ideas among countries.

In addition to trade being the fundamental contributor to globalization, foreign direct investment (FDI) is a crucial element of the service industry that has also played an important role in the rise of global trade. FDI over the past decades has risen at an impressive rate. Reports from the United Nations Conference on Trade and Development (UNCTAD) concluded that FDI has become an important engine of economic growth because those investments grew faster than GDP and international trade. Also, FDI flows are higher in comparison to technological flows, expressed through license fees, royalties, and related instruments (UNCTAD, 2018).

As can be seen in Figure 2.1, FDI's contribution to the global economy has been significant. It continued to increase until 2015 but then began to decline. In 2018, the world total of FDI was reported at $1.43 trillion. The fall was caused in part by a 22% decrease in the value of cross-border mergers and acquisitions (UNCTAD, 2018). Looking at the data for 2018, FDI flows were stable for the developing economies as a whole, where they received $671 billion. Flows to developing countries of Asia reached $476 billion. Such investments put this region as the largest FDI recipient in the world. FDI to Latin America and the Caribbean rose 8% in 2018 to reach $151 billion. FDI in structurally weak and vulnerable economies remained fragile. Flows to the LDCs fell by 17%, to $26 billion, whereas inward FDI flows to the developed economies fell sharply, by 37%, to $712 billion.

The many benefits that foreign direct investment can bring to a nation include bringing modern technologies, increasing production efficiency, and often promoting restructuring of enterprises. From the service sector's point of view, FDI contributes to human resources management by transferring knowledge, skills, and experience from the affiliate companies to the host country. This contribution is especially noted in areas of research and development, know-how, production organization, sales, and management skills. FDI also contributes by encouraging the development of domestic companies through subcontracting relationships. Multinational companies have helped countries access foreign markets that would otherwise be difficult to reach. Given that service era is upon us, it

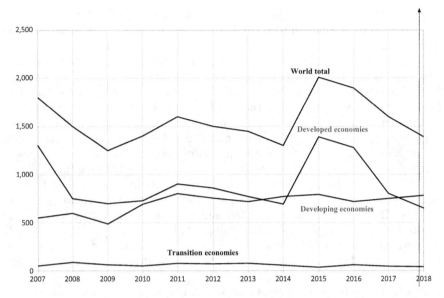

Figure 2.1   FDI inflows, global and by economic group, 2007–18 (billions of dollars)
Source: UNCTAD, FDI/MNE database (www.unctad.org/fdistatistics)

is imperative to have the tools offered by service leadership for human resource development and the overall growth of the economy.

Contrary to its benefits, FDI can also have some negative impacts. When foreign investors are expanding their markets in a host country, they can displace local competition by offering products at lower prices. Sometimes, this can lead to aggressive or 'hostile' acquisition of companies in the local market to decrease competition.

When investments are in capital-demanding production as opposed to labor-demanding production, unemployment may increase. This is especially so when there is a restructuring of production, streamlining of operations, or introduction of new technologies. Depending on the nature of the FDI, the impact on the labor force may be positive or negative. If a foreign investor is interested in the acquisition of local companies, the likelihood of increased unemployment is there. On the other hand, if the FDI is in the form of a new venture where local human and physical resources are used, then employment levels may increase.

Given the positive impact of FDI on the economy of a country, governments sometimes favor FDI and neglect local companies. Providing tax concessions and other infrastructural benefits to outside investors can create unfavorable conditions for local companies to compete. This harmful effect of FDI has been a major source of concern and even social protest that has hindered its expansion in some countries.

Globalization is a complex issue. While some argue that it reduces global poverty, others argue that it actually has increased wealth inequality worldwide (Alacevich & Soci, 2018; Mong, 2018; Mills, 2009).

Some voices in developed economies have argued that globalization has taken jobs overseas where labor is cheaper. This loss of jobs in the developed countries has created a hostile trade environment with the developing economies. According to conservative estimates from the Economic Policy Institute, granting China a most favored-nation status drained 3.4 million manufacturing jobs from the US (Scott, 2017). The labor force in countries such as the US are facing pay cuts and loss of jobs as their employers are searching for lower labor costs abroad. As was mentioned earlier in the discussion of FDI, some nations provide incentives such as tax benefits to foreign investors. Multinational corporations take advantage of tax havens offered and avoid paying taxes in their own country. In the process of globalization, multinational corporations have been accused of social injustice, unfair labor practices, mismanagement of natural resources, and environmental damage (Jorgenson & Givens, 2013; Dadush & Shaw, 2012; Hillman, 2008). Other arguments against globalization stem from the risks associated with losing copyright and other intellectual property, as well as the outright stealing of technology. The recent trade war between the US and China centered on intellectual property rights and how easy it is to copy and steal technology where substantial research and development funds have been used.

Furthermore, it has been argued that globalization is an economic storm that is affecting nations around the world (Collins, 2015). To counter this, leadership to adjust to these economic conditions with equanimity and thoughtfulness is needed. With the deindustrialization in some developed nations around the world, countries are looking for the next economic revolution. This may come from the service sector. This is where the values that are espoused in service leadership will enhance the capabilities of the service sector.

To better understand what is new in the 21st century, a set of data will be examined to highlight the changes that are being observed. To start, it is abundantly clear that services are taking away the spotlight from the industrial manufacturing story that dominated economic and social developments in the 20th century. Make no mistake, industrial manufacturing will continue, albeit in a different mode and capacity. Other than technological developments, one should also explore the causes of the shift to a service-driven economy.

## 2.2 Historical developments of the service economy

At each stage of human civilization, humanity has experienced different economic conditions. These have guided populations to acquire skills that were needed and necessary for survival and growth. As human civilizations progressed from hunter-gatherer communities to agriculture and later to manufacturing, *homo sapiens* developed tools and skills that responded to those environmental conditions. Now that we have entered the 21st century, there has been a dramatic shift from the industrial manufacturing to services to accomplish the goals of economic growth and development (Prakash & Mishra, 2014).

With increasing emphasis throughout the world on services and the contribution of the service sector to the GDP of economies (see Table 2.1), it is essential to have the higher-level leadership skills that can manage this economic reality. Service leadership training provides these skills.

In addition to the significant contribution of the service sector to the GDP of countries, it is also notable how the service sector has become highly integrated with virtually every other aspect of the present-day world economy. Service-sector roles have become a critical source of new local jobs, as well as an essential

Table 2.1 Contribution of the service sector to the GDP of the top 15 countries in 2017

| Rank | Country | Percent contribution to the GDP |
| --- | --- | --- |
| 1 | Gibraltar | 100.0 |
| 2 | Jersey | 96.0 |
| 3 | Barbados | 93.8 |
| 4 | Bermuda | 93.3 |
| 5 | Hong Kong SAR | 92.7 |
| 6 | Cayman Island | 91.3 |
| 7 | Turks and Caicos Islands | 90.6 |
| 8 | The Bahamas | 90.0 |
| 9 | British Virgin Islands | 87.8 |
| 10 | Macau | 88.7 |
| 11 | Malta | 88.1 |
| 12 | Luxembourg | 87.9 |
| 13 | Guernsey | 87.0 |
| 14 | Cyprus | 86.8 |
| 15 | Isle of Man | 86.0 |

ingredient in creating a commercial environment conducive to entrepreneurship. Under the conditions of globalization, service roles also provide a vital link to the wider world economies. On a global scale, the service sector is growing more rapidly than any other sector in the economy (Hoshmand, 2018).

It does not matter whether it is Hong Kong or New York, the employment generated by the service sector compared with the manufacturing sector is unprecedented. According to Economy Watch (2008), 87.7% of the workforce in Hong Kong was employed by the service sector. Similarly, looking at the employment generated by the service sector in the US between 1965 and 2013 (Bureau of Labor Statistics, 2016), an increasing growth over the decades is observed in Figure 2.2.

The prominent role that the service sector has taken in the economic development of nations has not always been welcome. Historically, the service sector has not received the positive attention seen in, for example, agriculture or manufacturing. Even Adam Smith in his book *The Wealth of Nations* questioned the social value provided by 'churchmen, lawyers, physician, musicians, etc.' Economists of the 20th century such as Baumol (1967) have argued that the service sector is resistant to improvements in productivity. His view is that 'the provision of services – such as restaurant meals, haircuts, and medical checkups – required face-to-face transactions. These did not lend themselves easily to standardization and trade, the source of growth in productivity and hence income.' More recently, an economist in a *New York Times* op-ed pointed out that 'it is better to produce "real things" than services' (Romer, 2012).

Given the transformational changes that nations have experienced in the last few decades, the perception of the service sector must change. Today, those jobs that Adam Smith thought useless are major players in the economy. Many service jobs use technology more efficiently and effectively and hence contribute to higher incomes for those engaged in this sector. Services that are coupled with

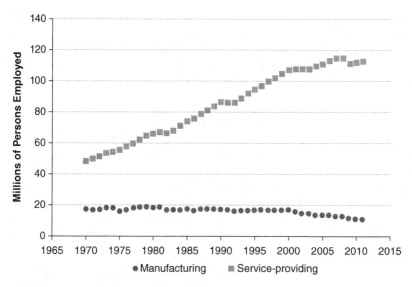

*Figure 2.2* Employment

*Source*: Bureau of Labor Statistics, Employment, Hours, and Earnings from Current Employment Statistics survey (National), http://data.bls.gov/cgi-bin/surveymost?ce (Accessed on 03/03/2016)

the manufacturing sector are now cocreators of value for both the suppliers and consumers. The ability to work cooperatively versus competitively has made it possible for these sectors to move economic development and growth forward.

Economic theorists of the 20th century, such as Nicholas Kaldor (1957), Ragnar Nurkse (1952), and Arthur Lewis (1955) posited that industrialization was the prime engine of employment and growth. This led nations to pursue policies that favored manufacturing. Given the realities of the time, the emphasis on manufacturing did contribute to growth in both developed and developing nations. However, in the 21st century the growing interdependence of the manufacturing and service sectors could put an end to the debate about favoring one sector over the other. The critical role that the service sector plays in the manufacturing supply chain is undeniable. The success of many chains depends on the central role of services, from research and development at the inception of the product to distribution and repair at completion.

Throughout the world, organizations and corporations are beginning to recognize the interdependence of the manufacturing and the service sectors. A movement is now emerging to shift from selling products to selling an integrated combination of products and services that deliver value to all involved in the supply chain. Some academics have referred to this development as the 'servitization of manufacturing' (Baines, Lightfoot, & Smart, 2011). Today, many manufacturing companies are incorporating services from other vendors to help them establish and maintain a relationship with their customers. Examples abound. An obvious one is DHL courier service, which through reliable delivery and a tracking system assures companies that products will make it to customers on time and with care. Their commitment is in their motto: 'Excellence, Simply Delivered.'

For developing countries where manufacturing still plays a significant role in the economy, developing state-of-the-art services could act as an economic development strategy. Such services are needed for manufacturing firms to connect to the global value chains and develop competitiveness in more skill-intensive activities (Flaaen, Ghani, & Mishra, 2013). Furthermore, countries can choose to use their comparative advantage, particularly in labor, to become exporters of some intermediate or final service products. With technological innovations, services may pose lower barriers to entry than capital-intensive industries.

Trade in services has the advantage over trade in goods by being offered without having to cross a national border. However, such services are affected by domestic regulations set across various sectors. International trade of services is sensitive to the national regulations that can affect the supply of such services. For developing countries and LDCs, service trade has become the new frontier as it allows these nations to enhance their participation in international trade. This in turn, can help these nations realize their development goals. Taken as a whole, this sector's positive impact on the economy can be used as an effective component of a comprehensive development strategy for nations around the world.

Some have argued that the 'service economy' is more often associated with more developed economies around the world (OECD 2005). Although it is commonly observed that an economy tends to shift to services as per capita income increases, why such a shift takes place in the first place and what kind of impact such a structural change has, especially on growth, is still debated. The data show that services play an increasingly important role in the global economy and the growth and development of countries. As noted by the World Bank (2012), services are becoming crucial in a country's development, including in achieving the Millennium Development Goals such as poverty reduction and access to basic services, including education, water, and health. Furthermore, the World Bank (2012) notes that the service sector's higher contribution to poverty reduction has been more significant than the contribution of growth from the agriculture or the manufacturing sectors.

The services sector is the largest of the world as 63% of total global wealth in 2017 came from services (World Fact Book, 2017). This impressive contribution would be even greater if the forward and backward linkages of the domestic services with the primary and the secondary sectors as well as its linkage with trade are considered. Inter-sectoral linkages, composed of backward and forward linkages, reflect the interconnectedness between the services sector and the other sectors of an economy. The mutual interdependencies that exist between the sectors contribute to the growth of other sectors in this symbiotic relationship. Backward linkages create additional demand for the output of upstream sectors, which, in turn, induces an increased upstream investment and an increased level of capacity utilization as well as a possible upstream technological upgrading. By contrast, a sector's forward linkages affect downstream sectors. Thus, decreasing costs of a sector's output can result in growth-inducing effects to downstream industries. These could include downstream investment, technological upgrading, or increased productivity and resource utilization.

Hirschman's (1959) theory of inter-industrial linkage analysis especially emphasizes the role of backward linkages for growth stimuli. He further argues that forward linkages cannot exist in a pure form since they are a result of the demand that emanates from existing backward linkages. Thus, the existence of demand is a condition for forward linkages. A service firm that purchases inputs from a local supplier is an example of a backward linkage. For example, a restaurateur purchases fresh produce from a local producer to satisfy his or her customers. On the other hand, a firm selling intermediate inputs to another firm creates a forward linkage. For example, when FinTech sells technologies to the financial sector, the financial institutions are capable of facilitating more investment potentials and economic growth. Keep in mind that while backward linkages induce economic development, forward linkages enable economic development.

The US was the largest beneficiary from the services sector valued at around US$15.53 trillion (World Fact Book, 2017). The same source also notes that the services sector is the leading sector in 201 countries/economies, with some 30 countries receiving more than 80% of their GDP from the services sector. The services sector now accounts for over 70% of total employment and value added in OECD economies. It also accounts for almost all employment growth in the OECD area (OECD, 2005). Approximately $8.9 trillion of goods are transacted across borders, and $2.10 trillion of services are provided across borders (Hill, 2009).

Services are the driving force of the European economies. They account for more than two-thirds of the EU GDP and create nine out of ten jobs in the economy (Corugedo & Ruiz, 2014). These authors argue that although well-functioning services are key for growth, they are not yet delivering their full potential. This indicates that the service sector's contribution to the overall economy could be even higher than its expected.

In the largest middle-income countries also known as the BRICS group (Brazil, Russia, India, China, and South Africa), the contribution of the service sector is shown in Table 2.2. In 2017, the service sector accounted for half to two-thirds of each country's economy. For all BRICS economies, industry was the second-largest sector, followed by agriculture.

When a comparison of the export of services between 2012 and 2017 on such goods-related services, transportation, travel, and 'other services' in the various regions of the world are made, their growth as shown in Table 2.3 has been significant. Observing such an increasing trend in the contribution of service sector in the economy is therefore an appropriate strategy to further understand how to enhance and maintain the role of service strength through service leadership training. In the chapters to follow, there will be discussions on how service leadership training can be used to achieve the goals of the service sector.

The data show that in addition to the higher growth rate of service industries in production, employment, consumption, and trade, the proportion of services in intermediate inputs for other industries' production has gone up. This is

Table 2.2 Value added (% of GDP) of the various sectors in BRICS in 2017

| Country | Services | Industry | Agriculture |
| --- | --- | --- | --- |
| Brazil | 63.1 | 18.5 | 4.6 |
| Russian Federation | 56.2 | 30.0 | 4.0 |
| India | 48.7 | 26.3 | 15.5 |
| China | 51.6 | 40.5 | 7.9 |
| South Africa | 61.5 | 25.9 | 2.3 |

Source: World Development Indicators (NV.SRV.TOTL.ZS; NV.IND.TOTL.ZS; NV.AGR.TOTL.ZS). Retrieved on May 24, 2019.

Table 2.3 Trade in services by category and by group of economies

Developing economies

| Service category | Exports | |
|---|---|---|
| | Value (billions of US$) | |
| | 2012 | 2017 |
| Total services | 1,328 | 1,579 |
| Goods-related services | 48 | 52 |
| Transport | 305 | 317 |
| Travel | 438 | 521 |
| Other services | 538 | 689[b] |

Developing economies: Africa

| Service category | Exports | |
|---|---|---|
| | Value (billions of US$) | |
| | 2012 | 2017 |
| Total services | 104 | 109 |
| Goods-related services | 2 | 2 |
| Transport | 28 | 28 |
| Travel | 44 | 44 |
| Other services | 29 | 34 |

Developing economies: Americas

| Service category | Exports | |
|---|---|---|
| | Value (billions of US$) | |
| | 2012 | 2017 |
| Total services | 164 | 185 |
| Goods-related services | 4 | 4 |
| Transport | 30 | 29 |
| Travel | 64 | 88 |
| Other services | 66 | 64 |

Developing economies: Asia and Oceania

| Service category | Exports | |
|---|---|---|
| | Value (billions of US$) | |
| | 2012 | 2017 |
| Total services | 1,060 | 1,285 |
| Goods-related services | 42 | 46 |
| Transport | 246 | 259 |
| Travel | 329 | 389 |
| Other services | 442 | 590[b] |

Developing economies: Transition economies

| Service category | Exports | |
|---|---|---|
| | Value (billions of US$) | |
| | 2012 | 2017 |
| Total services | 125 | 122 |
| Goods-related services | 9 | 7 |
| Transport | 42 | 42 |
| Travel | 29 | 29 |
| Other services | 45 | 45 |

Developed economies

| Service category | Exports | |
|---|---|---|
| | Value (billions of US$) | |
| | 2012 | 2017 |
| Total services | 3,092 | 3,650 |
| Goods-related services | 97 | 124 |
| Transport | 572 | 573 |
| Travel | 645 | 760 |
| Other services | 1,778 | 2,193 |

[b] break in the series. Find the data on UNCTADstat

*Source*: United Nations, Statistical Office of the European Union, International Monetary Fund, Organisation for Economic Co-operation and Development, UNCTAD, World Tourism Organization, World Trade Organization (2012). *Manual on Statistics of International Trade in Services 2010*. ST/ESA/M.86/Rev. 1. United Nations publication, Sales No. E.10.XVII.14, Geneva. https://stats.unctad.org/handbook/Services/ByCategory.html Retrieved on July 1, 2019

reported under 'other services' in the table and is consistent for both developed and developing economies. It has been argued that as income rises, demand for manufactures increases at diminishing rates, whereas demand for services rises rapidly (Kniivilä, 2008).

Trade in services for those nations that have been isolated from the world's market of goods may provide an opportunity to connect with the world economy. In turn, this can contribute to a nation's GDP and generate foreign exchange that is crucially needed in the economic development of a country. Sub-Saharan nations of Africa may consider what India has done by capitalizing in the export of IT services to increase employment and generate income. Other labor-intensive services such as tourism have also become a strategy for many developing countries. Other important elements of service imports for developing countries relate to the improvement of services in the local markets by expatriates who bring with them best international practices, better skills, technologies, and capital investments.

Finally, given the multifaceted contribution of services to the national economy and trade, it is important to design and implement a services-driven development strategy, one that has a coherent and comprehensive policy framework that ensures links with other policy areas and overall national development objectives. From a service leadership perspective, this means creating an 'ecosystem' that supports and facilitates policies. Undoubtedly, nations would have to face structural challenges in the process of strengthening the potential of services to foster employment, productivity, and innovation. Such effort will need to build on sound macroeconomic fundamentals and involve a combination of changes in policies.

## 2.3  Structural changes in how an economy moves

Structural transformation in economic terms means reallocation of economic activity across the broad sectors of agriculture, manufacturing, and services. The previous section discussed how overtime, economies have moved from an agrarian society to an industrial one and now to a service-driven economy. The theoretical discussion about structural change began with Lewis's model of structural transformation. Lewis (1955) argued that there is a need for countries to transform their economies, away from agriculture, which has low labor productivity toward industrial activities with high labor productivity.

In his arguments, Lewis pointed out that agriculture generally underemploys the labor force and the marginal productivity of labor is virtually zero. Hence, transferring labor out of agriculture does not reduce productivity in the economy. Labor that is released from the sector would be employed in the more productive, urban, industrial sector. With such movement of labor into the industrial sector, firms begin the process of profit accumulation. When capital accumulates, further economic development takes place, and this creates sustainable economic growth for the economy. The model while highly influential had its critics too.

Earlier than Lewis, Fisher (1939) proposed the idea that economic progress leads to the emergence of a large service sector, and this follows the development of the primary and secondary sector. Later, Clark (1940) also made a similar argument, and the Fisher-Clark model posited that structural change must happen for economic progress to occur in capitalist economies. It is important to recognize that the Fisher-Clark model is still relevant in explaining the importance of a large sector like service as an indicator of economic development and growth. This model argues that there are two essential reasons why a service sector will emerge beyond agriculture and industrialization. First, services such as finance, leisure, and tourism have high income elasticity of demand. Hence, as income rises, demand for services increases and labor will be attracted to this sector. In Hong Kong, for example, service sector employment has reached a record level of 92.9% as mentioned in the preface of Shek and Chung's book (Shek & Chung, 2015, p. xix). The shift of labor from the manufacturing sector to services in Hong Kong as well as other industrialized countries has been phenomenal. Second, in comparison to the manufacturing sector, labor productivity in the service sector is lower as it is harder to apply new technology to many services. The implication of this is that over time, prices of services relative to the primary and secondary sectors will rise as suggested by Baumol (1967, 2001).

In addition to the classic works of Lewis and Fisher-Clark, an attempt was made by Fuchs (1968) to develop a general theory of economic development by looking at the service sector at its core. The analysis provided a comprehensive evidence for the Baumol hypothesis and found that service sector growth is mainly determined by the intermediate demand for services.

As noted from the previous discussion, the impact and contribution of the service sector to the economy is significant. What should be addressed now is how to continue the growth of this sector and what skills are needed to accomplish the structural changes in the economies to move forward.

Investing in human capital is the priority to make the most of this evolving economic opportunity in services. Three types of skills are increasingly important in labor markets: Advanced cognitive skills such as complex problem-solving, socio-behavioral skills such as teamwork, and skill combinations that are predictive of adaptability such as reasoning and self-efficacy. Building these skills requires strong human capital foundations and lifelong learning. All these skills are the fundamental pieces that are emphasized in service leadership.

Cognitive skills are the abilities needed to carry out any task from the simplest to the most complex. These include the ability to learn, process and apply knowledge, analyze, reason, evaluate, and decide. Such skills could be learned and practiced as one moves through the various stages of life. In today's world, one faces challenges that require higher levels of cognitive skill, such as advanced literacy and writing, quantitative and statistical reasoning, critical thinking, and processing of complex information. In addition to these hard skills, it is just as important to pay attention to socio-behavioral skills, the so-called soft skills that are critical to the service industry. These are essential to service leadership that will require more elaboration later. These include advanced communication and negotiation, empathy, lifelong learning, and adaptability.

Mankind has consistently wondered about where its talent for innovation might lead. In the 19th century, Karl Marx worried that

> The machine, which is the starting-point of the industrial revolution, replaces the worker, who handles a single tool, by a mechanism operating with a number of similar tools and set in motion by a single motive power, whatever the form of that power.
>
> (p. 497)

He argued that 'machinery does not just act as a superior competitor to the worker, always on the point of making him superfluous. It is the most powerful weapon for suppressing strikes.' In 1930, John Maynard Keynes warned that

> We are being afflicted with a new disease of which some readers may not yet have heard the name, but of which they will hear a great deal in the years to come – namely, technological unemployment. This means unemployment due to our discovery of means of economising the use of labour outrunning the pace at which we can find new uses for labour.
>
> (Keynes, 1930, p. 3)

From such pessimistic view of technology, one currently finds optimism that technology and innovation have transformed living standards. Life expectancy has gone up; basic health care and education are widespread; and most people have seen their incomes rise.

With such changes in technology and innovation, the role that service leaders can provide becomes even more critical. When traditional companies compared with those who use digital platforms, business organizations can grow and scale up faster and at a lower cost. Doing this requires leadership that understands how to manage resources and have a long-term vision. As pointed out in the World Development Report 2019, a traditional company such as the Swedish company IKEA, which was founded in 1943, waited almost 30 years before it began expanding within Europe. It took IKEA more than seven decades to achieve global annual sales revenue of US$42 billion. On the other hand, the Chinese conglomerate Alibaba, using digital technology, was able to reach one million users in only two years and accumulate more than nine million online merchants and annual sales of $700 billion in just 15 years (World Bank, 2019). The trend in digital technology and how it can be used in a variety of settings is on the rise in all corners of the world. Globally, however, integrated virtual marketplaces are posing new policy challenges in the fields of privacy, competition, and taxation (World Bank, 2019, p. 6). These services, no matter where they take place, need ethical leaders who can direct and protect the privacy of individuals as they compete in a global environment.

## 2.4 The relationship of service economy to leadership

Having discussed how the world economy is in a transitional stage, the strategy and policy implications of this transition must be looked upon carefully. Given that services have forward and backward linkages to the agricultural and industrial sectors, service leaders have a responsibility to prepare frontline service providers with the skills needed to successfully implement their strategic goals.

The importance of the services sector is undisputed, but at the same time the challenge of managing intangible aspects and assets like interactions, experiences, and human resources is immense (Popli & Rizvi, 2015). Hence, the relevance of understanding employee behavior especially in terms of their service orientation seems critical to service performance. It must be recognized that the attitudes and behaviors exhibited by employees have a direct bearing on their job performance including service orientation, which are influenced by leadership styles prevalent in the organization.

With a global reach, the service sector has to be more flexible, adaptable, and strategic in its operation. The concept of the *3Cs* discussed in Chapter 1 certainly applies. Since services are heterogenous in nature, an organization's leadership must understand what the organization's overall service mindset is and is practiced by members of the organization. The leaders have a responsibility to inculcate these concepts among employees. Just as industrialization has contributed to the economy through innovation, services also have to be innovative and disruptive in nature for its continued contributions to the economy.

As mentioned earlier, service sector has forward and backward linkages to other businesses that contribute to the viability of the service sector. Examples of collaborators in the service sector include infrastructure services such as energy, telecommunications, and transportation; financial services that facilitate transactions and provide access to finance for investment; health and education services that contribute to a healthy, well-trained workforce; and legal and accountancy services that are part of the institutional framework required to underpin a healthy market economy. These services play a key role in the growth and productivity of any large and healthy economy.

Leadership, especially the service leadership standards and behaviors practiced in an organization, will have an impact on the company's sustainability and on the service sector as a whole. Broader than that, there is a connection between service leadership standards and behaviors with each organization's contribution to the broader economy.

## Key points to remember

Globalization has been a process of economic development over the centuries.

- From Adam Smith until now, the world has gone through many stages of globalization and development. From agrarian societies, to industrial revolution, and now to the service and information age, the world community has adapted to these transitions with the necessary skills. Some nations have been in the forefront of the change, and others have either been following the leaders or have stagnated in the process.
- The world is characterized by virtual communication, capital and labor movement, the flows of information at a pace that has not been seen before, and institutional deregulation, which have defined globalization.
- Theoretical discussions of this chapter have highlighted how different economies have transitioned from agrarian to manufacturing, and now, to services.
- The 21st century began with a revolution in technological development that has created a new set of challenges for the global economy. With technological changes, resources have shifted from certain sectors of the economy to services that connect the world in finance, education, health, leisure, travel, energy, transportation, and many others. These services require a new set of skills and even a mindset that is different from the command-and-control mindset practiced across the manufacturing sectors. This chapter elaborated on how service leadership training is needed in this new era and the tools needed to sustain the growth of the service sector.

## Case study

### Innovative sustainability

Being distinctive is a dynamic concept. Unless you are a monopoly, your competitors will catch up sooner or later if you remain stagnant. A business has to stay ahead of the game and continue to innovate to sustain its edge. Chung and Ip (2009) have created a term for this need. They call it 'innovative sustainability.' To understand this concept, a few examples from Chung's experience with DHL's competitive positioning will help elucidate the point. There were many years when DHL was the only cross-border international courier company in Asia. It focused on delivery and pickup services in the business districts in Hong Kong. For instance, it focused in Central and South Kowloon in Hong Kong. It did draw up a plan to cover all the outlying islands but did not implement it. When FedEx entered the market, within a week, DHL extended its services to the outlying islands. DHL knew it had to expand or suffer the consequences from the competition.

Innovative sustainability means anticipating the competitors' strengths and weaknesses and keep launching innovations that competitors cannot match. Being new to Hong Kong, FedEx had limited human resources and could not match DHL's new offer to respond immediately to customer calls. DHL started taking inbound calls 24 hours a day, 7 days a week and committed itself to immediately dispatching couriers to pick up any document from the customer. And if the customer's premises lay within predefined areas, the courier would arrive within three minutes of the inbound call.

There are some service areas with a perceived high cost of entry. New competitors will not even try to match the competition's standard in those areas. DHL started to cover remote cities that had very limited deliveries and pickups – places like Bali and Kathmandu. But one has to go to these places because some time or another, a customer's CEO will spend a few days there (for a conference, vacation, or on his or her way up Mount Everest). And the actual costs of operating in those places are often much lower than expected. Sometimes the firm could depend on only a couple, working from home, doing the delivery to customers. As for pickups, the customer could be asked to leave the document with the hotel front desk.

How does one develop distinctive propositions for different customer segments? Without innovative ideas on helping the customer, the firm will bear the consequence of failing.

*Source*: Adapted from Chung, P. and Ip, S. (2018). *Pillars of a service hub*. New York: Lexingford Publisher.

### Questions related to the case

1   What is meant by innovative sustainability?
2   How do you develop distinctive propositions for different customer segments?
3   What element of service leadership applies to this case?

## End of chapter questions

1 What theoretical concept best explains globalization?
2 What are the bases for transition of an economy from one sector to another?
3 Why was there an argument that marginal productivity of labor was lower in the service sector?
4 What countries in the world are moving faster in adopting services than manufacturing?
5 Explain why some nations have not been able to adopt the service model.
6 How can service leadership help in the sustainability of the service sector?

## References

Alacevich, M., & Soci, A. (2018). Inequality and globalization. In *A short history* (pp. 79–116). Washington, DC: Brookings Institution Press.

Baines, T., Lightfoot, H., & Smart, P. (2011). Servitization within manufacturing: Exploring the provision of advanced services and their impact on vertical integration. *Journal of Manufacturing Technology Management, 22*(7), 947–954.

Baumol, W. (1967). Macroeconomics of unbalanced growth: The anatomy of urban crisis. *The American Economic Review, 57*(3), 415–426.

Baumol, W. (2001). Paradox of the services: Exploding costs, persistent demand. In T. Ten Raa & R. Schettkat (Eds.), *The growth of service industries: The paradox of exploding costs and persistent demand* (pp. 3–28). Cheltenham: Edward Elgar.

Beynon, J., & Dunkerley, D. (Eds.). (2000). *Globalization: The reader*. London: Sage.

Bureau of Labor Statistics. (2016). Employment, hours, and earnings from current employment. *Statistics survey (National)*. Retrieved March 03, 2016, from http://data.bls.gov/cgibin/surveymost?ce

Central Intelligence Agency. (2017). *World fact book*. Washington, DC: CIA Publication. Retrieved June 11, 2019, from www.cia.gov/library/publications/resources/the-world-factbook/

Chung, P., & Ip, S. (2009). *The 5 dynamics of entrepreneurship*. Singapore: Cengage Learning Asia Pte Ltd.

Chung, P., & Ip, S. (2018). *Pillars of a service hub*. New York: Lexingford Publisher.

Clark, C. (1940). *The conditions of economic progress*. London: Palgrave Macmillan (Revised and reprinted in 1951).

Collins, M. (2015). The pros and cons of globalization. *Forbes*. Retrieved June 21, 2019, from www.forbes.com/sites/mikecollins/2015/05/06/the-pros-and-cons-of-globalization/#7bedcd10ccce

Corugedo, E., & Ruiz, E. (2014). *The EU services directive: Gains from further liberalization*. Washington, DC: IMF.

Dadush, U., & Shaw, W. (2012). *Globalization, labor markets and inequality*. Carnegie Endowment for International Peace. Retrieved June 29, 2019, from https://carnegieendowment.org/2012/02/02/globalization-labor-markets-and-inequality-pub-47028

Economy Watch Content. (2008). *Hong Kong economic structure.* Retrieved April 7, 2016, from www.economywatch.com/world_economy/hong-kong/structure-of-economy.html

Fisher, A. (1939). Production, primary, secondary and tertiary. *The Economic Record, 15*(1), 24–38.

Flaaen, A., Ghani, E., & Mishra, S. (2013). *How to avoid middle-income traps? Evidence from Malaysia* (World Bank Policy Research Paper No. 6427). Washington, DC: World Bank.

Fuchs, V. (1968). *The service economy.* New York, NY and London: Colombia University Press.

Goldstein, J., Rivers, D., & Tomz, M. (2007). Institutions in international relations: Understanding the effects of the GATT and the WTO on world trade. *International Organization, 61*(1), 37–67.

Hill, C. W. (2009). *International business.* New York, NY: McGraw-Hill.

Hillman, A. (2008). Globalization of social justice. *The Singapore Economic Review, 53*(2), 173–189.

Hirschman, A. (1959). *The strategy of economic development.* New Haven: Yale University Press.

Hoshmand, A. (2018). Service leadership at Hong Kong Baptist University: A new concept in general education. *International Journal of Disability and Human Development, 17*(1), 45–52.

Irwin, D. (2007, April 9). GATT turns 60! *Wall Street Journal.* Retrieved June 21, 2019, from www.wsj.com/articles/SB117607482355263550

Jorgenson, A., & Givens, J. (2013). Economic globalization and environmental concern: A multilevel analysis of individuals within 37 nations. *Environment and Behavior, 46*(7), 848–887.

Kaldor, N. (1957). A model of economic growth. *The Economic Journal, 67*(268), 591–624.

Keynes, J. (1930 [1963]). Economic possibilities for our grandchildren. In *Essays in persuasion* (pp. 358–373). New York, NY: W.W. Norton & Co.

Kiniivilä, M. (2008). Industrial development and economic growth: Implications for poverty reduction and income inequality. In D. O'Connor & F. Kjollerstrom (Eds.), *Industrial development in the 21st century* (pp. 295–332). New York, NY: ZED Books.

Lewis, A. (1955). *The theory of economic growth.* Homewood, IL: Richard D. Irwin.

Mills, M. (2009). Globalization and inequality. *European Sociological Review, 25*(1), 1–8.

Mong, A. (2018). *A better world is possible: An exploration of Western and Eastern utopian visions.* Cambridge: James Clarke & Co Ltd.

Moudoukoutas, P. (2011, September 10). The good, the bad, and the ugly side of globalization. *Forbes.*

Nurkse, R. (1952). Some international aspects of the problem of economic development. *The American Economic Review, 42*(2), 571–583.

OECD. (2005). *The service economy.* Annual report is prepared by the Public Affairs Division, Public Affairs and Communications Directorate of OECD, Paris, France.

Popli, S., & Rizvi, I. (2015). Exploring the relationship between service orientation, employee engagement and perceived leadership style: A study of managers in the private service sector organizations in India. *Journal of Services Marketing, 29*(1), 59–70.

Prakash, L., & Mishra, S. (2014). Not your father's service sector. *Finance and Development, 51*(2), 51–54.

Ricardo, D. (1817). *On the principles of political economy and taxation*. London: John Murray Publisher.

Robertson, R. (1992). *Globalization*. London: Sage.

Romer, C. (2012, February 4). Do manufacturers need special treatment? *New York Times*.

Schirato, T., & Webb, J. (2003). *Understanding globalization*. London: Sage.

Scott, R. (2017). *Growth in U.S.-China trade deficit between 2001–2015 cost 3.4 million jobs*. Washington, DC: Economic Policy Institute.

Shek, D., & Chung, P. (2015). *Promoting service leadership qualities in university students: The case of Hong Kong*. Singapore: Springer.

Smith, A. (1776). *An inquiry into the nature and causes of the wealth of nations*. London: William Strahan and Thomas Cadell Publishers.

UNCTAD. (2018). *World investment report, 2018*. United Nations Conference on Trade and Development. Retrieved June 26, 2019, from https://unctad.org/en/PublicationsLibrary/wir2018_overview_en.pdf

World Bank. (2019). *World development report 2019: The changing nature of work*. Washington, DC: The World Bank.

World Bank Presentation. (2012, July). *Role of services in economic development*. Geneva: World Bank.

World Trade Organization. (1994). *WTO legal texts; General Agreement on Tariffs and Trade 1994*. Retrieved June 21, 2019, from www.wto.org/english/docs_e/legal_e/legal_e.htm

World Trade Organization. (2019). *Annual report 2019*. Retrieved June 24, 2019, from www.wto.org/english/news_e/news19_e/anrp_04jun19_e.htm

# Leadership reorganized

## 3.1 Systematic change in the workplace

The work environment today is tremendously different from what it was just decades ago. The changes have been mostly in the form of organizational structure, cultural change, gender diversity, as well as the very nature of work itself. Some organizations, such as Apple Computer, Microsoft, Google, and others, have introduced new concepts in the work environment. Those changes have not been simply for the sake of change to be different, but rather substantial in nature. These organizations have recognized the benefits of restructuring the work environment to increase productivity and creating environments for collaboration, cost management, innovations and sharing, and better employee experience. The role of leadership in this context is as critical as the changes that have come into play. Each of these will be discussed to establish the connection between the changes and the role that leaders play in this environment (service habitat), using the terminology of service leadership.

### Efficiency and increased productivity

There is no doubt that the basis for efficiency and productivity is tied with the technological developments toward the end of the 20th century. Changing the habitat to take advantage of technology in providing a service has optimized time management. Such optimization has given the service provider an ability to engage more fully in tasks that lead to innovation and creativity. The level of expectation of clients and coworkers has also been affected as a result of technology in the workplace. Keeping everyone constantly connected has implications for how an employee values such connectivity. The role of a service leader is to show care by not overburdening the employee.

### Increased collaboration

Another aspect of the role of technology in the workplace is how communication takes place with members of the habitat. An important aspect of service leadership is the ability to communicate effectively with employees and clients, now that technology has made it possible for us to communicate with leaders and coworkers anytime and anywhere. This enables us to affect the time and space of service operations. One of the elements of service leadership has to do with moving the decision making to the lowest level of the organization. With this dramatic increase in communication and collaboration comes a heightened level of flexibility, allowing coworkers to facilitate continued partnership no matter where each individual may be. Such facilitation and working as a team contribute significantly to the service provided. This is particularly important in the provision of international trade services.

### Improved cost management

Every business, whether producing physical products or service, aims at achieving profitability. A significant impact of technological developments in the workplace has been how productivity in finance is achieved. The fiscal health of a business is directly tied with the innovative technological equipment and software entering the work environment. The ability of a service provider – be it trade, finance, health care, leisure, etc. – to reach its clients on time and respond to their service needs means cost reduction and increased profitability. The care and ethics involved in delivering such services contribute significantly to cost reductions and improved profitability. Research has shown that companies that invested heavily in the employee experience earned more than four times the average profit and twice the average revenue compared with those that did not (Morgan, 2019).

### A better employee experience

Undoubtedly, a happy employee will deliver a more positive service to clients. In many ways, technology has facilitated in the work environment or habitat of an organization, and its contribution to the employee's overall experience has been significant. It is important for us to recognize how technology shapes an organization's culture and how it affects its employees. Some forward-looking service organizations are investing in employee experience solutions as they realize how effective those will be in delivering the services needed (Raelin, 2008).

In addition to the technology changes in the service habitat, the cultural changes that have come to the work environment of the 21st century must be recognized.

As was noted in the previous paragraphs, the work environment of the 21st century has been partly shaped by the changes in technological developments. They are parallel to the changes in the organizational dynamics that have contributed to the growth of diversity in the workplace. In the last several decades, organizations have been struggling to accommodate cultural diversity in the work environment. Most often, a management approach has been to expect employees who come from a different cultural background to adapt to the culture of the majority in the organization (Amaram, 2007) without recognizing many issues that tie directly to cultural diversity.

Issues of social justice, moral, ethical, and social responsibility of organizations to their employees have given rise to the search for a new paradigm that better addresses these concerns than simply expecting employees to accept assimilation as a concept of diversity. In this environment of globalization, service organizations in particular must pay attention to the legal obligation they have in protecting the civil rights of individuals working in their firms. If not, they risk facing legal consequences for their actions. Furthermore, as organizations have sought to be competitive in the global market, cultural diversity has helped set them apart from those who still insist that assimilation to the cultural environment of the majority in the organization is an effective strategy.

Globalization, with its multicultural implications, has become an indispensable factor in strategic competitiveness. IBM, Exxon, Coca-Cola, and Dow Chemical, for example, derive at least half of their revenues from other countries. For the first time since World War I, immigrants make up the largest share of the recent growth in the population and the labor force (Amaram, 2007).

## 3.2 Visions of leadership

Studies on leadership have a long history. One of the earliest studies on leadership, Galton's *Hereditary Genius* (1962) emphasized a basic concept that informed popular ideas about leadership (Zaccaro, 2007). Galton believed that leadership is a unique quality of extraordinary individuals who are born with exceptional abilities and such traits were immutable and cannot be developed. This concept of trait was further developed by other leadership scholars that will be discussed in this section.

The most common conceptualizations of leadership include four main elements. Leadership is a process that entails influence, which occurs within a group setting or context, and that involves achieving goals that reflect a common vision (Shaw, 2007; Hunt, 2004; Northouse, 2004).

Leadership theories have certain characteristics that are common to all. Each of these theories emphasizes what constitutes leadership and how leaders should behave to move their organization forward. The intention is not to say that these characteristics are not important or relevant. However, it is in how and where these leadership theories are more effective. Each theory will not be looked upon in detail but will provide a synopsis for comparison. Table 3.1 shows different leadership models referred to over the past few centuries and how they have been applied in various sectors, including the service sector.

Looking at each of these theories, one begins to see that the individual leaders are given more attention in the leadership process than looking at leadership as a collective responsibility of the group or organization. The philosophy supporting

Table 3.1 Theories of leadership

| | |
|---|---|
| Great man theories | One of the earliest theories of leadership where it is argued that leaders are exceptional people, born with innate qualities, who are destined to lead. The use of the term 'man' in this theory was intentional because until the latter part of the 20th century, leadership was thought of as a concept that is primarily male, military, and Western. In this leadership style, certain qualities like charm, persuasiveness, commanding personality, a high degree of intuition, judgment, courage, intelligence, aggressiveness, and action-orientation contribute to being recognized as a leader. Individuals such as Mahatma Gandhi, Abraham Lincoln, Nelson Mandela, and others fall in this category. It is argued that those men would have become leaders in any case because they were inherently endowed with leadership traits and skills.<br><br>A weakness of this theory, apart from the improbability of inherent traits, is the belief that some people become great and successful leaders independent of their environmental situations. |
| Trait theory of leadership | This theory is a modification of the great man theory, which argues that leadership qualities or traits can be acquired. They need not always be inborn. The theory states that there are certain identifiable qualities or characteristics that are unique to leaders and those good leaders possess such qualities to some extent. Leadership qualities may be inborn, or they may be acquired through training and practice. Two specific traits – intelligence and personality – are the driving force in this type of leadership. It is argued that good leaders have the intelligence to recognize the context and content of their position in order to grasp the dynamics of environmental variables, both internal and external. At the same time, they are aware of how their actions affect their activities and have a good perspective of the present and future dimensions of their organization.<br><br>The personality dimension includes qualities such as emotional integrity, stability and maturity, self-confidence, decisiveness, strong drive, optimism, achievement orientation, purposefulness, discipline, and skill in getting along with others.<br><br>The criticism of this theory is based on various studies that show that the trait theory cannot hold good for all sets of circumstances. There is a lack of uniformity among the researchers as to what traits should be included in this theory. The theory also fails to account for the influence of other factors on leadership.<br><br>No evidence has been given in the literature about the degree of the various traits because people have various traits with different degrees.<br><br>The turning point was Stogdill's (1948) survey of 25 years of research, in which he concluded, 'A person does not become a leader by virtue of the possession of some combination of traits.' |
| Behavioral theories | Behavioral theories of leadership focus on the study of specific behaviors of a leader. Behavioral theorists argue that a leader's behavior is the best predictor of his or her leadership influences and hence is the best determinant of his or her leadership success. Studies that were conducted in Ohio State University (1943), and University Michigan (1950s) both identified specific elements of behavior that defined this leadership style. |

*(Continued)*

Table 3.1  (*Continued*)

| | |
|---|---|
| | These studies showed that there were two groups of behaviors that were strongly correlated. These were defined as people-oriented behavioral leaders and task-oriented leaders. |
| | The people-oriented leaders focused their attention on behaviors that ensured inner needs of the employees by encouraging, observing, listening, and mentoring and coaching them. |
| | On the other hand, the task-oriented leaders focus their behaviors on the organizational structure and the operating procedures so that they can keep control of the activities of the organization. These leaders deem activities such as initiating, organizing, clarifying, and information gathering as essential to their leadership. |
| Situational leadership | This approach sees leadership as specific to the situation in which it is being exercised. Depending on the situation, a leader may use an autocratic approach, while others may need a more participative approach. This theory proposes that there may be differences in required leadership styles at different levels in the same organization. |
| | This type of leadership is premised on the notion that effective leadership requires a rational understanding of the situation and an appropriate response to it. This implies 'the one best way to lead.' This theory evolved from a task-oriented versus people-oriented leadership continuum (Conger, 2011; Lorsch, 2010; Bass, 2008). The continuum represented the extent that the leaders focus on the required tasks or on their relations with their followers. |
| Contingency or situational theory leadership | This theory of leadership shifted the emphasis away from 'the one best way to lead' to a context-sensitive leadership. This is a refinement of the situational viewpoint and focuses on identifying the situational variables such as people, task, organization, and other environmental variables that best predict the most appropriate or effective leadership style to fit the particular circumstance. |
| | It has to be kept in mind that the earlier theories of leadership emphasized how a leader should lead. In the context of situational leadership, the relationship of the leader with the followers and an interdependency of the roles is important. Here, the solo leader becomes a team leader, in which the capacity of the leader to follow and be a servant is essential. |
| | Robert Greenleaf (1970) introduced the concept of servant leadership. His basic premise was that the leader's duty is to serve his or her followers. This shift from a desire to lead to a desire to serve is rooted in the conscious choice that brings one to aspire to lead. There is some similarity between the concept of servant leader and service leadership in that both emphasize ensuring that the needs of those who serve an organization receive the highest priority. In essence, those who are served by leaders grow as individuals, become healthier, wiser, freer, more autonomous, and more likely themselves to become service leaders. |
| | Servant-leadership, similar to service leadership, encourages collaboration, trust, foresight, listening, and the ethical use of power and empowerment. A servant leader leads by setting an example for others to follow and place emphasis on strong interpersonal relationships (Liden, Wayne, Zhao, & Henderson, 2008). |

| Transactional theory of leadership | Transactional leadership is based on the notion of transaction or exchange. In this case, there is something of value that the leader possesses or controls that the follower wants in return for his or her services. Most often, this style of leadership is found in contracting scenarios where both leader and the led understand and agree about which tasks are important. A distinction that can be made in this style of leadership and those mentioned earlier is that a transactional leader is driven by making sure everything in the organization moves smoothly. |
|---|---|
| | In this leadership style, often referred to as management style, leaders guide or motivate employees to achieve the goals of the organization by clarifying roles and tasks. They are not concerned about how to strategically guide his or her organization to a leadership position in the market. |
| | As stated, this approach emphasizes the importance of the relationship between leader and followers, focusing on the mutual benefits derived from a form of 'contract' through which the leader delivers incentives such as rewards or recognition in return for the commitment or loyalty of the followers. |
| | James MacGregor Burns (1978, p. 4) argued that transactional leadership fails to raise the aspirations of subordinates. He suggested that the transactional relationship can be seen as a bargaining process and continued by maintaining the transaction process. |
| | The characteristics that define a transactional leader can be summed as a leader who revels in efficiency, tends to be inflexible, opposes change, emphasizes short-term goals, and favors structured policies and procedures. |
| Transformational theory | This theory was first put forward by Burns (1978), who posited that 'transforming leadership is a relationship of mutual stimulation and elevation that converts followers into leaders and may convert leaders into moral agents.' He suggested that transformational leaders know how to shape, alter, and elevate the motives, values, and goals of the followers to achieve the goals of his or her organization. |
| | Transformational leaders create a shared vision and a strong identification with team members that is based on more than just rewarding completion of project activities (Kouzes & Posner, 2003; Keegan & Den Hartog, 2004; Bass, 1985). |
| | Bass (1985, p. 169) elaborated further on the concept of transformational leadership by stating that personality differences of leaders would affect exhibiting transactional and transformational leadership behavior. |
| | As Howell and Avolio (1993) stated, 'Leaders described as transformational concentrate their efforts on longer term goals; place value and emphasis on developing a vision and inspiring followers to pursue the vision; change or align systems to accommodate their vision rather than work within existing systems; and coach followers to take on greater responsibility for their own development, as well as the development of others' (pp. 891–2). |
| | It is apparent from the literature that this style of leadership creates and fosters an environment that builds trust and confidence and encourages individual development along with a shared vision |

*(Continued)*

Table 3.1  (*Continued*)

for the organization (Bass, 1985, 2008). It was pointed out by Jin (2010) that transformational leadership integrates the elements of empathy, compassion, sensitivity, relationship-building, and innovation. Some have argued that the transactional/transformational school of thought is now acknowledged as a dominant approach in the study of leadership (Dulewicz & Higgs, 2005; Vera & Crossan, 2004).

In sum, transformational leaders are models of integrity who set clear goals, have high expectations, encourage others, provide support and recognition, stir the emotion of people, and get people to see beyond their self-interest.

service leadership is in line with transformational theory, as the coming chapters will show.

Lately, a school of thought gaining increased recognition is that of 'distributed or dispersed' leadership (Badaracco, 2001; Raelin, 2003, 2009, 2016, 2019). What Raelin has suggested is to move away from the earlier theories of leadership to 'the new paradigm of leaderful practice,' with the stated intention of casting leadership in a new light to change both thinking and practice. Raelin redefines leadership as a collective practice embedded in communities where there is mutual sharing of the processes required to accomplish leadership (Raelin, 2013). This anti-individualistic stance is in tune with the recent work by a number of influential academics and consultants on the idea of 'dispersed' or 'distributed' leadership (Vanderslice, 1988; Wheatley, 1999; Bennis, 2004).

This leadership style encourages a shift in focus from the attributes and behaviors of individual leaders to a more open and systemic approach to leadership, in which a collective social process emerges through the interactions of multiple actors (Uhl-Bien, 2006). Using this perspective, it is argued that distributed leadership is not something done

by an individual to others, or a set of individual actions through which people contribute to a group or organization . . . but rather it is a group activity that works through and within relationships, rather than individual action.

(Bennett, Wise, Woods, & Harvey, 2003, p. 3)

Furthermore, Bennett et al. identified three elements of distributed leadership that other leadership experts also agree on. They are:

- Leadership is an emerging property of a group or network of interacting individuals.
- There is the openness to the boundaries of leadership.
- It has to be recognized that a variety of expertise is distributed across the many, not just a few.

This approach, with its foundations in sociology, psychology, and politics rather than management science, views leadership as a process that is diffused throughout an organization rather than lying solely with the formally designated 'leader.' The emphasis thus shifts from developing 'leaders' to developing 'leaderful' organizations with a collective responsibility for leadership (Raelin, 2003, 2006; Mortona, Treviñob, & Zapata-Cantúc, 2019).

## 3.3 Tools needed for transformation

### 3.3.1 *Logic*

Depending on the nature of an organization, the ability of a leader to lead depends on how he or she uses logic to understand the culture of the environment. As Rooke and Torbert (2005) point out,

> Most developmental psychologists agree that what differentiates leaders is not so much their philosophy of leadership, their personality, or their style of management. Rather, it's their internal 'action logic' – how they interpret their surroundings and react when their power or safety is challenged.

Based on the research by Rooke and Torbert (2005) and those of others such as Cook-Greuter (2002), the following seven 'action logics' define the style that leaders apply to transform their organizations. These are the opportunist, diplomat, expert, achiever, individualist, strategist, and alchemist leaders. Briefly, each of these styles of leadership will be discussed and what research shows about their respective successes or failures will be highlighted.

### The opportunist style

As the title indicates, leaders in this category focus on those opportunities that accomplish their goals and see the world and people around them to be exploited for achieving their goals. These individuals are manipulative, untrustworthy, and egocentric. Research shows that this style of leadership is least productive in organizations.

### The diplomat style

Similar to the opportunist style, the diplomat style is also least productive as a leadership tool. In this style, the leader tends to please higher-level management by avoiding conflicts. Those who practice this style of leadership are not suited for top leadership positions as they tend to avoid conflict.

### The expert style

Those who follow this style of leadership exercise control of the group by improving their personal and professional life through the acquisition of knowledge in their field. Individuals who use this type of action logic are often associated with such fields as accounting, investment analysis, marketing research, software engineering, and consulting. The difficulty leaders of this style have to contend with has to do with their assumption that they are always right. This creates problems when others see alternative solutions, and these leaders are not too comfortable with collaboration or accepting others' opinion. They also see no value in emotional intelligence.

## The achiever style

This style of 'action logic' recognizes that many of the ambiguities and conflicts of everyday life are due to differences in interpretation and ways of relating. Leaders in this category know that creatively transforming or resolving clashes requires sensitivity to relationships and the ability to influence others in positive ways. Achievers are also capable of reliably leading a team to implement new strategies to achieve short- or long-term objectives of the organization.

## The individualist style

An important characteristic of individuals who follow this type of leaderships is their recognition that neither their own individualist 'action logic' nor any of the other action logics are 'natural,' having recognized that all are constructions of oneself and the world. These individuals are able to communicate effectively with those who may have action logic that is different from theirs. Individualists are aware that there may be a possible conflict between their principles and their actions, or between the organization's values, hence creating problems in the implementation of those values.

## The strategist style

Leaders in this category focus their attention on organizational constraints and perceptions, which they believe are discussable and transformable. Strategists sets the stage to create shared visions across different action logics – visions that encourage both personal and organizational transformations. They also recognize that organizational and social change is an iterative developmental process that requires awareness and close leadership attention. What makes strategists different from other action logic is their ability to handle people's instinctive resistance to change. As a result, these leaders are highly effective change agents.

## The alchemist style

Leaders who display this type of 'action logic' are charismatic individuals who have high moral standards and are able to fit easily at all levels of management. Alchemists are capable of motivating their subordinates to achieve the goals of an organization. Their ability to reinvent themselves and multitask and perform excellently at each task sets them apart from the strategists. They focus intensely on the truth. These individuals have the ability to capture a moment in their organizations and turn it to a symbol that has a profound impact on the hearts and minds of the people they lead.

What Rooke and Torbert (2005) found is that those leaders whose 'action logic' is similar to the opportunist, diplomat, or expert perform below average on their corporate or personal tasks. Compared to the achievers, they were significantly less effective in implementing organizational strategies. Furthermore, they found that the individualists, strategists, and alchemists consistently showed effective leadership in implementing organizational strategies.

These transformational leadership strategies capture styles of leadership that predominate management leadership. What is important to remember is that among the tools of leadership, emotional intelligence plays a critical role in the success of these strategies. The next section discusses the importance of emotional intelligence in being a leader.

### 3.3.2 Emotional intelligence

When discussing various leadership styles, it is important to delve into some characteristics that are essential in leadership. Most often, technical skills and knowledge of the leader do appear to be recognized as essential. However, the challenges that a leader faces in leading an organization go beyond the technical skills. The ability of the leader to successfully coach teams, manage stress, deliver feedback, and collaborate with others is just as important as the technical skills needed in their leadership position. These soft skills are referred to as emotional intelligence skills. Leadership literature shows the important role that emotional intelligence plays in everyday life.

Early researchers such as Thorndike (1920) had recognized that the traditional concepts of intelligence did not fully consider what he believed to be important, that is, a person's ability to recognize his or her own and others' intentions and motives and act accordingly. He classified intelligence into three facets, namely, abstract intelligence, mechanical intelligence, and social intelligence. He believed that social intelligence plays a critical role in a person's daily interactions. Service leadership emphasizes *care* as a pillar of service, and hence social intelligence becomes a necessity. Later research by Wechsler (1940), Guilford (1967), Gardner (1983, 1998, 2005), Goleman (1995, 1998a, 1998b, 2001) elaborated on this concept.

In 1990, Salovey and Mayer coined the term 'emotional intelligence' as a subset of social intelligence. They defined emotional intelligence or emotional quotient as 'the ability to engage in sophisticated information processing about one's own and others' emotions and the ability to use this information as a guide to one's thinking and behavior' (Mayer, Salovey, & Carouso, 2008). That is, individuals high in emotional intelligence or emotional quotient pay attention to, use, understand, and manage emotions, and these skills serve adaptive functions that potentially benefit themselves and others (Mayer, DiPaolo, & Salovey, 1990).

Goleman's contribution in the area of emotional intelligence has been significant. From his early work on this topic (1995), and the extension of the concept to the leadership field (1998a), he proposed a four-branch model (2001), which was further classified with 20 emotional competencies. His model includes the following:

- *Self-awareness:* Emotional self-awareness, accurate self-assessment, and self-confidence.
- *Self-management:* Self-control, trustworthiness, conscientiousness, adaptability, achievement drive, and initiative.
- *Social awareness:* Empathy, social orientation, and organizational awareness.

- *Relationship management:* Developing others, influence, communication, conflict management, leadership, change catalyst, building bonds, and teamwork and collaboration.

These competencies are at the center of the service leadership model where it is believed that service leaders have to recognize the importance of these competencies as they lead their organizations forward. The next chapter will discuss the service leadership method and how it ties with the concept of emotional intelligence. Social scientists have made significant contributions to the field of leadership by encouraging leaders and those who wish to pursue leadership roles to recognize the interaction of hard and soft skills as tools that will facilitate effective leadership in an organization. The following section will distinguish between tools and relations.

### 3.3.3 *Tools vs. relations*

A distinction should be made between the tools and relations in leadership. In service leadership, the emphasis is placed on relationships and how effective they are in achieving organizational goals. Building a trust-based relationship with people within and outside the organization and the significant contribution it makes has been supported in the literature. How relationship-building leads to the growth and sustainability of a firm will be discussed in more detail in Chapter 4. Now, your attention should turn to the tools needed to achieve success by a service provider. Effective leadership is a synthesis of proper planning (Marta, Lertize, & Mumford, 2005), intelligence (Hedlund et al., 2003), creativity (Mumford, Connelly, & Gaddis, 2003), critical thinking (Marcy & Mumford, 2010), and wisdom (McKenna & Rooney, 2008). It is in large part a decision about how to marshal and deploy these tools effectively.

### Leadership planning

Most textbooks on leadership will have a chapter on planning, specifically on strategic planning. The intention is not to delve in the planning process but to highlight its effectiveness in creating a shared vision and strategy that can be used to guide the firm in order to be able to identify the favorable prospects and opportunities at hand and avoid any unwanted effects of negative external factors influencing the situation.

The idea behind such planning is to give an organization the tools to achieve certain goals and maintain competitiveness in the industry. The process involved often starts with bringing together a group of people, usually top executives with other management people and sometimes employees, to develop a planning document that will highlight broad organizational goals and other elements as deemed appropriate by the top executives. Whether such planning document is used to implement major goals is often doubtful. So, what is the purpose of such exercise other than some benefit of giving employees the impression that there is a planning document that may guide the organization to achieve its goals? What must be considered in the context of service leadership is the link between planning and doing service leadership. When planning is done solely as an exercise to bring people together and develop the notion of teamwork among the members of an organization, it loses its purpose. In a service organization, the planning process developed by the leadership must incorporate the values that are collectively agreed on by the leadership and its employees and allow each member of the habitat to implement the plan. The reason behind planning is to create a blueprint on how to handle change in the organization when needed. Given that demand for services is dynamic and changes with time, the plan should allow a service firm to control its own direction in this process. This planning document should delegate responsibility to the members of the habitat to make swift decisions when the need arises. It also could serve as a monitoring tool to guide the allocation of resources for achieving future goals of the service firm.

## Leadership intelligence

In discussing leadership intelligence, the emphasis is not on conventional intelligence in its narrow sense, but rather on how intelligence is applied in leadership situations successfully. The notion of successful intelligence is based on how one frames the concept of success given the cultural context. Literature shows that there are two ways of looking at intelligence in leadership: One is academic, and the other is practical intelligence (Neisser, 1979; Hedlund, 2003).

Academic intelligence is the ability to recall and recognize but also to analyze, evaluate, and judge information, whereas practical intelligence is the ability to solve everyday problems by utilizing knowledge gained from experience in order to purposefully adapt to, shape, and select environments. Hence, it involves changing oneself to suit the environment (adaptation), changing the environment to suit oneself (shaping), or finding a new environment within which to work (selection). A service leader should use these skills to

1    Manage oneself.
2    Manage others.
3    Manage tasks (Sternberg, 2003, p. 388).

Other forms of intelligence, such as emotional intelligence and its impact on leadership, are previously discussed in Section 3.3.2.

## Leadership creativity

Creativity is an important quality of leadership. When leaders have this quality, followers refer to them as persons who are inventive and have imagination, vision, originality, and progressiveness in their thinking. These qualities along with practical intelligence inspire others to follow them and achieve the goals of the firm.

Some of the attributes of creative leaders include the ability to redefine problems, take sensible risks, tolerate ambiguity, overcome obstacles in their activities, trust in their ability to complete tasks, and continue to grow intellectually rather than stagnate.

Research has shown that creativity often involves defying conventional wisdom and that it is relatively domain specific. Additionally, creativity is weakly related to academic intelligence, but certainly it is not the same thing as academic intelligence (Sternberg, 2003, p. 393).

A question that is raised often is how do *I* become a creative leader? Having stated some of the attributes of creative leaders earlier, it would be helpful to suggest some steps that may serve as a guide for a service leader.

- High tolerance for ambiguity or uncertainty is essential. To achieve this, set aside time to think about knowledge and contemplate how to use it.
- Have exposure to different experiences. That is why leaders are encouraged to participate in a variety of experiences within the firm.
- Read more and contemplate on the readings.
- Have confidence in your abilities to achieve goals.
- Maintain high levels of energy in your work and personal life.
- Don't be afraid to fail but have the stamina to get back up fast and try again.
- Let your passion for making a change and a difference be visible to those around you.

An effective leader needs creative ability to come up with ideas, academic ability to decide whether they are good ideas, practical ability to make the ideas work and convince others of the value of the ideas, and wisdom to ensure that the ideas are in the service of the common good rather than just the good of the leader or perhaps some clique of family members or followers (Sternberg, 2003, p. 396).

## Leadership critical thinking

Another tool that enhances a service leader's ability to achieve the goals of the firm is critical thinking.

> [This] is the use of those cognitive skills or strategies that increase the probability of a desirable outcome. It is used to describe thinking that is purposeful, reasoned, and goal-directed – the kind of thinking involved in solving problems, formulating inferences, calculating likelihoods, and making decisions. . . . [I]t's the kind of thinking that makes desirable outcomes more likely.
>
> (Halpern, 2014)

In the context of service leadership, an element of being a leader is that critical thinking is encouraged by the leadership at all levels of the organization. It does not mean that only leaders of a service organization should use critical thinking in their decision making. The effectiveness of a service organization is measured by how frontline employees use critical thinking in making decisions that will facilitate customer demands. When decision-making responsibility is pushed to the lowest level of the organization, the employees are empowered to make the right decisions that are driven by *character* and *care*.

## Leadership wisdom

It can be argued that a leader could have all of the previously mentioned attributes and still lack wisdom. In Chapter 1, character was discussed as one of the pillars of service leadership, and wisdom is an important element of character. Lack of wisdom has ramifications in being a service leader.

The concept of wisdom has a long history. The Greek philosophers paid significant attention to the idea of wisdom. The Platonic dialogues offered the first intensive analysis of the concept of wisdom. These dialogues elaborated on three different senses of wisdom: Wisdom as

1  *Sophia* – found in those who seek a contemplative life in search of truth.
2  *Phronesis* – the kind of practical wisdom shown by statesmen, legislators, and chief executive officers in the business world.
3  *Episteme* – in those who understand things from a scientific point of view (Robinson, 1990).

Applying the notion of *phronesis* is more in line with what a service leader seeks. This implies that the wisdom garnered by a service leader is through practical experience as well as epistemic knowledge.

The tools needed for being a service leader has been highlighted in this chapter. The next chapter will discuss the elements of relationship-building in the service ecosystem.

## Key points to remember

- When literature is reviewed, one finds an evolving series of 'schools of thought' from 'Great man' and 'Trait' theories to 'Transformational' leadership (see Table 3.1). While early theories tend to focus on the characteristics and behaviors of successful leaders, later theories begin to consider the role of followers and the contextual nature of leadership. Service leadership falls into the latter group.
- A variety of leadership styles, such as the opportunist, diplomat, expert, achiever, individualist, strategist, and alchemist, are used to engage followers to allow a leader to transform an organization.
- The concept of emotional intelligence and its use in providing service has a significant role.
- Goleman identifies the following to be critical in leadership:
    - Self-awareness: Emotional self-awareness, accurate self-assessment, and self-confidence.
    - Self-management: Self-control, trustworthiness, conscientiousness, adaptability, achievement drive, and initiative.
    - Social awareness: Empathy, social orientation, and organizational awareness.
    - Relationship management: Developing others, influence, communication, conflict management, leadership, change catalyst, building bonds, and teamwork and collaboration.

In discussing the role of a service leader, the following tools are recognized as effective in leading:

- Leadership planning.
- Leadership intelligence.
- Leadership creativity.

- Leadership critical thinking.
- Leadership wisdom.

## Case study

### Decentralize authority and leadership responsibility

An ingredient of a healthy service habitat is distributed leadership under strong governing principles. There has never been a question of highly centralized authority in service businesses. Services are provided on the spot and in real-time in many locations. There are simply too many variables to define a clear-cut process that works in all circumstances. Field commanders need to make many localized decisions.

Key decisions are made every minute by these field leaders, and together they shape the strategy of the company. Top service businesses understand this and incorporate this reality into their service habitat. They decentralize authority and encourage leadership responsibility at the local level.

DHL serves as an example in this case study. Picture one hundred clients, all of whom want their packages picked up or delivered 'right away'. Courier companies using predetermined routes (and hence daily pickup and delivery times for each client) will never be flexible enough to meet last-minute client requests. But you cannot have a senior manager planning the daily route in real-time to orchestrate the optimal path, even with the support of a supercomputer. There are simply too many uncertain variables like traffic and delays at a client's office. You will have to rely on the intelligence and dedication of the leading courier on the ground for that route to make the right choices. He or she may choose to 'go out of the way' to help out a customer in a time-crunch situation and, for that matter, choose not to let a customer's demands get out of hand. He or she may even rearrange the usual route to give a specific customer more time to prepare an urgent package. Then the courier may even spend an extra minute (in an extremely busy day) to talk with a receptionist about her shipping needs for next week (so he or she can plan ahead).

Top service businesses also encourage field leaders to assume ownership of the job at hand. A field leader cannot escalate and hope a superior officer at headquarters will somehow mysteriously solve his problem on the ground. Taking ownership also includes building rapport with all the key stakeholders on the ground. DHL calls this the 'doorman approach.' Each field leader has to take seriously the potential influence of good relations with everyone who passes through the 'door' of his daily professional life. An airport supervisor at DHL needs to treat all aircraft operators and junior customs officers with courtesy and good humor. These relationships will turn out to be extremely valuable in some stressful situations (such as cargo overbooking). Building bridges to other helpful people should happen before the flood, not after.

Finally, field leaders need to go beyond the day-to-day operation and assume strategic leadership. At DHL, this is accomplished through the annual budgeting process.

Together, each year draw up strategic guidelines going forward. Given these guidelines, the budget is then prepared bottom-up, starting at the supervisor level. This becomes an opportunity for a supervisor to learn strategic thinking: How he or she addresses customer needs, plans for service improvements, maintains leadership against an emerging competitor, and deals with escalating costs.

*Source*: Adapted from Chung, P. and Ip, S. (2018). *Pillars of a service hub*. New York: Lexingford Publisher.

### Questions related to the case

1 What benefits do firms get from a decentralized decision-making system?
2 Why did DHL choose this approach in meeting the needs of the customers?

### End of chapter questions

1 Leadership concepts have been changing through time. What factors contribute to this?
2 Can the great man theory of leadership be applied in the service environment? Why and why not?
3 What distinguishes transactional theory of leadership from transformational theory of leadership?
4 What are the differences between the trait theory of leadership and the situational theory of leadership?
5 What tools are needed to transform an organization using the manufacturing mindset to a service mindset?

### References

Amaram, D. (2007). Cultural diversity: Implications for workplace management. *Journal of Diversity Management*, 2(4), 1–6.

Badaracco, J. (2001). We don't need another hero. *Harvard Business Review*, 79(8), 120–126.

Bass, B. (1985). *Leadership and performance beyond expectation*. New York, NY: The Free Press.

Bass, B. (2008). *The Bass handbook of leadership: Theory, research, & managerial applications* (4th ed.). New York, NY: Free Press.

Bennett, N., Wise, C., Woods, P., & Harvey, J. (2003). *Distributed leadership*. Nottingham: National College for School Leadership.

Bennis, W. (2004). Share the power. *CIO Insight*, 37, 27–29.

Burns, J. M. (1978). *Leadership*. New York, NY: Harper & Row.

Conger, J. (2011). Charismatic leadership. In A. Bryman, D. Collinson, K. Grint, B. Jackson, & M. Uhl-Bien (Eds.), *The Sage handbook of leadership* (pp. 86–102). Thousand Oaks, CA: Sage.

Cook-Greuter, S. (2002). *A detailed description of the development of nine action logics adapted from ego development theory for the leadership development framework*. Retrieved from October 2, 2019, from http://nextstepintegral.org/

wp-content/uploads/2011/04/The-development-of-action-logics-Cook-Greu
ter.pdf

Dulewicz, V., & Higgs, M. (2005). Assessing leadership styles and organisational context. *Journal of Managerial Psychology, 20*(2), 105–123.

Galton, F. (1962). *Hereditary genius.* USA: Collins.

Gardner, H. (1983). *Frames of mind.* New York, NY: Basic Books.

Gardner, H. (1998). A multiplicity of intelligences: In tribute to Professor Luigi Vignolo. *Scientific American*, 1–10.

Gardner, H. (2005, May 25). *Multiple lenses on the mind.* Paper presented at the ExpoGestion Conference, Bogota, Colombia.

Goleman, D. (1995). *Emotional intelligence: Why it can matter more than IQ.* New York, NY: Bantam.

Goleman, D. (1998a). *Emotional intelligence.* New York, NY: Bantam.

Goleman, D. (1998b). What makes a leader? *Harvard Business Review, 76*, 93–102.

Goleman, D. (2001). Emotional intelligence: Issues in paradigm building. In C. Cherniss & D. Goleman (Eds.), *The emotionally intelligent workplace.* San Francisco, CA: Jossey-Bass.

Greenleaf, R. (1970). *The servant as leader.* San Francisco, CA: Robert K. Greenleaf Publishing Center.

Guilford, J. (1967). *The nature of human intelligence.* New York, NY: McGraw-Hill.

Halpern, D. (2014). *Thought and knowledge: An introduction to critical thinking.* New York, NY: Psychology Press.

Hedlund, J., Forsythe, G., Horvath, J., Williams, W., Snook, S., & Sternberg, R. (2003). Identifying and assessing tacit knowledge: Understanding the practical intelligence of military leaders. *Leadership Quarterly, 14*, 117–140.

Hoshmand, A. (2015). The role of service leadership in the university's GE curriculum: The HKBU experience. In D. Shek & P. Chung (Eds.), *Promoting service leadership qualities in university students: The case of Hong Kong.* Singapore: Springer.

Howell, J., & Avolio, B. (1993). Transformational leadership, transactional leadership locus of control, and support for innovation: Key predictors of consolidated-business performance. *Journal of Applied Psychology, 78*, 891–902.

Hunt, J. (2004). What is leadership? In J. Antonakis, A. T. Cianciolo, & R. J. Sternberg (Eds.), *The nature of leadership* (pp. 19–47). Thousand Oaks, CA: Sage.

Jin, Y. (2010). Emotional leadership as a key dimension of public relations leadership: A national survey of public relations leaders. *Journal of Public Relations Research, 22*(2), 159–181.

Keegan, A., & Den Hartog, D. (2004). Transformational leadership in a project-based environment: A comparative study of the leadership styles of project managers and line managers. *International Journal of Project Management, 22*(8), 609–617.

Kouzes, J., & Posner, B. (2003). *Credibility: How leaders gain and lose it, why people demand it.* San Francisco, CA: Jossey-Bass.

Liden, R., Wayne, S., Zhao, H., & Henderson, D. (2008). Servant leadership: Development of a multidimensional measure and multi-level assessment. *Leadership Quarterly, 19*, 161–177.

Lorsch, J. (2010). A contingency theory of leadership. In N. Nohria & R. Khurana (Eds.), *Handbook of leadership theory and practice* (pp. 411–432). Boston, MA: Harvard Business Press.

Marcy, R., & Mumford, M. (2010). Leader cognition: Improving leader performance through casual analysis. *The Leadership Quarterly, 21*(1), 1–19.

Mayer, J., DiPaolo, M., & Salovey, P. (1990). Perceiving affective content in ambiguous visual stimuli: A component of emotional intelligence. *Journal of Personality Assessment, 54*, 772–781.

Mayer, J., Salovey, P., & Caruso, D. (2008), Emotional intelligence: New ability or eclectic traits? *American Psychologist, 63*(6), 503–517.

McKenna, B., & Rooney, D. (2008). Wise leadership and the capacity for ontological acuity. *Management Communication Quarterly, 21*, 537–546.

Morgan, J. (2019). *Employee's experience index.* Retrieved September 26, 2019, from https://thefutureorganization.com/employee-experience-index/

Mortona, F., Treviñob, T., & Zapata-Cantúc, L. (2019). A conceptual model of organizational culture and its implications in the service sector. *Multidisciplinary Business Review, 12*(1), 24–37.

Mumford, M., Connelly, S., & Gaddis, B. (2003). How creative leaders think: Experimental findings and cases. *Leadership Quarterly, 14*, 411–432.

Neisser, U. (1979). The concept of intelligence. In R. J. Sternberg & D. K. Detterman (Eds.), *Human intelligence: Perspectives on its theory and measurement* (pp. 179–189). Norwood, NJ: Ablex.

Northouse, P. (2004). *Leadership: Theory and practice* (3rd ed.). Thousand Oaks, CA: Sage.

Raelin, J. A. (2003). *Creating leaderful organizations: How to bring out leadership in everyone.* San Francisco, CA: Berrett-Koehler.

Raelin, J. A. (2006). Does action learning promote collaborative leadership? *Academy of Management Learning and Education, 5*(2), 152–168.

Raelin, J. A. (2008). *Work-based learning: Bridging knowledge and action in the workplace.* San Francisco, CA: Jossey-Bass.

Raelin, J. A. (2009). The practice turn-away: Forty years of spoon-feeding in management education. *Management Learning, 40*(4), 401–410.

Raelin, J. A. (2013). The manager as facilitator of dialogue. *Organization, 20*, 818–839.

Raelin, J. A. (Ed.). (2016). *Leadership-as-practice: Theory and application.* New York, NY: Routledge.

Raelin, J. A. (2019). Deriving an affinity for collective leadership: Below the surface of action learning. *Journal of Action Learning Research and Practice, 16*(2), 123–135.

Robinson, D. (1990). Wisdom through the ages. In R. J. Sternberg (Ed.), *Wisdom: Its nature, origins, and development* (pp. 13–24). New York, NY: Cambridge University Press.

Rooke, D., & Torbert, W. (2005). Seven transformations of leadership. *Harvard Business Review, 83*(4), 66–76.

Salovey, P., & Mayer, J. (1990). Emotional intelligence. *Imagination, Cognition, and Personality, 9*, 185–211.

Shaw, S. (2007). *Nursing leadership.* Oxford: Blackwell Publishing.

Sternberg, R. (2003). A model of leadership in organizations. *Academy of Management Learning & Education, 2*(4), 386–401.

Stogdill, R. (1948). Personal factors associated with leadership: A survey of the literature. *Journal of Psychology, 25*(1), 35–71.

Thorndike, E. (1920). Intelligence and its uses. *Harper's Magazine, 140*, 227–235.

Uhl-Bien, M. (2006). Relational leadership theory: Exploring the social processes of leadership and organizing. *Leadership Quarterly, 17*, 654–676.

Vanderslice, V. (1988). Separating leadership from leaders: As assessment of the effect of leader and follower roles. *Human Relations, 41*, 677–696.

Vera, D., & Crossan, M. (2004). Strategic leadership and organizational learning. *Academy of Management Review, 29*, 222–240.

Wechsler, D. (1940). Nonintellective factors in general intelligence. *Psychological Bulletin, 37*, 444–445.

Wheatley, M. (1999). *Leadership and the new science: Discovering order in a chaotic world* (2nd ed.). San Francisco, CA: Berrett-Koehler.

Zaccaro, S. (2007). Trait-based perspectives of leadership. *American Psychologist, 62*(1), 6–16.

# 4     Service leadership method

## 4.1 Dynamics of service leadership

### Why is this important? The necessity of the method

As stated in Chapter 2, the global economic environment has shifted dramatically toward services. As such, the tools necessary for the growth of the sector must take into account the cultural shift in decision making, the diversity that has permeated the work environment because of globalization, and many other factors. In the language of service leadership, a leader needs to attend to the service habitat with the highest *competence, character,* and *care.*

By now you probably understand the different models of leadership and their application in organizations that mostly emphasize products rather than service. This is not to say that those principles do not apply to the service sector; they do, in a limited sense. Given that the manufacturing mindset is rigid in nature and requires a commitment from the followers to adhere to the set of rules for the sake of consistency and efficiency, it is not consistent with the dynamic nature of service. Hence, a shift in paradigm is needed to move away from a command-and-control approach toward a more humanistic approach of a service mindset. It must be understood that service leadership focuses on leadership, rather than management – which in turn means a focus on people, rather than systems. The intention is to show that honoring the intrinsic, instinctive wisdom of established human cultural approaches has a significant impact on how a service is delivered.

The core tenet of service leadership, or the *3Cs,* was stated in Chapter 1. To be successful in the service sector of today, it must be understood that the role that a leader versus a follower plays is simply collaborative in nature and not a top-down approach. Earlier discussion pointed out that *competence*, *character*, and *care* are natural organic forces that people can easily connect with, understand, and exercise. These attributes, when used effectively, provide the reasons, guidelines, and platform for reducing conflict, service-recovery cost, and human-relations cost. The effect of reducing conflicts and costs for the workforce – and possibly for your customer base as well – is profitability. One of the costs that can be minimized is the cost of training new employees. Traditional measures of the losses incurred by employee turnover concentrate only on the cost of recruiting, hiring, and training replacements. In most service jobs, the real cost of turnover is the loss of productivity and decreased customer satisfaction (Heskett, Jones, Loveman, Sasser, & Schlesinger, 2008, p. 5). Proper recruitment of individuals who possess the element of *character* and *care*, reduces such costs. In the 21st century, turnover rates can and will go up as changes in the work environment provide opportunities and risks for those who seek an alternative career path.

According to the 2017 training industry report, companies spent an average of $1,075 per employee trained. While this may seem like a small sum, this is a $200 increase from the previous year. This translates, in cash dollars, to a nearly 33% increase in overall training expenditures in the US from 2016 to 2017 for a total of nearly $91 billion (Hansen, 2019). This is a cost that can be minimized if proper training is offered. In service leadership, emphasis is placed on the apprentice–master approach in training employees. Hence, this is a continuing process that enhances the capabilities of an employee to deliver service with the utmost care. The apprentice–master approach has the ability to turn an apprentice to a master when he or she is delivering the service. This progression continues throughout the organization in a geometric fashion. Once the apprentice masters the art of delivering a service, he or she will in turn teach the new employees what he or she has learned. This collaborative approach to learning has many benefits to an organization. It is an effective tool in team building, loyalty to the organization, and social development of the employee.

Under the normal circumstances, people have some level of *competence*, *character*, and *care*. Recognizing this at the hiring stage gives the firm a chance to assess the capabilities of a service provider and also help in identifying leadership potentials in the employee. Each firm can organizationally help its people develop a higher degree of awareness, intensity, and fluency within their own being. Raising the awareness of people's *competence*, *character*, and *care* can be interpreted as teaching, so in this sense, the effort to 'teach' the 3Cs is a key part of their being in the organization. Modeling such behavior by the leadership of a firm becomes the teaching approach in the organization. When it comes to complete, holistic leadership, the 3Cs come as a set. Competence, or skill, can be taught, but without the right character, an individual would not be able to function within a larger group. From a Confucian point of view, character is the combination of both morality and ethics. The circumstances that highlight each is stated by Confucius in the following way: The most dangerous time is when you're by yourself and facing your own ethics. Morality appears when you are by yourself, while ethics requires the presence of a second person next to you. Since this chapter deals with the reasonings behind service leadership, it will elaborate on how each of the 3Cs builds an effective service organization. The competent service leaders are individuals who naturally possess a service mindset, meaning they can easily understand a variety of situations. Additionally, due to their high-level social skills, they are able to use a variety of communication skills to convey the message to the entire organization.

In a world that is driven by profit motives, service organizations have to be mindful of not taking shortcuts in the quality of service or ethics involved to achieve the goals of the firm. This is why it is imperative that the character exhibited by the service organizations (leaders and followers) must take precedence over the hard skills that can be easily learned. Research shows that the long-term sustainability of profit in a firm is tied to the delivery of quality and ethical service (Adhikari & Adhikari, 2009; Bolton & Tarasi, 2006; Silvestro & Cross, 2000; Brooks, 2000). Specific research applying service chain to retail in the United Kingdom found that there is a strong correlation between profit, customer loyalty, customer satisfaction, service value, internal service quality, output quality, and productivity (Silvestro & Cross, 2000). To survive and grow in this volatile market today, firms cannot always depend upon the conventional ways to manage and grow the business by only going after the sales. Rather, they need to search for the innovative measures that effectively cater to the customers' needs, which will provide sustainable competitive advantage over a period of time (Florea, Tanasescu, & Duica, 2018).

Heskett et al. (2008) argue that there is a dynamic link in the service-profit chain that essentially leads to profit. It starts as

> employee satisfaction soars when you enhance internal service quality (equipping employees with the skills and power to serve customers). Employee satisfaction in turn fuels employee loyalty, which raises employee productivity (Awan & Tahir, 2015). Higher productivity means greater external service value for customers – which enhances customer satisfaction and loyalty.

A mere 5% jump in customer loyalty can boost profits 25%–85% (Reichheld, 2000). The study by Heskett et al. (2008, p. 1) shows how the fast-food giant Taco Bell found that its stores with low workforce turnover (a key marker of employee loyalty) enjoyed double the sales and 55% higher profits than stores with high turnover. This was accomplished by enhancing internal service quality – for instance, by giving employees more latitude for on-the-job decision making. This is what was precisely done by DHL, a courier service firm that achieved growth and profitability in a very short period of time (Chung, 2019).

Among the other dynamics of service leadership in an organization is the promotion of critical and independent thinking, and self-leadership. According to Ennis (2011), critical thinking is 'reflective reasoning about beliefs and actions. [Critical thinking] is reasonable reflective thinking focused on deciding what to believe or do.' Hence, leaders with critical thinking skills have the ability to understand the logical connections between ideas. They are able to identify the relevance and importance of arguments, detect inconsistencies or mistakes in reasoning, and make proper decisions.

As a prized attribute of service leadership, critical thinking is an essential tool to manage the complex organization of the 21st century. The ability of a service leader to model this skill for others in the service organization is critical.

Leaders who show critical thinking in their actions often:

- *Question assumptions* and are inquisitive about the circumstances of every proposition. They want to know *what* the problem is and *why* it has occurred.
- *Adopt multiple perspectives* in their decisions given that they work in a multicultural environment. This awareness and adaptability give them a better sense of how to deal with problems as they arise.
- *See potential* in scenarios that are the result of questioning assumptions and harnessing multiple perspectives. The creative bent of critical thinkers allows them to see opportunities where others see obstacles.
- *Manage ambiguity* in a global business environment that is affected by multiple factors. These critical thinkers know that they are operating in an environment where change is constant and rapid decisions are required.

Self-leadership is just as important as critical thinking for a service leader. As human beings, all of us have an inner-self and an outer-self. The inner-self has its roots in the upbringing and the value system that has guided us through life. These inner-self characteristics define who we are as individuals. The outer-self is what is observable by those with whom we interact. The ability to actively monitor and correct the unseen or inner-self by those who are around us is self-leadership. Leaders who are adept in the art of using intrapersonal qualities that define their inner-self to control the interpersonal action or outer-self are looked upon as having integrity and deserving trust. Hence, self-leadership is the ability to consciously influence your own thoughts and behavior in order to achieve personal goals or meet the objectives of an organization (Manz, 1986).

Just like any other skill, self-leadership can be learned. Some basic elements of self-leadership skills for a service provider are given next.

*Clear vision*: Being your own leader, your purpose or vision will be the foundation upon which you will build self-leadership. This means that you have to recognize what you wish to achieve in life, and how to go about achieving them. This process allows for reflection and action. As stated by Chung (2012), 'you are the entrepreneur of your own life.' Hence, remain committed to your vision.

*Take reasonable risks with the aim to succeed*: Challenging yourself to take on daring projects does allow the creative-self to come to fore. An individual with self-leadership does not get discouraged by past failures but focuses on success. Any challenging task requires a thoughtful approach with a reasonable amount of calculated risk.

*Reflect on personal life*: Earlier it was mentioned that when setting goals for self-leadership, it is just as important to also reflect on them. Allowing oneself to consider multiple perspectives in life leads to a better self-leader with empathy and care.

*Remain steadfast on your goals*: Keeping your vision alive is important. Learn not to be persuaded by self or others to move in the direction of any suggestion or ideas that are not in line with your vision. This means not tolerating negative aspects of your nature such as laziness, fear, and timidity to keep you from achieving your goals.

As part of self-leadership, taking care to attend to one's needs and development is essential. By doing so, individuals recognize how important this is for all those who follow them. Taking on the responsibility to lead others is why self-leadership is so essential.

Leadership tasks are often broad-based and include assisting team members in finding joy in their roles, teaching them self-leadership, encouraging them to be good colleagues, team leaders, and service providers while showing them how to be kind to others. In the next section, the interactions of the players in the service habitat will be elaborated on. In the earlier discussion, the 'why' of service leadership was stated. Now, let's turn your attention to the 'who' in service leadership.

## The players of service leadership (who)

The aim of service leadership is to provide service with *competence, character, and care*. So far, the discussion has been on how leaders and followers interact with each other and those whom they serve. Since service leadership emphasizes collaboration by all who are engaged in the delivery of service, every member of the habitat has a responsibility to each other and the client. The guiding post of moral decency, or values, for the self, group, organization, and network must be present for a service provider to build personal trust and respect in the community. All human relationships are built on trust and respect, and service leadership provides the connection to human relationships. Some of the principles behind the relative stability and success of service organization is their ability to build trust and be respected by those whom they serve. In this context, it is emphasized that those who are being served (customers and shareholders) are looking for their own interest in the transaction of service. They are seeking value in their relationship with the service firm that has different dimensions.

Keep in mind that principles and systems that are central to service leadership help organizations to focus on the dual creation of value: The creation of value for shareholders (via long-term firm profitability) and the creation of value or utility for customers (Vargo & Lusch, 2004).

As for the creation of value for shareholders of a service firm, it is no surprise that customer trust and satisfaction are linked to the growth and stability of a firm's future cash flows. A study by Anderson, Fornell, and Mazvancheryl (2004) reported that a positive association exists between a firm's current level of customer satisfaction and contemporaneous financial market measures such as Tobin's Q, stock and market-to-book ratio. The economic theory of investment behavior suggests that 'q' represents the ratio of the market value of a firm's existing shares to the replacement cost of the firm's physical assets. Hence, if q (representing equilibrium) is greater than one (q > 1), additional investment in the firm would make sense because the profits generated would exceed the cost of the firm's assets. If q is less than one (q < 1), the firm would be better off selling its assets instead of trying to put them to use. Subsequently, Gruca and Rego (2005), in a robust model, reported that satisfaction increases shareholder value by increasing future cash flow and reducing its variability. What this suggests is that when customers are satisfied with the quality of the service delivered, the firm generates more revenue, and this in turn reaffirms investors' decision to further invest in the service organization, boosting its position in the market.

Research has also shown that service quality, customer satisfaction, trust, and commitment provide insights for service leaders on how relational processes create value for customers (Rust, Lemon, & Zeithaml, 2004; Berger et al., 2002). These relationships must be based on trust (Florea, 2014, p. 257) and how leaders collaborate with employees and customers (Schuh, Egold, & van Dick, 2012). To build strong, sustainable, and ethical relationships, the leader and the organization must have credibility in the community they serve. These relationships are created and maintained through employees, whose skills and competencies will determine the success or failure of the organization. To develop and have these unique skills, the organization must perceive them as a long-term investment and not as a cost (Florea & Mihai, 2015, p. 229).

In another study, it was found that a business unit was able to achieve a 270% increase in business unit profits above target by implementing some straightforward customer relation management procedures (Ryals, 2005). These studies further support the notion of *care* as it applies to customer relations and satisfaction. Regardless of which leadership laws shape and influence a company's trajectory, it's imperative for them to learn how to design for the future while maintaining the initial success and underlying philosophy.

As major players in the delivery of service, leaders must continually assess their role in the organization and how they can achieve the goals of the firm. As stated by Maxwell (2011), there are five levels in the process of maximization of leadership potentials. The similarity between the concept of service leadership and Maxwell's levels to achieve Maslow's self-actualization of a leader will be highlighted.

*Position:* As a starting point to leadership, an individual is given the position to lead an organization. Generally, people follow this leader because of the leader's position. This leader may not have the necessary qualification to lead, but circumstances have given him or her this opportunity. Therefore, someone in this position has little influence over his or her followers and may not have their trust or respect. To be respected and trusted, this leader has to acquire those necessary and basic skills to leadership. These skills have been alluded to in Chapter 1.

*Permission:* Another context of leadership is where a leader is recognized by the followers and the leader knows that he or she has 'permission' to act as leader. This position gives the leader an increased ability to garner more trust from and develop better relationships with his or her followers. Part of the followers' motivation is their own, but it's also due to their leader believing in them. The followers are on board with their leader and offer their trust and support to achieve their goals.

*Production:* At this level of leadership, the leaders must have those skills to make people become more productive and show measurable results under their leadership. Leaders with the ability to build good interpersonal relationships are able to obtain this level as they can achieve positive results with a team of people who trust and believe in them. This type of leader is much loved by their team, creating the possibility that if the leader leaves, the team is in danger of falling apart.

*People Development:* As stated in Chapter 1, an element of service leadership is for the leader to break the hierarchical mold and allow all members of the team to have a say in the decision-making process. By doing so, the leader sets an example of how to develop others through this process. The leader believes in the importance of training the team and understands why it's necessary to delegate work to them. The team members then develop confidence in self-development, which must be clearly communicated to them. These leaders put the growth of others first and recognize how crucial this is to the success of an organization. The mentor–apprentice relationship fits into this category of leadership style.

*Pinnacle:* At this top level, people choose to follow the leaders because they respect them as persons. These are the George C. Patton type of leaders who become legends and leave behind a legacy of supreme leadership education and innovation.

Looking at these five levels of leadership, you should be able to recognize the parallels between Maxwell's concept of leadership levels and the notion of service leadership method. Both, if followed correctly, will lead to self-actualization that Maslow had put forward.

In summary, the players of service leadership are all those individuals who are either delivering the service (leaders and employees of a firm) or receiving it (the customer). It should be recognized that the delivery component is a controllable factor by the service provider; however, the receiver of service remains an uncontrollable factor until the service provider has met the need and expectation of the recipient.

Leadership literature supports the emphasis that the values espoused in service leadership are a collective and integrated process that serves as a guiding post that must be followed for any service organization to succeed. Values are an individual's software, capable of encoding organic systems of thought and conduct in ways people can understand. And these values are expressed in an individual's behavior. When people are engaged with the right values and behavior to develop self-generating energy, they, in turn, encourage to spread goodwill and energy within the habitat. Leaders who are also players in delivering service must remember that in the service mindset, they must be humble, keeping in mind that they may not know everything but show that they are willing to learn. You may recall that an element of self-leadership was the awareness of not feeling arrogant. As the Delphic oracle said of Socrates, he was the wisest man in ancient Athens because he was the only one who knew how little he knew. This kind of humility enables one to allow the system dynamics to achieve their ends through their own spontaneous, bottom-up forms of organization.

The method of service leadership is to push decisions to the lowest level, allow mistakes and correct them, and the values subscribed by the firm should be an extension of family values. These practices generate employee loyalty, which in turn results in low turnover, institutional memory, and institutional partner relationships. Maintaining a continual sea of familiar, friendly employees facilitate and inspire people to find positive energy in their work and contribute effectively to the growth of the company. Another aspect of creating the kind of self-generating energetic habitat described earlier is to recognize employees' needs. Attending to their needs contributes significantly to achieving the goals of the organization (Onwuzuligbo & Amakor, 2019, p. 14). Other studies have also shown that firms have collapsed when they failed to consider employee needs (Noe, Hollenbeck, Gerhart, & Wright, 2004). Service leaders need to understand the key benefits of employee performance so that they can develop consistent and objective methods for evaluating employees. Doing so helps determine strengths, weaknesses, and potential leadership gaps in the service organization. Understanding how to lead with a full set of human needs is extremely important, particularly when leading those at different levels of development. As stated in Chapter 1, a service firm must consider Maslow's self-actualization process to achieve its goals. Having explored in this chapter the principles that enable you to achieve this, let's now discuss the interaction of the 3Cs.

### The components of service leadership (what)

As described in the previous section, the key ingredients behind a great service leader can be summed up as the person's *3Cs* of *competence, character,* and *care*. By making each one as strong as possible, the leadership potential can be found in the intersection of the *3Cs* as shown in Figure 4.1. This is also the building block for establishing and maintaining the level of trustworthiness in an organization.

Chapter 1 elaborated on the elements of each of the *3Cs*. What is emphasized here is to show how the interaction of these components leads to a service leadership mindset. Competence, or hard skill, is achieved through a variety of means such as schooling, apprenticeship, or experience. Often, this is the first step for getting a position in a firm. *Character* as defined by the 'values' expressed by a firm and its leadership is the tool that sustains the firm in the long run. It's not enough just to announce the values that the firm or its leadership subscribes to but rather show in action how those values are serving as the guiding principle for the firm. Authenticity is essential if employees are to avoid cognitive dissonance – a perception of a gap between the proclaimed values and those actually used. The all-too-common result of that can be disengagement or the decision to leave the firm.

The element of *care* is as critical as the *character* shown by the leaders of a firm. Hence, a leader must express authentic concern for everyone involved with the team, either within the group or those beyond it. In other words, leaders achieve greatness as a measure of how deeply they care and are not selfish – they care about the team, the group's collective success, and even how stakeholders and clients feel about the services they are receiving. They should be aware that employees will feel little commitment toward their organization if they cannot see any meaning to their involvement in it.

*Care* is expressed as compassion, not being selfish, and having empathy for others. The degree to which a service provider communicates care is what wins loyalty. Employee loyalty has a significant impact on how a service organization operates. An empirical study of 100 service companies concluded that employee loyalty is significantly related to and has a positive influence on company

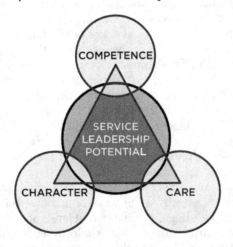

*Figure 4.1* The 3Cs and service leadership potential

*Source:* Adopted from 12 Dimension of a Service Leader, by Chung and Elfassy, 2016, p. 42.

performance (Tomic, Tesic, Kuzmanovic, & Tomic, 2018). Employee loyalty can be defined as employees' commitment to the success of the organization and the belief that working for this organization is their best option (Iqbal & Lodhi, 2015).

Consequently, nurturing loyalty, shown through care, has become a priority issue, not just for commercial companies, but for organizations of all types. It's true that a propensity toward mobility, even hypermobility, does exist these days. Whatever an organization does, there will always be some 'natural' attrition. Career plans shift, families move, exciting opportunities attract. To keep turnover to an acceptable and controllable level, service leaders need to make their organizations attractive to employees of all ages.

On a professional level, *care* can help drive a team toward excellence when no other reason may be there. This is referred to as the 'psychic income.' People with great levels of care are passionate about what they are doing, expressed as a commitment to the organization's mission as extended to the group.

A good example of a business leader who displays strong competence on all three is the legendary value investor Warren Buffett, from Berkshire Hathaway Inc. Through his actions and writing, it can be seen that he is strong on all three. Equally legendary is Microsoft founder Bill Gates, who has also proven to be well-rounded.

The potential benefit of a service mindset, which lies in the intersection of the *3Cs*, can be applied not only in business but also in other disciplines such as politics. For example, centrally planned economies are effective at delivering on the functional needs and capacities of a society. Where they fall short is around supporting the character and care of the population. Within this system, people are no less motivated by self-interest than those in the market economies, but they aren't as driven by selfless care. They surely care about their survival and the ability to feed the population (although even this isn't necessarily true when, for example, one looks at North Korea), but the care needed to uphold the rights of the individual is much weaker. It can be observed now that with decades of centrally planned practices in the execution and delivery, the system isn't as utopic as imagined.

Both *character* and *care* are more important in the context of service leadership than competence because they serve as a barometer of trust and care in the community an organization serves. This is important because it highlights that even if the job gets done, things will fall apart if those inside and outside question the character or integrity of the firm. This will manifest as anxiety about the motives of the firm, which will have negative consequences.

The concept of *character* and *care* are tied directly with the psychology of leadership that will be discussed next.

## 4.2 Psychology of leadership

The field of psychology deals with the inner soul of an individual and tries to explain the driving force behind an individual's actions. Some of those actions are looked upon as leadership capabilities of an individual. The discussion in the previous chapters has shed light on what constitutes leadership. One of those factors that define leadership is the ability to influence others to perform tasks that are given to them. As suggested by Cialdini (2001, p. 72), it is about 'getting things done through others.' There are several social and contextual factors affecting a leader's ability to influence others. In the context of service leadership, the culture of the habitat, the nature of the institution within which leadership takes place, as well as the gender of the leader (Haslam, Reicher, & Platow, 2011) play a critical role.

Leadership style has a profound impact on how the follower is influenced by the leader. Evidences from the literature shows that transformational leadership approach, which is similar to a service leadership mindset, has more beneficial outcomes on worker execution than transactional leadership (Mohiuddin, 2017).

You may recall that transformational leaders possess charismatic abilities; they induce moral values and try to develop the capabilities of the employees. Similar to service leadership, transformational leadership influences the follower to commit to the goals of the organization. Consequently, the employees put forward all their efforts to bring up the organizational standards on par with the global values. At the same time, the service leader also influences employees to be innovative and take bold initiatives and stands firm in collaboration with the popular will of all the units of the organization (Salman, Riaz, Saifullah, & Rashid, 2011).

The format of the leadership style mainly rests upon the level of trust, motivation leading to a decentralized system in which an individual can perform to his or her maximum beyond personal interests (Udoh & Agu, 2012). An excellent example of this is found in DHL, Inc., where the firm, having used a decentralized system in which responsibility for decisions were made at the local and lower levels of operation, was able to achieve a phenomenal growth in a short period of time. DHL is among a handful of companies that managed to expand from nothing to 120 countries within its first 15 years. Eventually, the network would expand its services to more than 220 nations and territories (Chung, 2019, p. 9).

Given the realities of today, the context that leaders operate in is the global community. The culture of the organization, in this global community, is shaped by how the leader sees his or her role in the organization. The national and societal culture of the country affects organizational culture (Hofstede, 2011).

From a service leadership perspective, the culture of the organization is shaped when leaders see their role as a collaborator in achieving the objective of the firm. Hence, they are able to influence those inside the firm and build trust with the outside community. The importance of trust in an organization was discussed earlier, but here interest lies in how trust plays a role in motivating followers to work together for a common goal. The nature of the habitat is affected not only by the people within the habitat but also those external to it. Hence, attempting to influence people who have a different cultural value is not an easy task.

When discussing the psychology of leadership as it pertains to services, it is imperative for the service organization to create an environment or habitat that grooms a culture of positive emotion, engagement, relationships, meaning, and achievement (PERMA), as proposed by Martin Seligman (2018, 2011). His conceptual model of psychological well-being and happiness (Schwartz & Sharpe, 2006) has implications for service providers. Using the five core elements can effectively help individuals within an organization to grow and in turn help achieve its goals. Seligman's premise is that people work toward a life of fulfillment, happiness, and meaning.

As service providers, the strength in each of PERMA's areas can help individuals find happiness, fulfillment, and meaning. PERMA has also been used to develop programs that help individuals develop new cognitive and emotional tools (Slavin, Schindler, Chibnall, Fendell, & Shoss, 2012). Service leadership suggests that the model can be taken even further and used as a framework for institutional leadership and culture change to help all those involved in the delivery of service reach their full potential. Each of the five core elements will be discussed briefly.

*Positive emotion:* Positive emotion is a cornerstone of the well-being model. Experiencing positive emotions such as hope, compassion, contentment, empathy, gratitude, joy, or love is considered the most essential element contributing to well-being conditions (Webster, 2014). To be able to create positive emotions, service providers need to: (1) Create a work environment or habitat that is less stressful to employees. This ties with meeting the needs of the employee. (2) Allow for transparency in decision making. This implies that real and meaningful input from stakeholders is utilized whenever possible; timely and complete explanations for changes in policies and procedures are provided.

*Engagement:* (1) Service leadership is driven by creating opportunities for all to engage fully in their work through reduction of non-valued work, reduction of unneeded policies, and streamlining of administrative procedures. (2) Promoting reflection is another mode of engagement. Employees must be encouraged to truly engage with their clients beyond the delivery of service so that a long-term relationship can be established with them.

*Relationships:* (1) Developing programs to increase opportunities for meaningful and productive relationships, such as mentorship for new employees, apprentice–master programs to engage those who have experience in the delivery of exceptional service, as well as small-group discussion sessions at all levels. (2) Promoting interdivisional and interdepartmental activities to achieve the goals of the organization.

*Meaning:* (1) Instituting programs in which service providers have the opportunity to reflect on their work to help revitalize the values and motivations for becoming a service leader in the first place as well as combat a culture of negativism and complaint. (2) Supporting employees of service programs to engage in activities and learning that help them find greater meaning and richness in their work.

*Achievement:* (1) Encouraging a culture of innovation and advancement is essential for the sustainability of a firm. Reducing barriers to individual initiative must be given attention. Avoiding micromanagement, delegating, and empowering employees are important. (2) Aligning incentives with institutional mission and values. (3) Celebrating and rewarding successes in achieving institutional missions and goals. Recognizing humanism and generosity of spirit is part of the concept of *care* in service leadership that must remain alive.

Individuals working in the service environment can reach their potential only if the institutional leadership is invested in creating multifaceted programs and working conditions in which individuals can truly flourish.

The PERMA formula leads to a happy person and creates groups of happy people – and joyful people in a people-service industry naturally deliver and provide better results. When energy is the giving force of service, a joyful person gives a better experience and offers a more satisfied customer at the same cost as a less satisfied customer, which is an essential element of reducing transactional costs.

For those who are in the service sector, Seligman (2011) offers means of incorporating these psychological factors into the equation of service so that all those involved in the delivery of service can develop their full potential. Far too many service organizations that apply the traditional approach to leadership not only fail to reach their potential as an organization, but their employees suffer unnecessarily from anxiety, burnout, and depression related to the unhealthy environment or habitat in which they work.

In summary, the players of service leadership are all those individuals who are either delivering the service (leaders and employees of a firm) or receiving it (the customer).

The components of service leadership are the *3Cs*. The intersection of the *3Cs* is where the service leadership potential is found. The elements of *character* and *care* are the two critical factors that distinguish service leadership from other forms of leadership.

### Key points to remember

To be successful in the service sector of today, it must be understood that the role that a leader versus a follower plays is simply collaborative in nature and not a top-down approach.

- Service leadership focuses on leadership, rather than management – which in turn means a focus on people, rather than on systems.
- Service organizations have to be mindful of not taking shortcuts in the quality of service or ethics involved to achieve the profit goals of the firm.
- Among the other dynamics of service leadership in an organization is the promotion of critical and independent thinking, and self-leadership.
- Leaders who show critical thinking in their actions often:

  *Question assumptions* and are inquisitive about the circumstances of every proposition.
  *Adopt multiple perspectives* in their decisions given that they work in a multicultural environment.
  *See potential* in scenarios that are the result of questioning assumptions and harnessing multiple perspectives.
  *Manage ambiguity* in a global business environment that is affected by multiple factors.

- Self-leadership is just as important as critical thinking for a service leader. The basic elements of self-leadership skills for a service provider are:

  - *Have a clear vision.*
  - *Take reasonable risks with the aim to succeed.*
  - *Reflect on personal life.*
  - *Remain steadfast on your goals.*

- The guiding post of moral decency, or values, for the self, group, organization, and network must be present for the service provider to build personal trust and respect in the community.

- Service quality, customer satisfaction, trust, and commitment provide insights for service leaders on how relational processes create value for customers.
- There are five levels in the process of maximization of leadership potentials:
  - *Position.*
  - *Permission.*
  - *Production.*
  - *People development.*
  - *Pinnacle.*

- PERMA stands for *positive emotion, engagement, relationships, meaning,* and *achievement* and has significant impact in the context of service leadership. These five elements play a critical role in how services could use the formula to achieve the goals and objectives of an organization.

---

## Case study

### A distinctive value proposition

Lindsey McAlister always knew that she would work in arts-related sectors. She says, 'Theatre is my life, my passion; it consumes every waking hour. When I am not making theatre, I am depressed and feel ill.' She began by working in the Arts Council of Great Britain and the Gulbenkian Foundation implementing the 'Arts in Schools' report. She then left the UK to do some traveling. She came to Hong Kong on a backpacking trip in her twenties. It was love at first sight. Within two hours of her arrival, she decided to give up the job waiting for her in the UK to stay in Hong Kong. She remembered the day like it was yesterday: 'That was the best decision I ever made in my life.'

After settling in Hong Kong, she found that there were almost no opportunities for young people to express themselves through arts in a noncompetitive environment. That became her true passion. She herself experienced some hurtful moments in her own schooling. Her music teacher barked at her to stop singing because 'it made her ears bleed.' Her dance teacher said she danced like a baby elephant. But she persisted in spite of these comments. She developed a strong belief in empowering young people through the arts.

'Looking back,' she mentioned, 'those experiences had a huge impact on what I do today. I never want any young person I work with ever to have to suffer lack of respect. Everything I do is about empowering young people, giving them self-confidence, self-esteem and encouraging them to be the best they can be.'

She tried to start up a platform for youngsters to create noncompetitive arts. But she had never had any experience in fundraising. She started cold-calling many companies in Hong Kong in an attempt to raise funds for the initial project. Things did not work out. Eventually someone introduced her to Mr. Chung (2018, p. 89), who had founded a group called Business for Art. Mr. Chung supported her, and she founded the Hong Kong Youth Arts Foundation (HKYAF) in 1993.

She started working with English-speaking students in Hong Kong and gradually expanded the program to local schools. HKYAF is now one of the biggest youth arts events in the world, reaching 800,000 youth audience through projects, exhibitions, and performances. Around 90,000 students participate in these events each year; only a quarter of them come from international schools.

HKYAF stands out from the other youth-related arts companies and festivals in two ways: First, creating youth art in a noncompetitive environment, and second, a commitment to high-quality arts.

Although HKYAF does not receive any direct funding from the government, it still pays full market rate for professional artists to work with students to create high-quality artworks. That is why the artworks are so much more professional than 'ordinary' school projects. For example, there are 100 schools participating in Arts in the Park each year. HKYAF pays for 12 professional artists to work with these schools. For each of these 100 schools, HKYAF makes sure a professional artist will visit the school at least eight times to help prepare the student artists. There was a night parade in year 2014, for which HKYAF brought in the Lantern Company from the UK to work with local artists to create dazzling illuminated giant puppets and costumes.

Though a nonprofit organization, HKYAF is still one of the best examples of a distinctive value proposition. Successful companies in the service sectors need a distinctive value proposition, that is, what specific benefit(s) it provides for its customers. A distinctive value proposition is a proposition that stands out. In this context, there is a Chinese saying that states 'Offer something extra, excel in a competitive market, avoid exceptional competitors.' In modern strategic terms, this means choosing your customer segment carefully and trying to stand out from your competitors in that segment by doing more or doing better than your competitors.

*Source:* Adapted from Chung, P., & Ip, S. (2018). *Pillars of a service hub.* New York, NY: Lexingford Publisher.

### Questions related to the case

1   What is meant by value proposition?
2   How does value proposition help the firm achieve its goals?
3   Should there be a difference in the value proposition between a for-profit and a nonprofit business?
4   What principles of service leadership apply to this case?

### End of chapter questions

1   Who are the players of service leadership?
2   What is the role of a service leader in interacting with employees and those outside the firm?
3   Why does employee loyalty lead to customer satisfaction?

4    How does Seligman's conceptual model of psychological well-being and happiness help a service organization?
5    What does PERMA stand for? How is its application helpful in services?

## References

Adhikari, B., & Adhikari, B. (2009). Managing customer relationships in service organizations. *Administration and Management Review, 21*(2), 64–78.
Anderson, E., Fornell, C., & Mazvancheryl, S. (2004). Customer satisfaction and shareholder value. *Journal of Marketing, 68*(3), 172–185.
Berger, P., Bolton, R., Bowman, D., Briggs, E., Kumar, V., Parasuraman, A., & Terry, C. (2002). Marketing assets and the value of customer assets: A framework for customer asset management. *Journal of Service Research, 5*(1), 39–54.
Bolton, R., & Tarasi, C. (2006). Managing customer relationships. In N. K. Malhotra (Ed.), *Review of marketing research* (pp. 3–38). Bingley, UK: Emerald Publications.
Brooks, R. (2000). Why loyal employees and customers improve the bottom line. *The Journal for Quality and Participation, 23*(2), 40–44.
Chung, P. (2012). *Service reborn: The knowledge, skills, and attitude of service companies*. New York, NY: Lexingford Publishing.
Chung, P. (2019). *Designed to win: What every business needs to know to go truly global*. Levanto, Italy: Leaders Press Publishing.
Chung, P., & Elfassy, R. (2016). *The 12 dimensions of a service leader: Manage your personal brand for the service age*. New York, NY: Lexingford Publishing.
Chung, P., & Ip, S. (2018). *Pillars of a service hub: Lessons learned from world-class service companies based in Hong Kong*. New York, NY: Lexingford Publishing.
Cialdini, R. (2001). Harnessing the science of persuasion. *Harvard Business Review, 79*, 71–80.
Ennis, R. (2011). Critical thinking: Reflection and perspective – part I. *Inquiry, 26*, 1.
Florea, N. (2014). Implementing a model of strategic communication to obtain organizational performance. *Revista Academiei Fortelor Terestre, 3*(75), 256–266.
Florea, N., & Mihai, D. (2015). Improving organization performance through human capital development using a regression function and MATLAB. *Journal of Science and Arts, 3*(32), 229–238.
Florea, N., Tanasescu, D., & Duica, A. (2018). Enabling customer-centricity and relationship management using net promoter score. *Valahian Journal of Economic Studies, 9*(23), 115–126.
Gruca, T., & Rego, L. (2005). Customer satisfaction, cash flow, and shareholder value. *Journal of Marketing, 69*(3), 115–130.
Hansen, M. (2019). *What's the real cost of training new employees?* Retrieved October 6, 2019, from https://elearningindustry.com/cost-of-training-new-employees-real
Haslam, S., Reicher, S., & Platow, M. (2011). *The new psychology of leadership: Identity, influence and power*. New York, NY: Taylor and Francis Group.
Heskett, J., Jones, T., Loveman, G., Sasser, W., & Schlesinger, L. (2008, July–August 1–13). Putting the service-profit chain to work. *Harvard Business Review*.

Hofstede, G. (2011). Dimensionalising cultures: The Hofstede model in context. *Online Readings in Psychology and Culture, 2*(1), 1–26.

Iqbal, T., & Lodhi, R. (2015). Employee loyalty and organizational commitment in Pakistani organizations. *Global Journal of Human Resource Management, 3*(1), 1–11.

Manz, C. (1986). Self-leadership: Toward an expanded theory of self-influence processes in organizations. *Academy of Management Review, 11*(3), 585–600.

Maxwell, J. (2011). *The five levels of leadership: Proven steps to maximize your potential.* New York, NY: Center Street.

Mohiuddin, Z. (2017). Influence of leadership style on employees performance: Evidence from literatures. *Journal of Marketing and Management, 8*(1), 18–30.

Noe, R., Hollenbeck, J., Gerhart, G., & Wright, P. (2004). *Fundamentals of human resource management.* Boston, MA: McGraw Hill, Irwin.

Onwuzuligbo, L., & Amakor, I. (2019). Corporate turnaround and employee needs a study of selected firms in Nigeria. *International Journal of Academic Accounting, Finance & Management Research, 3*(7), 10–18. Retrieved October 14, 2019, from www.researchgate.net/publication/334831563_Corporate_Turnaround_and_Employee_Needs_a_Study_of_Selected_Firms_in_Nigerian

Reichheld, F. (2000, November). Loyalty-based management. *Harvard Business Review.*

Rust, R., Lemon, K., & Zeithaml, V. (2004). Return on marketing: Using customer equity to focus marketing strategy. *Journal of Marketing, 68*(1), 109–127.

Ryals, L. (2005). Making CRM work: The measurement and profitable management of customer relationships. *Journal of Marketing, 69*(4), 252–261.

Salman, Z., Riaz, A., Saifullah, M., & Rashid, M. (2011). Leadership styles and employee performance. *Interdisciplinary Journal of Contemporary Research in Business, 3*(6), 257–267.

Schuh, S., Egold, N., & van Dick, R. (2012). Towards understanding the role of organizational identification in service settings: A multilevel study spanning leaders, service employees, and customers. *European Journal of Work and Organizational Psychology, 21*(4), 547–574.

Seligman, M. (2011). *Flourish: A visionary new understanding of happiness and well-being.* New York, NY: The Free Press.

Seligman, M. (2018). PERMA and the building blocks of well-being. *The Journal of Positive Psychology, 13*(4), 333–335.

Silvestro, R., & Cross, S. (2000). Applying service chain to retail in UK. *Journal of Service Industry Management, 11*(3), 244–268.

Slavin, S., Schindler, D., Chibnall, J., Fendell, G., & Shoss, M. (2012). PERMA: A model for institutional leadership and culture change. *Academic Medicine, 87*(11), 1481.

Tomic, I., Tesic, Z., Kuzmanovic, B., & Tomic, M. (2018). An empirical study of employee loyalty, service quality, cost reduction and company performance. *Journal of Economic Research, 32*(1), 827–846.

Udoh, B., & Agu, O. (2012). Impact of transformational and transactional leadership on organizational performance. *International Journal of Current Research, 4*(11), 142–147.

Vargo, S., & Lusch, R. (2004). Evolving to a new dominant logic for marketing. *Journal of Marketing, 68*(1), 1–17.

Webster, A. (2014). A flourishing future: Positive psychology and its lessons for education. *Independent School, 74*, 40–46.

# 5 Dynamics of service leadership (the promise)

## 5.1  Increased return on investment (ROI)

When discussing increased ROI in a service firm, the emphasis must be on creating value for employees, shareholders, and the customers. Doing so would follow a natural path to the firm's growth. Since employees are the generators of revenue, it is incumbent upon the leadership to create value for its employees. Creating value for employees takes the form of investments in their development and ensuring they have jobs. Similarly, the firm has to create value for shareholders by becoming a trustworthy firm in the community that consistently delivers on its obligations. Hence, creating value comes in the form of increased stock prices, which ensure the future availability of investment capital by shareholders to fund future development and operation of the firm. Creating value for customers is through the delivery of quality service that is done efficiently and satisfies the need of customers. This helps the firm to develop a long-term relationship with the customer and ensure its revenue stream.

To have a better picture of what is meant by the ROI in services, it would be appropriate to start the discussion on the dynamics of service leadership from two perspectives. The first being the macro view of services, and the second being the micro view of services that drives the organizations toward its goals.

From the macroeconomic perspective, Chapter 2 elaborated on how the service sector has evolved to its present-day configuration, and its major contribution to the growth of the GDP and national economies. It was shown that societies went through a transformation from being based mainly on agriculture (for centuries) and industry (in the 20th century) to having a majority of economic activities located in the service sector (in the 21st century). The transformation that has taken place around the world over the last few decades has often been characterized as the rise of the service economy. In all of these transitions, technology, in one form or another, has been the driving force. Technological progress and changes in economic policy have facilitated the services industry's access to foreign markets via different paths: Exports, FDIs, and offshoring. The rise of the service economy has implications for management trends and specifically for leadership.

From the microeconomic perspective, factors that service leaders have to consider in leading their organizations are highlighted. As the principles of service leadership states, transforming an organization requires leaders to be effective in their communication and strategic in their execution. This means that the elements of the 3Cs have to come together. One element of this is self-leadership, which was elaborated on in the previous chapter. Regardless of circumstances, a service leader will allow members of the organization to take their own personal journey so that they can explore their inner 'self' and at the same time find their voice in the organization. It is through this effort that the firm is able to increase its ROI in its people. Consequently, the contribution of the leader and the follower will enhance the reputation of the firm in the community, and this can lead to greater 'value-added' to the firm.

The five steps necessary in achieving the goals of a service organization and generating the revenues needed for its success and sustainability are discussed next.

*Step one*: Recruit the right individuals who are capable of making productive contributions through talent, skills, knowledge, ethics, and a caring attitude toward self and others. This individual is the one person in the service habitat who understands that people come first, then the organization. This applies not only in the hiring of an employee but the leader of the organization too.

*Step two*: Hire an experienced leader with character and a caring attitude who is capable of integrating skills in a team-led environment (the service habitat) to achieve the objectives of the organization. The experienced leader begins his or her growth by learning the constructs in the mission statement of the service organization to find his or her voice, then, influences others to find theirs. The competent leader understands organizational behavior across different units of the organization and organizes people and resources for developing effective strategies to achieve the desired goals of the firm.

*Step three*: Effective implementation of a clear and compelling vision by all involved in the service organization. This implies outlining specific cognitive abilities such as a disciplined, synthesizing, creative, respectful, and ethical mind to be followed by all members of the habitat.

*Step four*: Delivering the highest standard of service by every member of the organization. Each member of the firm knows that an extraordinary organization is one that is driven by extraordinary people who make a distinctive impact and deliver superior performance over a long period of time as members of the service habitat.

*Step five*: A service mindset leader is an individual who employs strategic approaches to achieve the goals of the service organization by being humble and professional at the same time. All successful service organizations have a single component in common: They have a service leader at the helm who knows the disciplines of strategic agility and flawless execution. It is important to remember that distributed leadership is top-down and bottom-up, so it's not only that a lone leader has a service leadership mindset, but that everyone in the organization has a shared mindset.

Regardless of ROI, it is important to understand that no matter what measures are placed on the leadership development programs, one must strive to improve results for internal and external customers. Creating value for customers helps sell products and services, which in turn provides a consistent revenue stream from the customer.

Value creation in today's companies is increasingly represented in the intangible drivers (Kuźnar, 2016, p. 76). Some of the major intangible drivers discussed in earlier chapters include technology, innovation, intellectual property, alliances, management capabilities, employee relations, customer relations, community relations, and brand value.

To achieve an expected ROI, the service leader must consider the following:

1   *Set clear expectations*:
    Communicating with all members of the habitat on expected outcomes that are based on character and care principles of the organization. By doing so, the team will understand their roles and what is expected of them. The organization must demonstrate a consistency of purpose and allow the decision making to percolate to the lowest levels of the organization.

2   *Define the context*:
    The service leader has a responsibility to define the context of the service (the 'why' of service) and the strategy to achieve the objectives of the organization, by being involved in the daily routines of the service and working side by side with members of the organization. Learning by doing is just as important to the success of the firm as spending resources to train individuals in the context of service.

3   *Nurture commitment*:
    Once an employee is hired, the process of commitment to the basic philosophy of the firm begins. A service leader creates a trust-filled environment that is supportive of individual initiatives and encourages members to participate as a member of the habitat by sharing their ideas with the group. Members of the habitat understand that their service is valuable to the organization and their own careers. When the leadership provides the environment and the employees recognize that their skills can grow with the service organization, their commitment grows, and contribution to the overall effectiveness of the organization increases revenue.

4   *Engage in empowerment*:
    A service leader must initiate the process of empowerment by making members of the habitat feel that they can exercise authority and have resources in the accomplishment of the organization's mission. This responsibility has to be understood by all members of the firm, where they understand their boundaries. This process paves the way for the members of the service organization to feel that the trust bestowed on them is to make the firm more effective in serving the customer.

5   *Insist on collaboration*:
    Since service leadership is driven by collaboration, it is imperative for the service leader to engage with his or her team in a collaborative mode. This requires sharing ideas on the group processes, how to solve problems, improve service processes, and goal setting. By doing so, the firm will function in ways that benefit the service receiver and ultimately increase the firm's ROI.

6 *Encourage innovation:*

The success and sustainability of a firm depend on how the leadership encourages change and innovation in the process of service delivery. Being helpful to the members of the habitat by rewarding those who take a reasonable risk to make service improvements and value creative thinking, transformational thinking, unique solutions, and new ideation is critical to increase the performance and revenue of the firm. Innovation does not occur in a vacuum. The service firm should consider allocating resources for professional development to stimulate new thinking among its employees.

7 *Develop coordination mechanisms:*

Service delivery depends heavily on a coordinated team effort. A simple mistake in the delivery of service has major implications for the firm. As stated by Chung (2012), a service receiver will remember one mistake more than a thousand occurrences of good delivery. A service leader has to pay attention to how such coordination takes place in the organization to eliminate a mistake in the service. This leader has to ensure that proper configurations or reconfigurations have been made and planned for across departments and that the team understands the concept of developing a customer-focused process-centric orientation that moves away from traditional departmental thinking. Well-organized coordination efforts contribute to cost reductions and improved ROI.

8 *Recognize cultural shifts:*

In the discussion in Chapter 2, it was mentioned that the service environment of the 21st century has affected a firm's cultural environment, that is, behavior internally and externally. The service leader must recognize that the team-based, collaborative, empowering, and enabling organizational culture of today is different from the traditional hierarchical organization. Such recognition implies that the firm's leadership is willing to reward, recognize, appraise, hire, and develop plans that motivate and manage the people it employs. When such an environment exists in a service organization, it generates more ROI from the workforce.

In the context of creating value for all the constituencies of service, it would be helpful to introduce the concept of service-dominant (S-D) logic that was put forth by Vargo and Lusch (2004). S-D logic states that intangibility, exchange processes, and relationships are central. There are similarities in the basic philosophy of S-D logic and what is put forward in the service leadership model. Because of its relevance, Table 5.1 summarizes the main ideas.

From Table 5.1, it is apparent that the creation of service is an interactive process that requires a deliverer and a recipient. Given that the notion of excellent service is very subjective, it is incumbent on the leader to educate his or her employees to the standards of excellence that define the organization. One of the pillars of service leadership is *care* that hones on the delivery of quality service to the customer. Hence, if an organization fails to fully consider the notion of care, the organization will have to contend with the negative consequence of their actions.

Table 5.1 S-D logic foundational premises

| Foundational premise | Explanation and comment |
|---|---|
| Service is the fundamental basis of exchange. | The application of operant resources (knowledge and skills), 'service,' as defined in S-D logic, is the basis for all exchange. Service is exchanged for service. |
| The customer is always a cocreator of value. | This implies that value creation is interactional. |
| All social and economic actors are resource integrators. | This implies that the context of value creation is networks of networks (resource integrators). |
| Value is always uniquely and phenomenologically determined by the beneficiary. | Value is idiosyncratic, experiential, contextual, and meaning-laden. |

Source: Vargo & Lusch, 2008, p. 7.

## 5.2 Trust building within and outside the organization

In the discussion in Chapter 2 about a leader's character, emphasis was placed on trust as an important element of leadership. Since trust plays a critical role in the dynamics of service leadership, it is of value to discuss it further here. Trust is an outcome of future activities of others based on their interest and moral commitment to engage. At the initial stage, engagement between parties occurs even though both parties lack complete information about the interest or motives of the other. Trust develops when it is recognized that the other party shares the same interests and is morally committed to being trustworthy. The degree of trust in any relationship will be affected by the formal constraints governing the relationship (Oskarsson, Öberg, & Svensson, 2009, p. 309; Dirks & Skarlicki, 2004).

To build trust among members of the organization (its service habitat), a service leader must show behavioral consistency in his or her action, provide accurate and open communication, and more importantly, demonstrate concern for the employees.

Researchers have elaborated on the role of trust within and outside of an organization, and how it affects the functioning of an organization. Morrow, Hansen, and Pearson (2004) and Johnson and Grayson (2005) have indicated that trust has a cognitive and affective dimension that must be carefully considered when leading. From a service point of view, cognitive trust is knowledge-driven, in which a customer develops confidence in the provider of service based on competence (an aspect of service leadership that was discussed in Chapter 1) and reliability of the service provider. Affective trust, on the other hand, depends on the perceived security and strengths of the relationship that exists between partners. This suggests that trust is developed when the level of care and concern shown by the partners is mutual. In service leadership, a combination of cognitive and affective trust to achieve the goals of a service organization is emphasized. As can be noted from the foregoing discussion, cognitive trust is an objective process while affective trust is a subjective process of evaluating a relationship. In this context, it has been observed by Morrow et al. (2004) that affective trust has a positive effect on nonfinancial indicators of performance while cognitive trust may have a positive effect on financial performance.

Helping service providers to recognize this is one of the dynamic elements of service leadership. Some researchers have opined that trust, like loyalty, is specific to the relationship and not merely to a particular exchange episode (Singh & Sirdeshmukh, 2000). The higher the customers' trust toward retailers, the greater the display of customer loyalty (Liang & Wang, 2006). The key factors to establishing a long-term relationship between a service provider and its customer are competence, empathy, reliability, promptness, and making decisions on the spot for the customer. It was pointed out earlier that a service's inherent intangibility introduces an element of risk for the consumers because they lack information on the service provider's ability to deliver on their expectations. Such risk can be ameliorated by the service provider through consistent delivery of quality of service. Research has demonstrated that the need for trust arises in any situation characterized by a high degree of risk, uncertainty, and/or a lack of knowledge or information on the part of the interaction participants (Schoorman, Mayer, & Davis, 2007; Mayer, Davis, & Schoorman, 1995, p. 710).

Building trust within organizational settings often deals with the following three perspectives:

1 The first major theme has been its constructive effect with respect to reducing transaction costs within organizations.
2 The role trust plays in spontaneous sociability among organizational members.
3 There has been appreciation of how trust facilitates appropriate (that is, adaptive) forms of deference to organizational authorities (Kramer & Cook, 2004, p. 2).

It is noted that the merit of trust as a social resource is related to the disenchantment with traditional organizational theories of managerial 'command and control.' Those theories that emphasized authority and hierarchy were prevalent in the manufacturing age and are less applicable to the flatter and less centralized organizational forms in the service age. As one would expect, the socially differentiated character of service organizations is contrary to the conventional notions of organizing and managing social relations that are prevalent in the hierarchical systems.

In the context of deference to organizational authority, Dirks and Skarlicki (2004) note that much of the theory and research to date on trust in leaders is typically relationship-based or character-based. Relationship-based trust of followers is driven by how followers construe their relationship to a leader. This type of relationship is built upon a shared identity, recognition of a common background, and a history of cooperative interaction. Hardin (2002) refers to this type of relationship-based trust as 'encapsulated interest,' where leaders and followers exist in an exchange relation, in which positive sentiments and the behaviors foster reciprocal behavior that results in the building of mutual trust over time. Character-based perspectives focus on leaders' characteristics, specifically, how the followers perceive the level of trust they have in the character of the leaders in such matters as the leaders' fairness, trustworthiness, or competence, which Chapter 1 discussed. A study done in Sweden shows that perceptions of duly enforced and fair institutions positively influence employees' trust in their superiors, which, in turn, leads to more cooperative behavior and an increased willingness to enter into less formalized contracts (Oskarsson et al., 2009, p. 296). As it is proposed in the framework of service leadership, a workplace environment (the service habitat) that fosters trust will lower transaction costs and is crucial to design institutions that are perceived as fair (Chung, 2019).

Building trust takes time and effort, and a service leader should be familiar with the driving forces behind building trust inside and outside of the organization. No matter what service is delivered, the contribution of trust is undeniable in the proper functioning of a firm. Examples abound on the nature of trust in the service sector (Wang & Emurian, 2005; Yoon, 2002). Using qualitative data from interviews and focus groups involving patients and physicians, Cook et al. (2003) found that patients trust physicians who demonstrate care, empathy, and respect for them as individuals, not just as 'cases.' Service leadership's concepts of *care* and empathy precisely deal with how service firms can build trust with those who receive the service whether the constituency is internal or external.

Another view of building trust within an organization relates to the psychological safety individuals feel working for a firm. Edmondson (1999, 2019) defines psychological safety in terms of individuals' perceptions of the degree of interpersonal threat in their group or organizational environments. This implies that individuals within the habitat feel a sense of security when they take risks, make personal self-disclosures, propose new ideas, or report mistakes. Hence, psychological safety is a form of trust that should be imbedded in a service organization. To achieve psychological safety in the service organization, the leader must be accessible and solicit feedback from all members of the habitat. This modeling of openness does create a sense of safety that employees desire.

The following factors contribute to building trust with the constituency outside, namely, the customers:

1   Competence.
2   Ability to customize solutions.
3   Promptness.
4   Reliability.
5   Empathy.
6   Politeness.
7   Perceived similarity between service representative and customer (Moorman, Deshpandé, & Zaltman, 1993; Coulter & Coulter, 2002).

These factors related to both economic and psychological reasoning. Having recognized the importance of these factors in the delivery of service, it would be essential for service leaders to have a deep understanding of the processes by which consumers maintain relational exchanges with them, and how these processes in turn influence loyalty of the customer. Since services are inherently intangible and heterogeneous, and performance ambiguity poses challenges for forming and sustaining customer relationships, the service leader must ensure that there is consistency in the delivery of service to the customer and recognize the stages of relationship that evolves. In the early stage of relationship-building, the customer has a certain degree of risk due to the intangible nature of the service and not knowing what to expect in terms of the service outcome.

Uncertainty (and hence risk) is reduced when the service receiver has repeated exposure to the service provider over time. That exposure could be positive or negative and hence will affect the level of trust developed (Pi, Liao, & Chen, 2012). In service leadership, it is suggested that both economic and psychological factors that shape customer loyalty be incorporated in the relational exchange. Research has shown that similarity with customers' values and empathy and politeness of the service provider have a greater effect on trust when customers are in the early stages of a particular service relationship (Coulter & Coulter, 2002, p. 45). In the same context, they suggested that the service provider should concentrate upon the service 'extras' that allow them to differentiate themselves from competitors.

Across its early stages of development in the 1970s, the global courier DHL made a commitment to its customers that it will deliver packages within a day anywhere (Chung, 2019). This is how it differentiated itself from other competitors in the market, which made DHL a global leader in a very short period of time. Service leadership emphasizes the importance of interpersonal skills and other qualities in building trust with the customer, which were discussed in Chapter 1.

Another approach to building trust with customers is in the application of agency theory (Mitnick, 1973; Ross, 1973) to services. Since this conceptual model explicitly considers the role of trust in consumer–provider exchanges, its relevance for building trust with the customers is important. Agency theory offers a solid foundation because it construes relationships in terms of principal–agent problems of adverse selection and moral hazard and uses assumptions that are compatible with the nature of most service exchanges (Singh & Sirdeshmukh, 2000).

The agency theory points out that due to information asymmetry and the possible opportunism by the provider of service, consummation of service exchanges may be hindered. The notion of information asymmetry implies that one partner in the exchange has a greater quantity and/or quality of information. But when it comes to uncertainty in the exchange process, both, of course, have incomplete information when making decisions. The information domain is usually constrained by the nature and quality of service delivered. In most instances, the information asymmetry is in favor of the service provider, as it is aware of what it is delivering. However, the customers only have the expectation of what may be delivered. Service leadership promises to remove the information asymmetry by making sure that the customers receive what they asked for and the quality of service matches the expectations.

Opportunism follows from the notion that partners in the exchange are motivated by self-interest and are likely to exploit the situation if they can, to further their self-interest (Singh & Sirdeshmukh, 2000, p. 151). This situation applies to both internal and external constituencies of the service provider. As such, this assumption is less about the object of exchange (e.g., service offered and consumed) and more about the character of partners involved in the exchange. Since character is one of the pillars of service leadership, the dynamic role that it plays in the exchange transaction would hinder opportunism, thus creating trust that is needed by the service provider.

## 5.3 Autonomy of decision making

Service providers, just like any other business organization, are driven by profit motives and sustainability. How to achieve this in a highly competitive environment is important to service leaders and their shareholders. There are many avenues to achieve this goal. Price adjustments and cost reduction, for example, are often seen as appropriate measures. Given that the nature of services being intangible and heterogenous, it can lead to problems in the delivery of service. How such problems are handled depends on the culture and structure of the organization. Organizations with a service leadership mindset emphasize the employees' autonomy of decision in solving problems. Keep in mind that training employees in the values and culture of the organization is essential in this context.

Before discussing this further, it would be of value to return back to the notion of transaction cost, which is part of the reality of service organizations, and why it is believed that when delegation of responsibility is moved to the lowest level and the service members are given the autonomy of making decisions on the spot, the transaction cost will be minimized.

Earlier, it was mentioned how lack of information about the service and its quality contributes to the risk of opportunism. Therefore, the receiver of service may choose to minimize risk by signing an extensive contract with the service provider. This considerably increases the cost of a transaction.

The concept of transaction cost has its roots in the work of Coase (1937), who analyzed why firms exist and what determines the number of firms and what firms do. He spoke indirectly of the cost of using the market mechanism (price) for exchanging goods and services, without explicitly using the term transaction cost. He argues that in a service transaction, there is a cost via contracts that affects the firm's efficiency. Later, Williamson (1973) theorized that treating the firm as an avoider of negative (transaction costs) toward conceptualizing the firm as a creator of positive (knowledge) is why a firm exists in the economic system. He states that the determinants of transaction costs are frequency, specificity, uncertainty, limited rationality, and opportunistic behavior. The argument is basically about the efficiency of the firm. To look at the transaction cost from another perspective, it is argued that the cost of transacting is a function of the interplay between two assumptions of human behavior, namely, bounded rationality and opportunism (Oskarsson et al., 2009, p. 298).

It has to be understood that the players in the market (the supplier of the service and the receiver of the service) have limits to their rationality and constraints on their cognitive capabilities (bounded rationality) and a propensity, when given the chance, to act out of self-interest and, sometimes, even opportunistically. Transaction costs will rise as asset specificity increases and the circumstances surrounding the exchange become more uncertain (Hardt, 2009).

Based on an earlier argument on fairness and how it influences the behavior of employees in a service organization, it was stated that fair institutions can influence and expect individuals' propensity to act on the basis of moral commitments. In line with the previous discussion on transactions costs, the formal constraints governing the relationship should be perceived as fair and just by the actors to enable credible commitments and cooperative behavior (Farrell, 2004; Levi, Moe, & Buckley, 2004; Ostrom, 2000). Furthermore, it must be recognized that decisions are made by people not only on the basis of a single rational utility-maximizing utility function, but rather that individuals weigh their self-interest against their commitment to adhere to moral values in a dual utility function (Rothstein, 2001). In the context of service leadership, it is expected that individuals' behavior will be shaped by both of these avenues.

How does the previous discussion relate to the autonomy of decision making? From a service leadership's point of view, when the delegation of responsibility to deliver a service is given to the lowest level of the organization, there is a deliberate commitment on the part of the service organization to ensure minimizing the risk of opportunism. That uncertainty comes with the delivery of any given service. Such commitment is one of the *3Cs* – that of *care* – that drives service leadership. When a member of the service habitat is given the autonomy to make decisions on the spot, it reduces transaction costs, not only in dollar terms but also in psychological terms for the customer. The implication of this for the service provider is that in the long run, this would lead to a commitment and loyalty by the customer to the firm.

## Key points to remember

The basic premise of this chapter was to broaden the discussion of the *3Cs* by showing how dynamic service leadership is in its role in the growth and sustainability of a service firm.

- The discussion began by elaborating on the role of service leadership in increasing returns on investment (ROIs). Service firms have a responsibility to its shareholders, employees, and customers.
- The interplay of *competency, character,* and *care* shows how each contributes to creating an environment (the service habitat) that supports the long-term goals of the firm in terms of ROI.
- Shareholders expect the leaders and employees of the firm to create value in the delivery of service for the customers. They know that as a consequence of the actions taken by the firm, trust will be developed and revenue will be generated. There are five steps in this process:

  1   Recruiting the right people with *character* and *care*.
  2   Hiring individuals with experience in the delivery of service.
  3   Effective implementation of the firm's mission and strategy.
  4   Delivering the highest quality of service.
  5   A leadership at the helm that knows how to be humble and work collaboratively with employees to achieve the goals of the organization.

- Value creation in a service firm is driven by a number of factors that must be adhered to in order to succeed.
- The firm's leaders have to be clear in their expectation by defining the context of service to employees (the 'why' of service leadership), nurturing commitment by creating a habitat built on trust inside and outside of the firm. A most important piece in this process is empowering employees to take initiatives to improve the quality of services of the firm.
- When leaders are cooperative and collaborative in their action, the employees emulate that philosophy. In addition to the aforementioned factors, the leaders should also encourage innovation, develop systematic coordination

strategies, and recognize the cultural shifts that are taking place in the eco-system of service.

- Various approaches to building trust within and outside the firm were dis-cussed. It was elaborated how behavioral consistency, accurate and open communication as well as demonstrating concern for employees by the lead-ers help build trust.
- Service providers must remember that building trust with the customers has a cognitive and affective dimension. Paying attention to them allows the ser-vice provider with the tools needed to achieve customer loyalty and reduce transaction costs.
- From the employee's perspective, a habitat that is built on the notion of fair-ness and provides a sense of security does lead to developing trust.
- In the service leadership framework, the importance of the autonomy of decision making by the employees cannot be overstated. This does not mean that the leadership does not take responsibility for the actions of its employ-ees, but rather allows its employees to take appropriate action on the spot to deliver quality service.
- The apprentice–mentor approach that is applied in service leadership pro-vides the mechanism to train the employees on the nuances of quality ser-vice. Such quality service that is driven by the values that the service provider adheres to, and the moral commitment of the employee gives the customer a sense of trust where loyalty to the firm gets shaped.

## Case study

### Technological advances are transforming services

In the 1920s, the Ford Motor Company built the River Rouge assem-bly plant in Michigan. Coal and iron ore were brought in at one end and finished automobiles came out the other. Today, this would seem aber-rant, some sort of bizarre theme park, but in fact, at that point in time, the technology of scale made it an entirely rational way of working. There is a great similarity between banks today (service organizations) and the automobile industry that built that plant nearly 80 years ago. And that is, today's banks, like Henry Ford in the 1920s, are learning the techniques of mass production for the first time. There was a time when a bank would lend to a business or provide a mortgage, take the asset, and put it on their books much the way a museum would place a piece of art on the wall or under glass – to be admired and valued for its security and constant return. Times have changed. Banks now take those assets, structure them into pools, and sell securities based on those pools to institutional inves-tors and portfolio managers. In effect, they use their balance sheets not as a museum, but as parking lots – temporary holding spaces to bundle up assets and sell them to those investors who have a far greater interest in holding those assets for the long term. The bank has thus gone from being a museum where it acquired only the finest assets and held and exhibited them in perpetuity into a manufacturing plant that provides a product for the secondary market. Just as Henry Ford did 80 years ago, banks today are focusing on producing a standardized product at a predictable rate, under standard norms of quality, and are teaching their workforces to produce that product as quickly and as efficiently as possible. Technology has been key to this process. The reason that we see a service economy today and gather to talk about it and recognize its importance is because technology has allowed services to gain the operational leverage that manufacturing achieved 100 years ago. In addition to banks, health systems, telephone and telecommunication networks, and distribution and retailing firms are further examples of sectors that have been able to benefit from economies of scale. As a result, we are now living in a world where global-scale service companies exist for the first time, whereas we have seen global manufacturing companies for 50 years or more.

*Source*: Adopted from OECD 2000, p. 8.

## Questions related to the case

1   Given what is stated in this case, what elements of service leadership are missing?
2   How should the banks behave using the technology to serve the customer?
3   Does technology reduce transaction cost in the banking sector? If so, what is the added transaction cost from technology in the delivery of service to bank customers?
4   Technological enhancements will continue to advance. What mitigating circumstances have to be considered in using technology?

## End of chapter questions

1   Has executive leadership clearly communicated its expectations for the team's performance and expected outcomes?
2   Do team members understand why the team was created?
3   Is the organization demonstrating consistency of purpose in supporting the team with resources of people, time, and money?
4   Does the work of the team receive sufficient emphasis as a priority in terms of the time, discussion, attention, and interest directed its way by executive leaders?
5   Do team members understand their roles and responsibilities to achieve the goals set by members of the habitat?
6   Can the members of the habitat see the organization's goals, principles, posture, vision, organizational behavior, and values?
7   What is meant by 'encapsulated interest'?
8   How does the agency theory fit in with service leadership?

## References

Coase, R. (1937). The nature of the firm. *Economica*, 4(16), 386–405.
Chung, P. (2012). *Service reborn: The knowledge, skills, and attitude of service companies*. New York, NY: Lexingford Publishing.

Chung, P. (2019). *Designed to win: What every business needs to know to go global (DHL's 50 years)*. New York, NY: Leaders Press.

Cook, K., Yamagishi, T., Cheshire, C., Cooper, R., Matsuda, M., & Mashima, R. (2003). Trust building via risk taking: A cross-societal experiment. *Social Psychology Quarterly, 68*(2), 121–142.

Coulter, K., & Coulter, R. (2002). Determinants of trust in a service provider: The moderating role of length of relationship. *Journal of Services Marketing, 16*(1), 35–50.

Dirks, K., & Skarlicki, D. (2004). Trust in leaders: Existing research and emerging issues. In R. Kramer & K. Cook (Eds.), *Trust and distrust in organizations: Dilemmas and approaches* (pp. 21–40). New York, NY: Russell Sage Foundation.

Edmondson, A. (1999). Psychological safety and learning behavior in work teams. *Administrative Science Quarterly, 44*(2), 350–383.

Edmondson, A. (2019). *The fearless organization: Creating psychological safety in the workplace for learning, innovation, and growth*. Hoboken, NJ: John Wiley & Sons Inc.

Farrell, H. (2004). Trust, distrust, and power. In R. Hardin (Ed.), *Distrust*. New York, NY: Russell Sage Foundation.

Hardin, R. (Ed.). (2002). *Trust and trustworthiness*. New York, NY: Russell Sage Foundation.

Hardt, Ł. (2009). The history of transaction cost economics and its recent developments. *Erasmus Journal for Philosophy and Economics, 2*(1), 29–51.

Johnson, D., & Grayson, K. (2005). Cognitive and affective trust in service relationships. *Journal of Business Research, 58*(4), 500–507.

Kramer, R., & Cook, K. (2004). *Trust and distrust in organizations: Dilemmas and approaches*. New York, NY: Russell Sage Foundation.

Kuźnar, A. (2016). *Value creation in the service economy*. Warsaw, Poland: Szkoła Główna Handlowa w Warszawie Publisher.

Levi, M., Moe, M., & Buckley, T. (2004). The transaction costs of distrust. In R. Hardin (Ed.), *Distrust*. New York, NY: Russell Sage Foundation.

Liang, C., & Wang, W. (2006). The behavioural sequence of the financial services industry in Taiwan: Service quality, relationship quality and behavioural loyalty. *Service Industries Journal, 26*, 119–145.

Mayer, R., Davis, J., & Schoorman, F. (1995). An integrative model of organizational trust. *Academy of Management Review, 20*(3), 709–734.

Mitnick, B. (1973). *Fiduciary rationality and public policy: The theory of agency and some consequences*. Paper presented at the 1973 Annual Meeting of the American Political Science Association, New Orleans, LA.

Moorman, C., Deshpandé, R., & Zaltman, G. (1993). Factors affecting trust in market research relationships. *Journal of Marketing, 57*, 81–101.

Morrow, J., Hansen, M., & Pearson, A. (2004). The cognitive and affective antecedents of general trust within cooperative organizations. *Journal of Managerial Issues, 16*(1), 48–64.

OECD (2000). *The service economy*. Paris: OECD.

Oskarsson, S., Öberg, P., & Svensson, T. (2009). Making capitalism work: Fair institutions and trust. *Economic and Industrial Democracy, 30*(2), 294–320.

Ostrom, E. (2000). Collective action and the evolution of social norms. *Journal of Economic Perspectives, 14*, 137–158.

Pi, S., Liao, H., & Chen, H. (2012). Factors that affect consumers' trust and continuous adoption of online financial services. *International Journal of Business and Management, 7*(9), 108–119.

Ross, S. (1973). The economic theory of agency: The principal's problem. *American Economic Review, 63*(2), 134–139.

Rothstein, B. (2001). The universal welfare state as a social dilemma. *Rationality and Society, 13*, 213–233.

Schoorman, F., Mayer, R., & Davis, J. (2007). An integrative model of organizational trust: Past, present, and future. *Academy of Management Review, 32*(2), 344–354.

Singh, J., & Sirdeshmukh, D. (2000). Agency and trust mechanisms in consumer satisfaction and loyalty judgments. *Journal of the Academy of Marketing Science, 28*(1), 150–167.

Vargo, S., & Lusch, R. (2004). Evolving to a new dominant logic for marketing. *Journal of Marketing, 68*(1), 1–17.

Vargo, S., & Lusch, R. (2008). Service-dominant logic: Continuing the evolution. *Journal of the Academy of Marketing Science, 36*(1), 1–10.

Wang, Y., & Emurian, H. (2005). Trust in e-commerce: Consideration of interface design factors. *Journal of Electronic Commerce in Organizations, 3*(4), 42–60.

Williamson, O. (1973). Markets and hierarchies: Some elementary considerations. *American Economic Review, 63*(2), 316–325.

Yoon, S. (2002). The antecedents and consequences of trust in online-purchase decisions. *Journal of Interactive Marketing, 16*(2), 47–63.

# 6 Joyful leadership

## 6.1 Elements of joyful leadership

The world of work can be rigid, demanding, stressful, and tiring, or it can be a happier experience with a joyful disposition. How one turns all of those negative elements of work into a positive experience is at the core of this chapter. In service leadership, the notion of care for self and others is seen as an important element of well-being. Chung and Elfassy (2016) suggest that one's emotional state of mind, of which happiness is an element, is as rich, varied, and diverse as the 'competence' of service leadership that was discussed in Chapter 1. They correctly point out that everything one does thrives or crumbles, depending on the emotional state. The emotional states of happiness, delight, or bliss have been discussed in the psychological research (Seligman, 2000, 2002, 2018; Scorsolini-Comin, Fontaine, Koller, & Santos, 2012; Lyubomirsky, Sheldon, & Schkade, 2005; Argyle, 2001).

Before discussing the impact of joyful leadership and a joyful work environment, it is appropriate to take a look at the notion of happiness and well-being from different perspectives. Several concepts such as 'happiness,' 'bliss,' and 'delight' are used in the literature to shed light on what makes for a better life (Lalatendu & Pradhan, 2017; Seligman, 2018). In an attempt to determine the link between happiness and quality of life, practitioners have turned their attention to exploring interventions that can improve long-term happiness among employees (Sheldon & Lyubomirsky, 2007). The emphasis on the notion of *care* in service leadership ties directly with happiness in the work environment (habitat). Interestingly, an important question that provokes today's behavioral researchers is what makes people joyful. Various postulates that contribute to joyfulness include (1) positivity inside an individual that predisposes a person to be joyful; (2) environmental condition (habitat) or social setup that gives one joy; (3) interactions with situations that create a joyful atmosphere; and (4) behavioral choices of individuals that influence them to derive joy from circumstances.

Warr and Clapperton (2010) stated that 'contentment' as a form of joyful experience is based on two approaches: (1) Hedonic – emphasizing subjective internal experiences, for example, job satisfaction; or (2) eudemonic – fulfillment of higher-order needs, for example, self-actualization for the attainment of one's well-being as was discussed in Chapter 1. The concept of hedonic drive promotes positive emotion, whereas the eudemonic approach provides an incessant motivation to derive happiness. According to Joshanloo (2014), to a great extent, the Western notion of happiness is based on hedonism, while the Eastern concept tends toward eudemonism. Hedonic concept claims that happiness lies in achieving delight and avoiding suffering and emphasizes physical pleasure. On the other hand, the eudemonic concept claims that happiness is experienced when a person acts nobly in harmony with his or her conscience and emphasizes inner well-being (Ryan & Deci, 2001).

No matter what the driving force behind happiness is, researchers have recognized the complex nature of happiness and how to measure it. Much of the theoretical research has shifted from happiness to well-being (Seligman, 2002, 2000). Some have suggested that happiness may be a personality trait or characteristic more stable than those of genetic origin and there are others who argue that happiness lies in reducing stress through the satisfaction of goals and needs (Snyder & Lopez, 2009). Extensive research by psychologists on emotions and their impact on how individuals live their lives has shown that happiness is a learned optimism (Seligman, 1991, 2018). Seligman recounts his journey through the studies about learned helplessness and highlights several benefits of the people considered optimistic. Optimists tend to assume that the problems experienced are temporary and due to external causes, and hence they don't consider themselves to be a failure in their activities. Furthermore, optimists are more entrepreneurial and have better health. Seligman postulates that happiness could be analyzed according to three different elements: Positive emotion, engagement, and meaning. Positive emotion entails sensations such as pleasure, excitement, ecstasy, and comfort among others. Engagement refers to a loss of self in an activity in which the person has little awareness of his or her true sensations, only reports feeling much pleasure and being in a position of constant openness. The third element is meaning, and it relates to the search for a purpose in life. A meaningful life consists of belonging and serving something you believe is greater than the self (Seligman, 2004). As human beings, positive institutions have been created to provide consistency for this search, such as religion, political parties, family, and diverse social groups. In service leadership, through the concept of *character* and *care*, all the three elements of positive emotion, engagement, and meaning when serving self and others are employed.

The concept of authentic happiness attests that people make choices estimating how much happiness (satisfaction in life) they can achieve individually by choosing a path that maximizes their satisfaction (Seligman, 2011). By doing so, an individual maximizes his or her satisfaction regardless of interactions and interpersonal relationships with others. It is here that the well-being theory makes advances, as it incorporates the need for social relationships for development and the feeling of being happy and accomplished. In other words, social relationships have greater importance, overtaking the consideration of well-being as something solely individual. This is where the joy of work and its connectivity with others contribute to happiness and well-being no matter what service is being offered.

Given the nature of happiness as being complex, transient, and difficult to measure, researchers have opted to look at well-being as a more accepted psychological construct (Seligman, 2011). In defining well-being, Seligman started from the classic definition of health proposed by the World Health Organization in 1946, which states that in the absence of illness, a person is considered healthy. He adds the presence of positive emotions, which leads to a situation of effective well-being of a healthy person.

Counseling, psychotherapy, and related services certainly have their place. It would be naïve to think that all leaders are emotional rocks, but the true service leader owns his or her mental states, can feel and process his or her vulnerabilities, and finds practical strategies to manage these states. For this purpose, let's discuss the catchall notion of well-being and happiness as the optimal state when looking at joy in the workplace.

The overall emotional state of a person dictates how that individual relates to work and others around them. For some people, they're at their best when they have the edge of stress pushing them forward. Others seek or create conflict around themselves to find the fuel to move forward. From the service leadership perspective, conflict would not describe these people as happy, but for them, conflict and turbulence fulfill a need that brings satisfaction. For example, a parent may find that his or her child consistently argues and resists when the underlying motivation is a desire to establish an emotional connection. Being a parent really is a solid building block and battleground for service leadership and managing a child's tantrums or sudden bursts of conflicting emotions is great service leadership training (even if it can make your hair turn grey).

Well-being and happiness do not only mean the sense of joy one feels when something goes well but rather the many different emotions that one experiences that are positive and create an optimal state of mind. It is unrealistic for us to assume that one can maintain a state of euphoria in all of the activities in daily life. One may be in a blissful state for a while, but all things must pass. Who among us would say they've never experienced pain or unhappiness? The Buddhist attitude, for example, is that life cannot avoid suffering.

In discussing well-being, it is not suggested that there is a magic trick to achieve never-ending happiness, but rather engage you in developing strategies that increase how often and how long you remain happy. The greatest benefit is that the happier you are, the more people around you will be uplifted. Rather than dragging down the energy, it's much better to lift the energy of the room and even be the life of the party. Happiness and optimism can be infectious, much the same as unhappiness and pessimism can infect and spread like a virus throughout your network.

In a service moment, it's clear that the happier the server is, the better and more impactful the service will be. For those who have worked a service job in retail, a common expectation is that the server leaves his or her personal problems at the door. The moment the server enters the role, his or her face and mood are the company they represent. For the more analytical type of person who never considered what it means to be a service provider, this may sound soft or vague. A chemist or meteorologist might find explorations of this dimension frivolous, especially around his or her level of happiness. This may work if you're in a lab or reviewing meteorological models and data, but once you have to deal with other people, this dimension can make all the difference.

There are definite, clear advantages and effects on a group's quality of engagement and bottom line when a team is made up of happy people. Whether you're in the executive suite or on the front line, being emotionally stable and happy enhances productivity. Research has shown that human happiness has powerful causal effects on labor productivity (Oswald, Proto, & Sgroi, 2015). In their empirical research, it was found that a rise in happiness leads to greater productivity in a paid piece-rate task. Furthermore, since happiness in a workplace carries with it a return in productivity, their findings have consequences for firms' promotion policies and how they structure internal labor markets and thus may be of interest to management scholars and human resources specialists.

More generally, psychologists have shown that positive emotion influences the capacities of choice and innovative content (Isen & Reeve, 2005). Argyle (2001) points out that little is understood about how life satisfaction affects productivity but that there is (some) evidence that happier service providers achieve career goals by remaining with firms that create a happy habitat for its employees. A recent study by Chamberlain and Zhao (2019) asked: Can companies help to achieve high customer satisfaction by investing in employees and ensuring that those who deliver goods and services are themselves satisfied with their jobs? Their study showed that there is a strong statistical link between employee well-being and customer satisfaction among a large sample of some of the largest companies today. A happier workforce is clearly associated with companies' ability to deliver better customer satisfaction – particularly in industries with the closest contact between workers and customers, including retail, tourism, restaurants, health care, and financial services.

Another study suggests that self-confidence enhances the motivation to act, so their framework is consistent with the idea that there can be a connection between mood and productivity (Benabou and Tirole (2002). Furthermore, Amabile, Barsade, and Muellur (2005), and Baas, De Dreu, and Nijstad (2008) uncover evidence that happiness provokes greater creativity. At a minimum, a team whose members manage their happiness dimension will connect more strongly with other team members and clients.

From the service leadership perspective, the leader's emotional state sets the tone for everyone in the habitat. If the leader has toxic qualities and a bad disposition, this will be a big hurdle for people who are in the front line of service. Like a virus, these qualities will spread and can end up dragging down the emotional state of people in the entire habitat.

The best way to understand happiness is to appreciate the absence of unhappiness. This may appear abstract, but let's see what insights are here. As a start, make an inventory; list the things, large and small, that make you unhappy and see if you can reduce the frequency and power they have in your life. For example, often one finds oneself unhappy when others have done something wrong to him or her. It is realistic that one may not be able to have control over others' behavior. So, the alternative to being unhappy with them is to forgive them for what they had consciously or inadvertently done. This can be managed by the individual in the comfort of one's own space. It does allow us to free ourselves from a lot of tension and unhappiness.

This approach is no substitute for real psychotherapy or pharmacological treatment if it's called for, but it is a strategy for reducing and removing the thoughts that bring unhappiness. Once this is achieved, you can start reaching small goals each day, goals that together result in a rolling sense of accomplishment. If you want to build on your momentum of happiness, build on the success of your small goals after you minimize the barriers that bring you unhappiness. In other words, this was happiness by design.

Herzberg, Mausner, and Snyderman (1959) stated that (positive) satisfaction and, as a consequence, happiness is due to good experiences and that these are due to 'motivators' – achievement, recognition, the work itself, responsibility, and advancement. He states that dissatisfaction is due to bad experiences caused by 'hygiene' factors – supervisors, fellow workers, company policy, working conditions, and personal life. Research on joy confirms Herzberg's finding that achievement is important, but it also finds that relationships with other people are even more important, and not just a source of distress as he found (Argyle, 1987).

Systematically identifying what makes you unhappy allows you to focus your energy and attention on thoughts and activities that enhance your quality of life. The chances are, no great epiphanies will come after going through this process. This exercise is about raising awareness of what's going on within you, and by doing this you'll clarify what makes you unhappy. Research explains how to increase happiness in your life by doing big and small things that make us happy (Lyubomirsky, 2008). The insight is that instead of focusing on getting or doing one big thing, and potentially waiting or denying yourself other joys in order to get it, do something smaller. The amount of happiness will be about the same, but cumulatively you will come out on top by having little highs more often.

As a practical approach, it is suggested spending ten to 15 minutes every morning to map out your day, to fit in as many small joys as possible. The act of planning it out and consciously scheduling where you put your energy will nudge you in the right direction and slowly but surely free you from what can bring you down. Plato's statement in *The Republic* that 'The just man is happy, and the unjust man is miserable' is grounded in the reality of today, too. A recent study finds a relationship between life satisfaction and a low tolerance for unethical conduct (James, 2009). In this study, which focuses on four Western countries (the US, Canada, Mexico, and Brazil), the results reveal a positive and generally significant effect of ethics on happiness, even after controlling for other factors known to be correlated with happiness. Furthermore, the study finds that cultural differences also affect how ethical issues have an impact on social well-being (happiness). For example, the relationship between ethics and happiness being stronger in Brazil than in other countries may be evidence of how strongly Brazilians feel about the importance of behaving ethically relative to respondents in other countries (James, 2009, p. 16).

Another insight worth considering is the notion of 'flow' in our activities. The core theory is that one can consciously bring up positive states through 'flow' experiences (Csikszentmihalyi, 2008). These so-called flow experiences come when one takes on a task that challenges one at the right level; just hard enough that one feels focused while doing it and the payoff feels great when the challenge is completed. If the task is too easy or too hard, engagement suffers, and one will miss out on the flow state because one becomes bored or frustrated. Flow activities can come from many sources, but if you can work them into your day, you will increase your sense of engagement, fulfillment, and happiness.

There's also those who argue that even if chasing flow experiences might help one feel good, it isn't necessarily a recipe for success. It has been pointed out that having and focusing on early-life passions is not the norm and it probably is not the right approach for everyone (Newport, 2012). Instead, Newport suggests strengthening your 'rare and valuable' skills to develop yourself into a 'craftsman,' and this focus can lead to a successful career. He asserts that to improve and grow, one must deliberately push oneself beyond the comfort zone, or whatever level needed to be in a flow state. In other words, one is more likely to succeed when one looks beyond the passions and focuses on what one is actually good at doing. What this implies is that after achieving these rare and valuable skills, then one can explore the passions in a more leisurely fashion.

It is important to keep in mind that happiness and ethics are related and have been discussed for millennia by philosophers, religious leaders, and other social scientists. This was elaborated on when the concept of ethics and 'character' of service leadership was discussed in Chapter 1. The argument has been that happiness is improved when individuals behave ethically. An effective strategy for managing our emotional state is to clarify what happiness means for us and what elements work or don't work and to focus on bringing in more positive experiences in the work environment or habitat. The next section discusses the creation of a joyful habitat.

## 6.2 Creation of a habitat for joyful leadership

The discussion thus far described service leadership as a set of attributes that every service provider must have in delivering service. What this implies is that the service leadership mindset is the driving force behind quality service. In this section, that context is broadened to include a physical space – a habitat – that encourages all aspects of service leadership. As Chung and Bell (2015) stated, 'a habitat is not necessarily a brick-and-mortar building, although many architects labor hard to influence people's perceptions and behaviors through the artful design of a business headquarters.'

No matter what description is given to a place where an exchange of ideas in an organization takes place, and the people within that environment find safety in thought and physical well-being, that place is referred to as a service habitat. Service leaders have variously described a habitat as their 'home base,' 'mothership,' or 'comfort zone.' It's where they go, literally or figuratively, to recharge, discuss strategies, receive new information, share insights, orient newcomers, and learn from experts and senior, experienced employees.

With technological advances of late, some global companies establish this kind of habitat through regular teleconferences that bring workers face-to-face in a private environment not shared by customers or competitors. Other companies keep their 'hive' of international locations all part of one habitat by frequent visits from top company leaders and regular exchange of work teams across borders.

A healthy service habitat is characterized by constant monitoring to prevent external and internal negative factors from contaminating the environment. The work of monitoring is everyone's business when it comes to sustaining a healthful habitat, not just a single manager (Etmanski, Fulton, Nasmyth, & Page, 2014). Employee focus groups, computer-based suggestion boxes, a dependable whistle-blowing capacity, and a culture of 'freedom-to-speak' across company hierarchies are all ways by which potential problems in the habitat can be caught in an early stage of contamination and remediated.

The power of a habitat to sustain and inspire its inhabitants can be demonstrated by taking a hard look at one-person businesses, often run out of a garage or home. Although these small operations may have the advantage of low overhead and high expertise, they typically lack the day-to-day relationships with other dedicated employees as found in a multimember habitat. To successfully sustain a business, the business needs resources like finance, for which it has to depend on financial institutions; acceptance of social norms, for which it has to depend on society; proper market conditions, for which it has to depend on the market; the delivery of services, for which it has to depend on the customers; and labor, for which it has to depend on society. These are just a few factors that affect the service habitat.

Perhaps for this reason more than any other, one-person operations often go out of business within a year. There's no one to discuss successes or failures with. No one steps forward with advice on how to solve a problem or congratulations on a particular success. In short, one of the virtues of the habitat is that it helps to satisfy the needs of humans as social beings. Within the confines of a well-monitored habitat, one feels safe to share doubts, ideas, fears, and experiences – that is, to learn from one another.

Service leaders take responsibility for the entire habitat of their service organization (Grint, 2005). The word 'habitat' stems from the natural world, referring particularly to a localized area containing all components necessary for the survival and perpetuation of the species it contains. In a business context, the habitat of a beauty salon would include not only an attractive and healthful physical environment (in terms of cleanliness, light, air, and so forth) but also the social environment, in which employees do not make work life uncomfortable for one another or for their clients, through gossip, bickering, and so forth.

This habitat would also include psychological factors, such as the management methods of the salon owner, as well as security factors, including health insurance, safe working conditions, and fair compensation.

A service leader often plays a key role in designing a work habitat, but his or her real work lies in monitoring and maintaining its health. Just as a habitat for fish can 'turn' quickly due to pH fluctuations or improper filtering, so a work environment can be 'unhealthy' in terms of interpersonal relations among employees or poor relationships with clients. A service leader acts quickly in the circumstances to identify the problems in the habitat and resolve them.

The service leader knows in advance that the company 'grapevine,' the private communication that passes among employees, will not automatically let him know what's wrong with the habitat. Through unobtrusive conversations and observation, the service leader can troubleshoot the ailing environment without asking any individual employee to be the informant who tattles to the boss on the other employees.

Since the employees are the first to be affected by a poor work habitat, the service leader works to develop a culture in which all members ('in the same boat together') consider themselves responsible for solving workplace problems. Some companies have opted to employ a third-party intermediary who can report problems without alienating themselves from the rest of the workforce.

Habitat, in the language of service leadership, and work environment as known in the business world, have a significant impact on productivity, creativity, and innovation just to name a few. When designing a service habitat, one should keep in mind that it is not only the physical space, but also the social and psychological environments that allow for easy interaction among members of the organization and with those in the outside community. The habitat supports its employees in their development through training, provides fair compensation and adequate workload, and most importantly develops a working environment that has a positive impact on the level of productivity in the organization.

Research has shown that the proper design of the habitat contributes to productivity. Smrita, Singh, Gupta, and Dutt (2010) found that the development of a good culture in the organization affects employees' level of motivation. Service leadership emphasizes that a major responsibility of a service leader is to create a culture of mutual respect and trust in the organization. McGuire and McLaren (2007) found that a working environment has a strong impact on employees' well-being and develops interaction, collaboration, and innovation and increase job satisfaction when there is less risk (Bakotic & Babić, 2013).

In the context of the relationship of the habitat with creativity, Haynes (2008) found that the behavioral components of a working environment have more impact than the physical components of the working environment. Furthermore, in the environment where the level of interaction is high, creativity and the transfer of transactional knowledge are substantial.

## Key points to remember

To complement the discussion on elements of service leadership, this chapter highlighted the contribution of happiness and well-being in the workplace (habitat) of service. Specifically, these elements were discussed:

- Happiness has many dimensions and its impact on the work environment or habitat is significant.
- Research has shown that joyfulness comes from a variety of sources such as:
  - Positivity inside an individual that predisposes a person to be joyful.
  - Environmental condition (habitat) or social setup that gives joy.
  - Interaction with situations that create a joyful atmosphere.
  - Behavioral choices of individuals that influence them to derive joy from circumstances.
- The leadership of an organization has the responsibility to create a culture of happiness in order to achieve its goals.
- 'Contentment' as a form of joyful experience is based on:
  - Hedonic desires that emphasize physical or psychological pleasures such as job satisfaction.
  - Eudemonic desires that emphasize fulfillment of higher-order needs of inner well-being.
- Some researchers have postulated that happiness could be analyzed according to three different elements:
  - Positive emotion: This includes pleasure, excitement, ecstasy, and comfort among others.

- Engagement: This involves the loss of self in an activity in which the person has little awareness of his or her true sensations.
- Meaning: This relates to the search for purpose in life. A meaningful life consists of belonging and serving something you believe is greater than the self.

- In service leadership, the emphasis is on the overall emotional state of a person and how that individual relates to work and others around him or her.
- Research has shown that human happiness has powerful causal effects on labor productivity. More generally, psychologists have shown that positive emotion influences the capacities of choice and innovative content.
- A happier workforce is clearly associated with companies' ability to deliver better customer satisfaction – particularly in industries with the closest contact between workers and customers, including retail, tourism, restaurants, health care, and financial services.
- The best way to understand happiness is to appreciate the absence of unhappiness.
- Another facet of happiness is that those who are happier tend to be more ethical in their activities.
- Cultural differences contribute to what is called happiness and joyful interactions.
- The design of a service habitat is critical to the success of a service firm. It refers to creating an environment where all members of the firm find safety in thought and action.
- Service leaders have variously described a habitat as their 'home base,' 'mothership,' or 'comfort zone.' It's where they go, literally or figuratively, to recharge, discuss strategies, receive new information, share insights, orient newcomers, and learn from experts and senior, experienced employees.
- A service habitat has significant impacts on productivity, creativity, and innovation, just to name a few.

## Case study

### Top chef in action

Le Petit Plat was always a hub of movement. From the moment the doors opened in the morning, Sharon and her staff would attend to all the details that made the restaurant special. One observation Sharon was especially proud of was when a reviewer noted that everyone in the restaurant was beaming, even in the thick of their evening dinner service.

Sharon made happiness within the restaurant a state she designed into the nature of the relationships and procedures. It wasn't that she insisted everyone smiled to customers and move with purpose and focus, but that there was a priority in the restaurant that it was a place where her staff wanted to be. Sharon was persistent about pushing her staff. She was demanding enough to make each shift a challenge, but she also ensured everyone was supported and had what they needed to deliver their best. In this climate, if someone lagged or tripped up to cause errors, everyone was in it for everyone else and the mistakes were corrected. Everyone could make mistakes; everyone could have a bad day. To maintain this climate of happiness, the team would have meetings to exchange war stories from the past week, what the mistakes were, and what might be the best solutions.

Sharon understood that by taking out the negative influences – either weeding out the wrong employees who brought people down or cutting out procedures that went against the team's harmony, she could make the restaurant into a great environment. Everyone would be proud of their work and each plate that came out of their kitchen, night after night.

*Source*: Adapted from Chung, P., & Ip, S. (2018). *Pillars of a service hub*. New York, NY: Lexingford Publisher.

## Questions related to the case

1  What did Sharon do to make her staff smile at customers and move with purpose and focus?
2  What did the team do to maintain a climate of happiness?
3  What is the leadership style that Sharon subscribes to?

## End of chapter questions

1  In the context of happiness, what do positive emotion, engagement, and meaning imply?
2  Give an example of how hedonic and eudemonic contentment contributes to a joyful work experience.
3  What is the relationship of eudemonic contentment to the self-actualization of Maslow?
4  What is meant by authentic happiness as put forward by Seligman?
5  How is service provider productivity tied to a happier work environment?

## References

Amabile, T., Barsade, S., & Muellur, J. (2005). Affect and creativity at work. *Administrative Science Quarterly*, *50*(3), 367–403.

Argyle, M. (1987). *The psychology of happiness*. London: Methuen.

Argyle, M. (2001). *The psychology of happiness* (2nd ed.). London: Routledge.

Awan, G., & Tahir, M. (2015). Impact of working environment on employee's productivity: A case study of banks and insurance companies in Pakistan. *European Journal of Business and Management*, *7*(1), 329–345.

Baas, M., De Dreu, C., & Nijstad, B. (2008). A meta-analysis of 25 years of mood-creativity research: Hedonic tone, activation, or regulatory focus. *Psychological Bulletin*, *134*, 779–806.

Bakotic, D., & Babić, T. (2013). Relationship between working conditions and job satisfaction: The case of Croatian shipbuilding company. *International Journal of Business and Social Science*, *4*(2), 206–213.

Benabou, R., & Tirole, J. (2002). Self-confidence and personal motivation. *Quarterly Journal of Economics*, *117*, 871–915.

Chamberlain, A., & Zhao, D. (2019, August 19). The key to happy customers? Happy employees. *Harvard Business Review* (Digital).

Chung, P., & Bell, A. (2015). *25 principles of service leadership*. New York, NY: Lexingford Publishing.

Chung, P., & Elfassy, R. (2016). *The 12 dimensions of a service leader: Manage your personal brand for the service age*. New York, NY: Lexingford Publishing.

Csikszentmihalyi, M. (2008). *Flow: The psychology of optimal experience*. New York, NY: Harper Perennial Modern Classic.

Etmanski, C., Fulton, M., Nasmyth, G., & Page, M. (2014). The dance of joyful leadership. In K. Schuyler, J. Baugher, K. Jironet, & L. Lid-Falkman (Eds.), *Leading with spirit, presence, and authenticity*. San Francisco, CA: Jossey-Bass.

Grint, K. (2005). *Leadership: Limits and possibilities*. Aldershot: Palgrave Macmillan.

Haynes, B. (2008). An evaluation of the impact of the office environment on productivity. *Facilities, 26*(5–6), 178–195.

Herzberg, F., Mausner, B., & Snyderman, B. (1959). *The motivation to work*. New York, NY: Wiley.

Isen, A., & Reeve, J. (2005). The influence of positive affect on intrinsic and extrinsic motivation: Facilitating enjoyment of play, responsible work behavior, and self-control. *Motivation and Emotion, 29*, 297–325.

James, H. (2009). *Is the just man a happy man? An empirical study of the relationship between ethics and subjective well-being* (Department of Agricultural Economics Working Paper No. AEWP 2009-07). Columbia, Missouri: University of Missouri.

Joshanloo, M. (2014). Eastern conceptualizations of happiness: Fundamental differences with Western views. *Journal of Happiness Studies, 15*(2), 475–493.

Lalatendu, K., & Pradhan, S. (2017). Joy at work: Initial measurement and validation in Indian context. *The Psychologist-Manager Journal, 20*(2), 106–122.

Lyubomirsky, S. (2008). *The how of happiness: A new approach to getting the life you want*. New York, NY: Penguin Books.

Lyubomirsky, S., Sheldon, K. M., & Schkade, D. (2005). Pursuing happiness: The architecture of sustainable change. *Review of General Psychology, 9*, 111–131.

McGuire, D., & McLaren, L. (2007). The impact of physical environment on employee commitment in call centres: The mediating role of employee well-being. *Team Performance Management, 14*(5–6).

Newport, C. (2012). *So good they can't ignore you: Why skills trump passion in the quest for work you love*. New York, NY: Business Plus.

Oswald, A., Proto, E., & Sgroi, D. (2015). Happiness and productivity. *Journal of Labor Economics, 33*(4), 789–822.

Ryan, R., & Deci, E. (2001). On happiness and human potentials: A review of research on hedonic and eudaimonic well-being. *Annual Review of Psychology, 52*(1), 141–166.

Scorsolini-Comin, F., Fontaine, A., Koller, S., & Santos, M. (2012). From authentic happiness to well-being: The flourishing of positive psychology. *Psicologia: Reflexão e Crítica, 26*(4), 663–670.

Seligman, M. (1991). *Learned optimism*. New York, NY: Knopf.

Seligman, M. (2000). Positive psychology: An introduction. *American Psychologist Association, 55*(1), 5–14.

Seligman, M. (2002). *Authentic happiness: Using the new positive psychology to realize your potential for lasting fulfillment.* London: Nicholas Brealey Publishing.

Seligman, M. (2004). *Authentic happiness: Using the new positive psychology for permanent accomplishment* (N. Capelo, Trans.). Rio de Janeiro, RJ: Objetiva.

Seligman, M. (2011). *Flourish: A visionary new understanding of happiness and well-being.* New York, NY: The Free Press.

Seligman, M. (2018). *Learned optimism.* London: Nicholas Brealey Publishing.

Sheldon, K., & Lyubomirsky, S. (2007). It is possible to become happier? (And if so, how?). *Social and Personality Psychology Compass, 1,* 129–145.

Smrita, S., Singh, A., Gupta, N., & Dutt, R. (2010). Impact of work culture on motivation and performance level of employees in private sector companies. *Acta Oeconomica Pragensia, 6,* 49–67.

Snyder, C., & Lopez, S. J. (2009). *Positive psychology: A scientific and practical exploration of human strengths* (R. C. Costa, Trans.). São Paulo, SP: Artmed.

Warr, P., & Clapperton, G. (2010). *The joy of work? Jobs, happiness, and you.* New York, NY: Routledge.

# Ethical dilemmas facing service leaders

## 7.1  Basic ethical principles

Ethics, to many, is a branch of philosophy that is sometimes referred to as moral philosophy. However, in its practical applications, the concept of ethics involves more than philosophy and touches other disciplines as well. It has to be kept in mind that ethics is distinct from other disciplines of science, social science, and arts. Ethics is more than dealing with factual knowledge in the way that the sciences and other branches of inquiry engage in. It deals with determining the nature of normative theories and applying these sets of principles to practical moral problems.

No matter what activities are performed, there are bound to be situations that require ethical judgment. Such judgment calls for the application of ethical principles that guide us in making decisions. What these ethical principles are and how they affect the service industry is of interest to us in this chapter. This section discusses the concept of ethics in historical terms as well as the ethical principles that have implications for the service sector.

### Early Western and Eastern philosophies on ethics

When did the concept of ethics come into being? Since ethics deals with the way humans interact with each other, there has to be a set of norms that will guide them on how to live in ways that are socially and morally acceptable. Thus, societies developed a set of moral codes that is called ethics. Given the nature of societies, whether in the East or the West, the principles all echoed the goodness of humans and their ability to be just. The intention here is to give an overview of these philosophical discussions and not get into the details of ethical developments in history. The reader is encouraged to look deeper into these principles elsewhere.

The basic premise of these philosophies of life is that humans have the capacity for being virtuous, moral, and just. How philosophers, through time, view the notion of virtue and morality depends on the school of thought.

Since its early inception, those who developed these moral codes knew that to be accepted by society, the codes must be tied to a divine origin. By connecting morality to a divine origin, the religious leaders became the interpreter and guardian of it. When looked at from this perspective, ethics appears to be not an independent field of study but rather a branch of theology. However, Plato in his dialogue *Euthyphro* argued otherwise by stating that there must be some standards of right or wrong that are independent of the approval of the gods (Singer, 2011, 2017). Protagoras (490 bc–420 bc), who was one of several Greek thinkers, stated that the foundations of an ethical system needed nothing from the gods or from any special *metaphysical* realm beyond the ordinary world of the senses (Duignan, 2011, p. 30).

The Greek philosopher Socrates argued that the standard of doing right or wrong depends on virtue. He believed that self-knowledge is sufficient for the good life and that knowledge leads to virtue. He pointed out that if knowledge can be learned, so can virtue. He thought that anyone who knows what virtue is will necessarily act virtuously. His argument was that individuals who behave badly either lack knowledge or are ignorant about the real nature of virtue.

Among his critical pronouncements was the statement that 'the unexamined life is not worth living.' What he suggested to us is that one needs to examine the essence of life, through knowledge, and what one wants from it. In all of these assertions, he did not suggest how one should live one's life. He further stated that one must seek knowledge and wisdom before private interests to be happy. In this manner, knowledge is sought as a means toward ethical action. One's true happiness is promoted by doing what is right.

Socratic ethics has a teleological character, that is, using a mechanistic explanation for human behavior is mistaken. Socrates's view on human action is that all of us aim toward the good in accordance with a purpose in nature.

Arguments contrary to Socrates's statement point out that there is a lot more that contributes to a person's happiness and well-being besides 'examining their lives.' Epicurus mentioned that factors such as life experiences, being with family, things to be thankful for, memories, and reaching success in life make one happy, and a happy life should most definitely be lived whether it is examined or not (Konstan, 2018).

Epicurus and Socrates have different approaches to the phrase 'analyzing life.' Epicurus made the point that contemplation and reflection on life bring more happiness.

Plato, like the other Greek philosophers of his time, believed that virtue is good for the individual and the community. He held that virtues are the requisite skills to happiness or well-being (eudaemonia). He maintained that a virtue-based eudemonic conception of ethics is the highest aim of moral thought and conduct. He accepted the key Socratic beliefs in the objectivity of goodness as well as the link between knowing what is good and doing it. He asserted that justice exists in the individual when the three elements of the soul – intellect, emotion, and desire – act in harmony with each other (Singer, 2019).

Aristotle, similar to Plato, held that the life of virtue is rewarding for the virtuous as well as beneficial for the community. His perspective on ethics differed from *deontological ethics*, which judges ethics by how well a person follows the laws and rules of society or *teleological ethics*, which states that if what you do leads to something good, you did the right thing. Aristotle introduced the notion of *virtue ethics*, which is based on the virtue of being human. There are two important distinctions between Aristotle's approach to ethics and his contemporaries. First, he did not consider ethics just a theoretical or philosophical topic to study. His argument was to understand ethics, one has to observe how people behave. Second, he believed that ethics is not about 'what if' situations, but rather what someone did and how his or her virtues affected his or her actions.

Aristotle also agreed with Plato that the highest and most satisfying form of human existence involves the exercise of one's rational faculties to the fullest (Singer, 2019). Early Western philosophy of ethics continues to be a driving force in the contemporary world. Similar to the philosophies discussed in the previous paragraphs, it would be important to highlight how the Eastern thinkers and philosophers looked at the concept of ethics.

The oldest Indian writing, the Vedas, describes ethics as an integral part of the philosophical and religious views about the nature of reality. Being the earliest body of Indian religious text (1500–700 bc), it codified the ideas and philosophies of Hinduism, which states how people ought to live.

The Vedic philosophy espouses that ultimate truth and reality are linked in such a way that a right moral order is built into the universe itself. Hence, humans ought to know what is real and to live rightly. Viewed from this perspective, ethics is traced to the very essence of the universe and is not without detailed practical applications. These applications are based on four ideals, or proper goals, of life: Prosperity, the satisfaction of desires, moral duty, and spiritual perfection – that is, liberation from a finite existence (Singer, 2019). These ideals serve as the basis for individuals to adhere to virtues such as honesty, modesty, purity of heart, nonviolence, charity, and rectitude. These ethical principles do not ask of the follower to simply conform to laws, but rather develop an inner desire for these virtues to achieve spiritual perfection. Among the many philosophical paths to moral living is the Jain philosophy of spiritual liberation. The means to achieve spiritual liberation is through nonviolence.

The relevance of Jain philosophy and its impact is noted in the Gandhian politics of the 20th century that focused on nonviolence, peace, morality, and ethics (Jain, 2019). The philosophy of nonviolence to achieve social justice, a moral principle, was practiced by Dr. Martin Luther King in the US and Nelson Mandela in South Africa.

Buddhism, another great ethical system, or social innovation in India, came about as a reaction to the codified Vedic philosophy. The philosophy of Buddhism is wholly characterized by the ethical principle seeking the meaning of life in life itself (Romesh, 2014). This tradition preaches nonviolence, nonabsolutism, and nonattachment as the core of living a meaningful life. Buddha's great achievement is the reformation of Hinduism and his deep understanding of karma and suffering. He viewed karma as the gateway to *nirvāna* (liberation) from all suffering.

At the core of this philosophy of life lies the eight paths, that when followed, will set free humans from all kinds of suffering. In service leadership, the interest

Table 7.1 Essence of Buddhist philosophy and its relationship with service leadership

|  | Pillars of Buddhism | Pillars of service leadership |
|---|---|---|
| **Wisdom** | Right view | Character |
|  | Right intention | Character |
| **Ethical conduct** | Right speech | Character |
|  | Right action | Character and competence |
|  | Right livelihood | Competence, character, care |
| **Mental development** | Right effort | Competence |
|  | Right mindfulness | Character and care |
|  | Right concentration | Competence and character |

is in how the ethical concept of Western philosophers and Eastern thinkers have shaped the behavior in the contemporary world. Just as an example, a look at the elements of the eight paths of Buddhist philosophy and its relationship with the basic pillars of service leadership are shown in Table 7.1. To live life in the best way, the Buddhist principles serve as a guide for a life without suffering. In service leadership, those elements of self-development that lead to the self-actualization of an individual for a better life are emphasized.

Similar to the Indian ethical philosophers, the Chinese moral philosophers and thinkers such as Laozi and Confucius made major contributions to the notion of morality and way of life.

Laozi (6th century bce), a legendary Chinese philosopher and thinker, advocated withdrawal from society, contemplation, and cultivation of internal virtues as an ethical behavior (Younkins, 2006). The Taoist philosopher, whose name can be translated as the 'Old Master,' wrote a manual of self-cultivation and government, as well as a metaphorical account of reality, called Daodejing, which is translated as 'Book of the Way and Its Power.' 'Daoism' designates both a philosophical tradition and an organized religion, which in modern Chinese are identified separately as *daojia* and *daojiao*, respectively (Chan, 2018). Dao philosophy emphasizes the naturalness or natural flow of things. Thus, it encourages humans to follow the course of nature and seek a path that provides the least resistance. Ultimately, take actions in conformity with nature and move forward in harmony with the universe. He also emphasized gentleness, calmness, and nonviolence to live a life of virtue. In a similar vein, Bejan and Lorente (2008) put forward the constructal theory, which states that a real system owes its irreversibility to several mechanisms, most notably the flow. The effort to improve the performance of an entire system or (organizations) rests on the ability to balance all its internal flow resistances, together and simultaneously, in an integrative manner (Ip, 2013).

These elements of Daoist philosophy have their place in today's world. Service leadership's concept of *character* and *care* also suggests that contemplation and cultivation of internal virtues are ethical behavior in the service environment.

Another major Chinese philosopher is Confucius, who was the more down-to-earth thinker, absorbed in the practical task of social reforms. Confucius thought that to be a virtuous man, an individual would have to be humane and thoughtful, motivated by the desire to do what is good rather than by personal profit.

Table 7.2 Confucian golden and silver rules of behavior

| Golden rule | Silver rule |
| --- | --- |
| **Be:** | **Don't be:** |
| • Kind. | • Cruel. |
| • Fair. | • Unjust. |
| • Respectful. | • Disrespectful. |
| • Wise. | • Foolish. |
| • Trustworthy. | • Untrustworthy. |
| • Loyal. | • Disloyal. |
| • Courageous. | • Cowardly. |
| • Incorruptible. | • Corruptible. |
| • Having a sense of shame. | • Shameless. |
| • Caring. | • Not caring. |
| • Self-correcting. | • Not correcting mistakes. |
| • Forgiving. | • Blaming. |

Source: Adapted from Fung Yu-Lan. (1966). *A short history of Chinese philosophy.* New York, NY: The Free Press.

Confucius's response to a question from one of his disciples about how to conduct one's entire life is if 'you do not want done to yourself, do not do to others.' (Ryff & Singer, 2008). Since this concept has appeared repeatedly in Confucian literature, it might be considered the supreme principle of Confucian ethics. Some of the basic Confucian ethical concepts and practices include benevolence or humaneness as the essence of being human and this manifests itself as compassion. It is basically the moral disposition of doing 'good' (Chan, 2018). The golden and silver rules of Confucian philosophy have compelling and usable approach to guiding behavior in service leadership. These rules are shown in Table 7.2.

Fung Yu-Lan, one of the great 20th-century authorities on the history of Chinese thought, compared Confucius's influence in Chinese history with that of Socrates in the West (Riegel, 2013).

### Modernity and concepts of ethics

Just as the philosophers in the medieval period both in the East and West had argued that central to the thesis of ethics is how humans relate rationally and logically in their interactions with others, the European philosophers of the modernity period (16th century and later) found themselves arguing about the notions of *reason* and *happiness* being the driving force for ethical behavior. This section will only highlight the arguments of some of these philosophers and how their views relate to the principles of service leadership.

Thomas Hobbes (1588–1679) believed that ethical norms are not to be found in God's cosmic plan but in the social and political agreements. He looked at ethics as part of human nature and political philosophy as the interactions of human beings. Hobbes's contention was that the concept of good and evil are related to human desire and aversion. This implies that what an individual desires is considered good, and any aversion to that desire must be bad.

Hobbes explained all of man's voluntary acts are aimed at pleasure or self-preservation (Lloyd & Sreedhar, 2018). He believed that human beings endeavor desperately to fulfill their desires for food, clothing, shelter, power, honor, glory, comfort, pleasure, self-aggrandizement, and a life of ease (Messerly, 2015). Chapter 1 discussed how service leadership leads to Maslow's self-actualization, and here the connection between Hobbes's self-preservation and self-actualization as a means to a self-actualized service leader is observed.

David Hume held that reason cannot be the basis of morality. His chief ground for this conclusion was that morality is essentially practical: There is no point in judging something good if the judgment does not incline one to act accordingly. Hence, the ethical behavior of a service leader can be judged as good, meeting Hume's notion of a moral person.

Utilitarian philosophers suggest that the argument over whether morality is based on reason or on feelings no longer serves the broader discussion of ethics. They, however, have argued that inquiry into which actions are right or wrong would be a better approach to the nature of morality. Service leadership also points out that individual actions of right or wrong on the part of the leader as well as those who are members of a service organization define its moral status.

Jeremy Bentham (1748–1832) is known as the father of modern utilitarianism. His utilitarian principle serves as the basis for a unified and comprehensive ethical system that applies, in theory at least, to every area of life. Utilitarianism, as a theory in normative ethics, suggests that a moral action is one that maximizes utility, or happiness, for the greatest number of people. In business, this is a common approach to moral reasoning as it considers costs and benefits of an action. Keep in mind that utilitarianism also has its limitations when values such as justice and individual rights are considered. Let us use the example given by the Center for Leadership and Ethics (2019), which highlights the notion of individual rights in making an ethical decision. Assume a hospital has four people whose lives depend upon receiving organ transplants: A heart, lungs, a kidney, and a liver. If a healthy person wanders into the hospital, his organs could be harvested to save four lives at the expense of one life. This would arguably produce the greatest good for the greatest number. But few would consider it an acceptable course of action, let alone the most ethical one.

John Stewart Mill (1806–73) in his essay 'Utilitarianism' offered some modifications to Bentham's position by stating that utilitarianism is compatible with moral rules and principles relating to justice, honesty, and truthfulness (Mill, 1861). Mill argued that a utilitarian should not attempt to calculate before each action whether that particular action will maximize utility. Taken as a moral principle, the utilitarian concept of honesty, justice, and truthfulness would parallel the *character* and *care* elements of service leadership.

Immanuel Kant (1724–1804), as an opponent of utilitarian ethics, put forward the concept of 'categorical imperative' (CI) as the basis of supreme morality. His notion of CI could be described as an objective, rationally necessary and unconditional principle that individuals must always follow despite any natural desires or inclinations to do otherwise (Johnson & Cureton, 2016). What this suggests is that all immoral actions are irrational because they violate the CI. The silver rule of Confucius, as shown in Table 7.2, explains better the concept of CI.

Other philosophers, such as Hobbes, Locke, and Aquinas, also subscribed to the standards of rationality being the requirement of morality. However, these standards are either instrumental principles of rationality for satisfying one's desires, as in Hobbes's approach to morality or external rational principles that are discoverable by reason, as in Locke's and Aquinas's views (Singer, 2019). Kant had argued that one's actions possess moral worth only when one does his or her duty for its own sake. The basis for this argument was the moral consciousness of human beings.

Much of the ethical developments in the 19th century revolved around the notion of right or wrong and how self-interest and community interests were juxtaposed. For the purpose of discussion, some of the 20th-century philosophers and their views on applied ethics that have ramifications for the service sector are highlighted here.

Since the beginning of the 20th century, ethical concepts have been developed in novel ways, and much attention has also been given to the application of ethics to practical problems (Singer, 2019). What should be kept in mind is that the concept of ethics and how it is viewed remains a point of contention up until now. There are those who question whether ethical judgments are truths or simply a reflection of the wishes of those who make them. Furthermore, could it be that ethical decisions are made based on one's self-interest to do good, or are they a rational thing to do even when self-interest is not the motive? This debate about the nature of goodness and the standard of right or wrong continues to engage philosophers of the East and the West on whether moral judgments are objective or subjective. No matter what school of thought one follows, the basic concern is how these ethical concepts are applied to practical problems societies face.

Applied ethics took center stage in the latter part of the 20th century. It is interesting to note that from Plato onward, moral philosophers have engaged in debates about practical questions, for example, the behavior of public servants, treatment of women, suicide, and many other similar issues. Aquinas (1225–74) pondered whether and when a war is just; whether a person should ever tell a lie; and whether it is appropriate for a woman to commit suicide to save herself from rape. Similarly, Hobbes (1588–1679) and Hume (1711–76) wrote on the ethics of suicide. The utilitarian philosophers such as Bentham (1748–1832) aimed at social reform, and Mill (1806–73) questioned the power of the state to interfere in the life of its citizens, put forth arguments on the status of women, and delved into the question of capital punishment.

Interestingly, the substantive discussion among philosophers about the practical application of ethical issues such as equality, war, justice, and civil disobedience reemerged in the 1960s when several events in the US (civil rights movement, the Vietnam war, along with student activism) took center stage.

These and many other issues that have risen in the 21st century have kept many philosophers busy finding practical ethical solutions for them. Given the depth and breadth of service economies, service leadership emphasizes practical approaches when ethical dilemmas surface.

## 7.2 Ethical dilemmas

The ethical dilemmas faced in the business world today are many. Only those ethical dilemmas encountered in the service sector will be discussed. Ethical dilemmas that service providers face arise when they have to choose between a moral and an immoral act in the performance of their duties. Service leaders have to contend with major issues related to finance, human resources, implementation of plans, competition in the marketplace, and many other day-to-day activities that require their decision. Such decisions are made on the basis of the leader's personal values and character, which was discussed in Chapter 1. Those elements of character contribute to the development of values and how they shape an individual's moral and ethical compass.

Similarly, employees must deal with many circumstances that contribute to their pressures to perform and help the company succeed as well as deal with personal temptations to take the easy way out. Other factors also play a role in creating ethical dilemmas for employees, such as pressure from management when making a profit is stressed above all else. An example of this type of pressure was seen when Enron's top officials asked employees to manipulate information and put their own interest above those of their employees and the public by breaching ethical norms. It was difficult to fathom how the leadership managed to fool regulators for so long with fake holdings and off-the-books accounting. Such leadership behavior led to the collapse of Enron in 2001, and once again, brought to surface the importance of ethical behavior of business organizations.

In a similar case, Wells Fargo Bank, the fourth largest bank in the US (Phaneuf, 2019), left ethics on the side by asking its employees to create over a million fraudulent accounts in their customers' names in order to meet steep sales goals set by the bank (see the case study at the end of this chapter). Such behavior cost the bank $185 million in fines and thousands of employees laid off (Maxfield, 2016). It will take many years before this bank recovers from such ethical misconduct.

Employees on their own also could, for the sake of recognition or ambition, sidestep ethics by falsifying sales numbers or taking credit for another person's work. Ethical norms can be breached when employees of different cultural backgrounds have been discriminated in the workplace, either in not getting recognition for their work or by being ignored for promotion (Nathwani & Bhayani, 2013). Not only is this unethical, but it is also illegal.

In addition to these internal ethical dilemmas in an organization, firms also have to be aware of unethical behavior when dealing with the outside business community. Often, a breach of ethics occurs when salespeople, to get the best deal in negotiating a price, lie to get a concession. Sometimes negotiators bribe their way to a good deal. Bribery is one unethical behavior that must not be accepted no matter how important the business opportunity is. The practice, while illegal in many countries, is still common in some parts of the world today.

When discussing ethical dilemmas, keep in mind that it is not exclusive to a particular service sector but rather inclusive of all service providers, be it finance, marketing, leisure and travel, logistics, food and beverage, or entertainment. The intention is not to ignore many more ethical issues that these sectors in particular face, but rather to highlight a few that broadly affect the service industry.

Any time a firm engages in disingenuous advertisements in which the receiver is in doubt about the content or validity, the effectiveness of the advertisement is diminished. Information misuse such as not disclosing correct information may lead the customer to make a wrong decision and will be costly. In those cases, the firm will lose not only a customer but credibility in the market. The use of negative emotions in marketing a service, for example, is unethical. Although the firm may be able to sell its service to the customer by creating fear in them, its impact may create murky communication between the firm and its customers.

Ethical dilemmas are faced by all service providers no matter where they operate. There has been much research devoted to developing management tools for service firms, such as for an advanced design of service delivery and customer-relationship building. Recent work by Chung (2019) shows how to design a system that effectively delivers service with ethics in mind.

The recent incidents of misuse, fraud, and other economically questionable transactions point out to us that service firms face many ethical challenges and pitfalls with potentially harmful consequences. Moreover, new issues and demand concerning the global responsibilities of the service firms are emerging (Rendtorff & Mattsson, 2009). Some cross-country ethical conflicts arise when dealing with production, negotiation, international marketing, advertisement, distribution, pricing, service, and supply chain management. The reason for the conflict in these areas has to do with the differences in values, and how the participants in cross-country activities view the ethical principles of right and wrong or being just. The earlier section of this chapter discussed how philosophers view what is right, wrong, or just.

Dunfee and Bowie (2002) distinguish three categories of moral expressions that service firms face – *benign*, *disputed*, and *problematic*. As the name suggests, the benign category does not pose particular problems since it deals with moral desires that are consistent with most ethical principles that most people agree with. The disputed category of ethical conflicts involves beliefs that are held across a particular social, political, or business community and are not easily validated by general consensus. The problematic category is more related to foreign settings and involves conflicts arising from different principles, depending on one's religious or social background. These are often inconsistent with universally recognized principles and therefore pose ethical conflicts (Ferro, 2004). To minimize the impact of problematic ethical cases in international dealings, it is suggested that service providers pay specific attention to these items: Bribery and corruption, gift-giving, contractual obligations, nepotism, violation of human rights, gender and racial discrimination, exploitation of child labor, employee theft, local safety and working standards, selling of untested or harmful products, and false or misleading advertisement.

These ethical dilemmas can be difficult for employees to deal with, especially if they don't know the company's official guidelines. Therefore, it is in the service firm's best interest to design an ethical system that best serves the interest of the firm and also provide ethical training to its employees. Helping employees identify unethical behavior and give them the tools with which to comply are the first steps in dealing with ethical dilemmas. More importantly, a service leader must lead by example, showing that the company takes ethics seriously and that violators will face consequences according to the organization's policies, including possible suspension or termination.

Another ethical dilemma that has received attention in the last few decades is the vast inequality in wealth between the leading industrialized countries and the developing countries of the world. The question that has been raised relates to moral obligations, if any, of the developed nations toward those that were falling behind economically. To understand the extent of income inequality, the Gini index is applied. Gini index or Gini coefficient is a measure of statistical dispersion intended to represent the income or wealth distribution of a nation's residents. Gini coefficient has a range of value from 0 (or 0%) to 1 (or

100%). A country with a value of 0 represents perfect equality (wealth distributed evenly), and those countries with a value of 1 represent perfect inequality (wealth held in few hands). The World Economic Forum (WEF, 2018) gathered data from the World Bank, the Organisation for Economic Co-operation and Development and other sources, and other indicators to create the Inclusive Development Index 2018, a snapshot of the gap between rich and poor.

According to the WEF index, income inequality has risen or remained stagnant in 20 of the 29 advanced economies while poverty increased in 17. Although most emerging economies have improved in these respects – 84% of them registered a decline in poverty – their absolute levels of inequality remain much higher (Ventura, 2018).

The WEF study shows that income inequality increased more rapidly in North America, China, India, and Russia than anywhere else in the world (WEF, 2018). Another study on income inequality highlighted the difference between Western Europe and the US as particularly striking: 'While the top 1% income share was close to 10% in both regions in 1980, it rose only slightly to 12% in 2016 in Western Europe, but it shot up to 20% in the United States' (Alvaredo, Chancel, Piketty, Saez, & Zucman, 2018).

When such disparity in income equality appears, do service firms operating in these environments have a moral obligation of not exploiting the underprivileged to get a maximum return on their investments? The next section will explore how the principles of personal ethics play a role in service leadership.

## 7.3 The principle of personal ethics and service leadership

Having reviewed some of the ethical principles, let's turn to the concept of personal ethics and how that applies to service leadership. Starting with a complex question, where do the individual ethical standards come from? Some would argue that parents' ethical code inevitably becomes an individual's own. Others would point to the influence of religion, philosophy, and even friendships in determining personal ethics. Without attempting to unravel the genesis of individual ethics, its crucial role for service providers and in all professional sectors is important. Doing what's right, although often difficult in times of organizational crisis or cutbacks, ultimately defines the leader who can be trusted. The emphasis that has been placed on the character of a leader along with his competence and care can guide the leader through turmoil in an organization.

It does not matter whether working in the public or private sector; there is bound to be situations in which the leader of an organization may find himself or herself in a scandal that threatens his or her career. Often the leader searches for a scapegoat and blames a subordinate for poor judgment when in reality, it is his or her own inadequacy in decision making that has created the problem. Many a job has been lost and careers ruined because of a leader who lacks integrity and moral leadership and does not take responsibility. Subordinates may choose not to confront the leader directly regarding an ethical breach, but they will surely lose their sense of loyalty to him or her. This defection results in absenteeism, lower quality work, and high turnover. On the other hand, when a subordinate sees an ethical leader who is just and fair, they will stand by that leader no matter how difficult the situation is.

From the service leadership perspective, the leader must clarify and perpetuate important ethical values and publicize and live by an organizational code of ethics. A code of ethics or 'value statement' outlines the mission and values of the business or organization, describes how its professionals ought to approach problems, states the ethical principles based on the organization's core values, and details the standards to which the professional is held. The five fundamental codes of ethics for any business organization are integrity, objectivity, professional competence and care, confidentiality, and personal behavior.

Doing the right thing as a service leader presumes that you know what the right thing is. Although moral knowledge can be encouraged by company codes of ethics and on-the-job mentoring, the leader's core commitment to a set of personal ethics is primarily something the leader brings to the job as an attribute of his or her character. The ultimate source of an individual's moral standards is complex indeed, involving both 'nature' and 'nurture.' (Chung & Elfassy, 2016). Some of the convictions about right and wrong appear to be innate as the nature of human beings. Others have been taught to us by parents, friends, teachers, religious influences, and the culture(s) in which an individual grew up and in which they continue to grow.

Personal ethics are always evolving and adapting as one faces new situations in life, makes decisions about those situations, and experiences the consequences of those decisions. But such daily ethical development notwithstanding, by early adulthood the personal code of ethics must be firmly established within the individual's character so as to have lasting professional and personal success.

Service leadership may not be possible, even with a well-developed personal code of ethics because no one trusts unethical people. Even if the unethical person has not directly affected us negatively, the tendency will be to be wary of such individuals. Individuals are driven to associate with people of integrity for ongoing business relationships.

What is true of individuals is no less true of companies. Newspaper, magazine, and Internet headlines in every country regularly report the moral breaches of companies that have purposely mis-manufactured or mislabeled products to increase profit; hidden the abysmal work conditions of their employees from public view; bribed their way to lucrative contracts; and turned a blind eye toward practices of gender, ethnic, and age discrimination in their hiring and firing practices. In spite of the noble ethical claims in a company's mission statement or code of professional conduct, the words of Socrates still apply: 'Know the wise man [or company] by the way he lives.' The sum total of a person's or company's ethical standards is measured in actions more than words.

## Key points to remember

Ethics, to many, appears to be a branch of philosophy, where it is sometimes also called moral philosophy. However, in its practical applications, the concept of ethics involves more than philosophy and touches other disciplines as well. What is essential to keep in mind is that philosophers of the East and West agree in the central goodness of humanity to be just and ethical.

- The basic premise of these philosophies of life is that humans have the capacity for being virtuous, moral, and just.

- Socrates argued that self-knowledge is sufficient for the good life and that knowledge leads to virtue. In service leadership, the importance of self-knowledge in the context of self-actualization is emphasized.
- Plato believed that virtues are the requisite skills to happiness or well-being (eudaemonia). He maintained that a virtue-based eudaemonistic conception of ethics is the highest aim of moral thought and conduct.
- Aristotle argued that the life of virtue is rewarding for the virtuous as well as beneficial for the community. His perspective on ethics differed from *deontological ethics*, which judges ethics by how well a person follows the laws and rules of society or *teleological ethics*, which states that if what you do leads to something good, you did the right thing.
- Similar to Western philosophers, the Eastern philosophers from Hinduism believed that ethics is an integral part of the philosophical and religious views about the nature of reality. They believed that ultimate truth and reality are linked in such a way that a right moral order is built into the universe itself.
- The Jain philosophy that Gandhi practiced focused on nonviolence, peace, morality, and ethics.
- The philosophy of Buddhism is wholly characterized by the ethical principle of seeking the meaning of life in life itself.
- Laozi (6th century bc), a legendary Chinese philosopher and thinker, advocated withdrawal from society, contemplation, and cultivation of internal virtues as ethical behavior. He wrote the manual of self-cultivation, which in the language of service leadership is self-development. He also emphasized gentleness, calmness, and nonviolence to live a life of virtue.
- Another major Chinese philosopher is Confucius, who thought that to be a virtuous man, an individual would have to be humane and thoughtful, motivated by the desire to do what is good rather than by personal profit.
- Philosophers of modern times include Hobbes, Hume, Bentham, and Mill.

  - Hobbes looked at ethics as part of human nature. His contention was that the concept of good and evil are related to human desire and aversion. This implies that what an individual desire is considered good, and any aversion to that desire must be bad.
  - Hume thought that morality is essentially practical: There is no point in judging something good if the judgment does not incline one to act accordingly.
  - Bentham's concept of utilitarianism suggested that moral action is one that maximizes utility, or happiness, for the greatest number of people.
  - Mill argued that utilitarians should not attempt to calculate before each action whether that particular action will maximize utility.

- Kant's concept of morality depended on his notion of 'categorical imperative.' He believed that all immoral actions are irrational because they violate the categorical imperative.
- Ethical dilemmas of the 21st century arise when service leaders and employees have to choose between a moral and an immoral act in the performance of their duties. For leaders, they must make moral decisions when dealing with finance, human resources, implementation of plans, competition in the marketplace, and many other day-to-day activities. Employees also may be

tempted to sidestep ethics by falsifying sales numbers or taking credit for another person's work.

- In international dealings, service leaders have to be cautious not to engage in unethical behavior in negotiation, international marketing, advertisement, distribution, pricing, service, and supply chain management.
- To minimize the impact of problematic ethical cases in international dealings, it is suggested that service leaders pay specific attention to these items:

  - Bribery and corruption.
  - Gift-giving.
  - Contractual obligations.
  - Nepotism.
  - Violation of human rights.
  - Gender and racial discrimination.
  - Exploitation of child labor.
  - Employee theft.
  - Local safety and work standards.
  - Selling of untested or harmful products.
  - False or misleading advertisement.

- From the service leadership perspective, the leader must clarify and perpetuate important ethical values and publicize and live by an organizational code of ethics.
- The five fundamental codes of ethics for any business organization are:

  - Integrity.
  - Objectivity.
  - Professional competence and care.
  - Confidentiality.
  - Personal behavior.

## Case study

### Wells Fargo fraud

Banking institutions have basic responsibilities to their customers in terms of keeping records of financial transactions, advising clients on meeting their financial needs, disbursing funds, and enforcing security from fraudulent activities. Customers place their financial resources in the banks based on the trust developed between the bank and the customer, as well as other factors.

Wells Fargo, the fourth-largest bank in the US, began its growth during the financial crisis in 2008 when the bank acquired Wachovia and become the third-largest bank by assets in the US at the time. A few years later, with growing revenue and soaring stock prices, the company was valued at nearly $300 billion (Macrotrend, 2019). Sadly, behind this success was a company culture that drove employees to open fraudulent accounts in an attempt to reach steep sales goals. Between 2011 and 2015, company employees opened more than 1.5 million bank accounts and applied for over 565,000 credit cards in customers' names that may not have been authorized. In 2017, the bank was brought into the public eye because employees fraudulently charged 800,000 car loan customers for unnecessary auto insurance, and the home mortgage division charged fees to customers for locking the rate on their mortgages when this was supposed to have no charges in the first place.

When the fraud was revealed, Wells Fargo had to pay a total of $185 million in fines and a settlement agreement with federal and local regulators. Additionally, in 2018, the Federal Reserve further sanctioned Wells Fargo by limiting its ability to grow in assets until the board of directors of the holding company fixed its risk management and governance problems. And finally, in April 2018, the Consumer Financial Protection Bureau (CFPB) and the Office of the Comptroller of the Currency (OCC) fined the company $1B in a settlement for the fraud committed by the car insurance and mortgage business (Premachandra & Filabi, 2018).

Considering that one of the largest multinational American banks had built its reputation on serving the needs of its customers, what could have caused such a major lap in ethical conduct by the institution? The answer lies in both the formal and informal internal systems and norms of the bank. Even though the senior management of the bank were informed of the violations, such warnings were dismissed by the leadership. Creating a culture of compliance to the wishes of the leadership, whose business model was flawed, encouraged employees' misconduct. Undoubtedly, the culture of the organization, at this stage of its growth, contributed significantly to such unethical behavior on the part of the leadership and employees.

As was pointed out in this chapter, the level of alignment between formal and informal systems within organizations plays a major role in the strength or weakness of the ethical culture in the habitat. Wells Fargo's culture placed a great value on short-term rewards at the expense of its customers. Additionally, the performance management system, in which incentives were tied to employees' sales outcomes, contributed to this unethical misbehavior. Organizations tend to use various strategies, including financial rewards for increased sales, to motivate their employees. However, strategies tied to financial rewards require constant monitoring. This was not the case in Wells Fargo's environment.

It has been pointed out that other systemic factors contributed to the scandal. These include:

1  Leadership's lack of response to the scandal.
2  Inadequate and proper training on ethical values of the firm when hiring new employees.
3  The decentralized nature of their management, which reduced accountability for more senior leadership (Premachandra & Filabi, 2018).

## Questions related to the case

1 Compare this case study with another conflict of interest.
2 In what ways does this case study demonstrate incentive gaming?
3 What factors played the most important role in leading so many Wells Fargo employees to cheat the bank's customers?
4 How were the problems at Wells Fargo expressed in their corporate culture or because of a few thousand 'bad apples'?
5 In what ways did company culture and compensation at Wells Fargo encourage incentive gaming? How did incentive gaming become entangled with conflicts of interest?
6 Who was more to blame, the low-level employees or the managers? Were both in a conflict-of-interest situation?
7 Many employees admitted that they knew that what they were doing was wrong but continued to open fraudulent accounts. Do you think their actions were in any way ethically justifiable? Why or why not? If you were in their position, what would you have done?

## End of chapter questions

1 Summarize the basic premise of the Greek philosophers with respect to morality and ethics?
2 How did the Eastern philosophers differ from the Greek philosophers?
3 How did ethics evolve during the period of modernity?
4 What were the concerns of 20th-century philosophers?
5 Does the concept of utilitarianism justify minor ethical infractions?
6 When do ethical conflicts evolve into ethical dilemmas?
7 What does service leadership offer in dealing with ethical dilemmas?
8 Do service organizations have an ethical responsibility in the inequality of income in developing countries?
9 What is a code of ethics, and how it would help a service provider?
10 Is it justifiable to negotiate a lucrative service contract when there are minor ethical problems?

## References

Alvaredo, F., Chancel, L., Piketty, T., Saez, E., & Zucman, G. (2018). *World inequality report: World inequality lab*. Paris: Paris School of Economics.

Bejan, A., & Lorente, S. (2008). *Constructal theory and applications*. New York, NY: Wiley.

Center for Leadership and Ethics. (2019). *Ethics unwrapped: McCombs School of Business*. Austin: The University of Texas.

Chan, A. (2018). Laozi. *Stanford Encyclopedia of Philosophy*. Retrieved from December 1, 2019, from https://plato.stanford.edu/entries/laozi/

Chung, P. (2019). *Designed to win: What every business needs to know to go truly global (DHL's 50 years)*. New York, NY: Leaders Press.

Chung, P., & Bell, A. (2015). *25 principles of service leadership*. New York, NY: Lexingford Publishing.

Chung, P., & Elfassy, R. (2016). *The 12 dimensions of a service leader: Manage your personal brand for the service age*. Hong Kong: Lexingford Publishing.

Duignan, B. (Ed.). (2011). *The history of Western ethics*. New York, NY: Britannica Educational Publishing.

Dunfee, T., & Bowie, N. (2002). Confronting morality in markets. *Journal of Business Ethics, 38*(4), 381–393.

Ferro, N. (2004). *Cross-country ethical dilemmas in business: A descriptive framework*. Mattei, Italy: Fondazione Eni Enrico.

Fung Yu-Lan. (1966). *A short history of Chinese philosophy*. New York, NY: The Free Press.

Ip, P. K. (2013). Daoism and business ethics. In C. Luetge (Eds.), *Handbook of the philosophical foundations of business ethics*. Dordrecht: Springer.

Jain, S. (2019). *Gandhi and Jainism*. New Delhi: International School for Jain Studies.

Johnson, R., & Cureton, A. (2016). Kant's moral philosophy. *Stanford Encyclopedia of Philosophy*. Retrieved December 6, 2019, from https://plato.stanford.edu/entries/kant-moral/

Konstan, D. (2018). Epicurus. *Stanford Encyclopedia of Philosophy*. Retrieved November 26, 2019, from https://plato.stanford.edu/entries/epicurus/

Lloyd, S., & Sreedhar, S. (2018). Hobbes moral and political philosophy. *Stanford Encyclopedia of Philosophy*. Retrieved December 2, 2019, from https://plato.stanford.edu/entries/hobbes-moral/

Macrotrend. (2019). *Wells Fargo total assets 2006–2019*. Retrieved December 16, 2019, from www.macrotrends.net/stocks/charts/WFC/wells-fargo/total-assets

Maxfield, J. (2016). Wells Fargo's fake-account scandal is still weighing heavily on its business. *The Motley Fool*. Retrieved December 15, 2019, from www.fool.com/investing/2016/12/24/wells-fargos-fake-account-scandal-is-still-weighin.aspx

Messerly, J. (2015). Summary of Hobbes' political and ethical theories. *Reason and Meaning*. Retrieved December 2, 2019, from https://reasonandmeaning.com/2015/05/01/hobbes-political-and-ethical-theories-in-two-pages/

Mill, J. S. (1861). Utilitarianism. *Frazer's Magazine, 64*, 391–406.

Nathwani, A., & Bhayani, S. (2013). Ethical issues of guerilla marketing. *Indian Journal of Applied Research, 3*(8), 438–440.

Phaneuf, A. (2019). Here is a list of the largest banks in the United States by assets. *Business Insider*. Retrieved December 2, 2019, from www.businessinsider.com/largest-banks-us-list

Premachandra, B., & Filabi, A. (2018). Under pressure: Wells Fargo, misconduct, leadership and culture. *Ethical Systems.org*. Retrieved December 17, 2019, from www.investopedia.com/articles/markets/093014/how-wells-fargo-became-biggest-bank-america.asp

Rendtorff, J., & Mattsson, J. (2009). Ethical issues in the service industries. *The Service Industry Journal, 29*(1), 1–7.

Riegel, J. (2013). Confucius. *Stanford Encyclopedia of Philosophy*. Retrieved November 30, 2019, from https://plato.stanford.edu/entries/confucius/

Romesh, K. (2014). Moral elements in the ethical code of Buddhism. *Public Philosophy and Democratic Education, 3*(2), 18–35.

Ryff, C., & Singer, B. (2008). Know thyself and become what you are: A eudaimonic approach to psychological well-being. *Journal of Happiness Studies, 9*, 13–39.

Singer, P. (2011). *Practical ethics*. Cambridge: Cambridge University Press.
Singer, P. (2017). *Ethics in the real world*. Melbourne, Australia: Text Publishing.
Singer, P. (2019). Ethics. *Stanford Encyclopedia of Philosophy*. Retrieved November 30, 2019, from www.britannica.com/topic/ethics-philosophy/Bioethics
Ventura, L. (2018, November). Wealth distribution and income inequality by country 2018. *Global Finance*. Retrieved December 12, 2019, from www.gfmag.com/global-data/economic-data/wealth-distribution-income-inequality
World Economic Forum. (2018). *The Inclusive Development Index 2018 summary and data highlights*. Retrieved December 12, 2019, from http://www3.weforum.org/docs/WEF_Forum_IncGrwth_2018.pdf
Younkins, E. (2006). *Lao Tzu's naturalistic metaphysics, ethics and politics*. Le Quebecois libre. No. 189. Retrieved December 1, 2019, from www.quebecoislibre.org/06/060820-4.htm

# 8 Entrepreneurial path in service leadership

## 8.1 Entrepreneurial developments in the service industry

Before embarking on the role of entrepreneurship in services, it would be of value to look at the historical developments of the concept in economic theory and its evolution and the role it plays in today's service economy.

Looking at the history of entrepreneurship in the academic literature, one finds a very interesting trajectory for the concept. The term *entrepreneur* generally refers to two main categories. The first is the small business dominated by the owner/manager and founder. More broadly, it refers to the small and medium enterprise (SME), or even a corporation. In the second category, the entrepreneur is a function in the economy, used in both a broad and a narrow sense (Elkjær, 2014). In either of these two contexts, entrepreneurs have played a major role in the economy.

Entrepreneurship received attention early on when Cantillon (1755) discussed the concept in his economic text. He theorized that in contrast to hired labor with individuals who negotiate a price for their contribution, the entrepreneur pays out costs to live with an insecure source of income. Jean-Baptiste Say defined the entrepreneur as a self-employed individual who engages in risky and profitable activities that create value (Say, 1971). In other words, his refinement of the term simply suggested that an entrepreneur is an individual who creates value by shifting resources from lower- to higher-valued activities.

Despite the attempts by Cantillon to recognize the role of the entrepreneur and to tie this to economic realities in the 18th century, the entrepreneur did not receive much attention in academic economic discussion until the late 19th century. Then, from the early 20th century onwards, there has been a rebirth of the concept of entrepreneurship within economic theory.

It was Schumpeter who suggested that the entrepreneur is a factor in explaining economic growth and explained the role an entrepreneur plays in the business cycle (Schumpeter, 1942 [1976]). Schumpeter believed that entrepreneurs fulfill a major role in innovation that leads to economic growth. His main contention was that innovation is the core element of economic change causing gales of 'creative destruction,' a term that he coined. According to him, innovation is a 'process of industrial mutation, that incessantly revolutionizes the economic structure from within, incessantly destroying the old one, incessantly creating a new one' (Schumpeter, 1942).

Schumpeter's basic realization was that economic growth resulted not from capital accumulation, but from innovations and 'new combinations' (Landström, 2005).

What Schumpeter called 'innovations' are technical inventions created by a few gifted individuals (entrepreneurs) who see opportunities that arise from downturns in business cycles. When economic conditions worsen, entrepreneurs look for opportunities that will create new business ventures to meet the unmet needs of the consumers. If they are successful with their inventions, other entrepreneurs will follow leading to economic recovery and growth. Schumpeter's view is often considered imprecise and speculative, in addition to being unsuitable for economic forecasting. Over time, Schumpeter modified his positions on the notion of entrepreneurship as being an individualistic desire. As a consequence, mainstream economists often have a skeptical attitude toward the entrepreneur, due mainly to the functional use of the entrepreneur concept (Elkjær, 2014).

Coase (1937), whose views differed from Schumpeter, stated that entrepreneurship is a vital source of endogenous change in the economy. He outlined the importance of investigating the structure of production and other important research and policy questions related to entrepreneurship. Coase stated that the firm arises because of an incentive for some to specialize in directing the effort of others. Those who lack competence or confidence in their judgment have a corresponding incentive to specialize in being directed (Langlois, 2005, p. 14). Some see entrepreneurs as promoters of economic development, while others focus on the role they play in the process of structural transformation.

Even though the concept of entrepreneurship and its role in economic growth was discussed in the 18th century by Cantillon, scholars in economics or management in the 19th century paid little attention to it. Several economists such as Mill, Say, and Marshall in the 19th century, in addition to Schumpeter (1942 [1976]), Knight (1921), Kirzner (1971), and Baumol (1968, 1990, 1993, 2010) throughout the 20th century, contributed significantly to the concept of entrepreneurship and its merit within economic theory. Economists consider the entrepreneur as a rational agent contributing to economic activity. Therefore, they decided to focus on market rather than human factors (Baumol, 1990). The missing awareness of the entrepreneur in economics is that psychological interest in the entrepreneur often does not fit with mainstream economic theory (Rocha, 2012).

What can be observed is that in the last few decades, there is renewed interest in entrepreneurship as researchers have explored its role in the theory of the firm that was put forward by Coase and other theorists. It is interesting to note that even with this renewed attention, the economic nature of the entrepreneur as a concept has not yet been fully identified in some theories of the firm. Throughout his career, Baumol urged his peers to pay attention to the instrumental role of entrepreneurship in economic renewal and growth. Hence, he took the position that the neoclassical conception of the entrepreneur should be looked upon as a functionary and as another factor of production separate from the standard triumvirate: Land, labor, and capital (Baumol, 1968). Other researchers have argued that if entrepreneurship is not explicitly incorporated into the theoretical models of economic growth, it will fail to take advantage of an opportunity to gain a greater insight into empirical analysis procedure (Acs and Storey, 2004).

Baumol (1990) highlights the role of institutions in guiding entrepreneurs into productive, unproductive, or destructive activities. Notably, most entrepreneurial activity benefits society, but not all of it, when ethical, legal, and social responsibilities are not in the mix (Eliasson & Henrekson, 2004). From the perspective of service leadership, there is agreement with Baumol and hence the emphasis on the ethical and social responsibilities of the entrepreneurs and entrepreneurial activities is crucial.

Another helpful view of entrepreneurship is provided by the 21st century management scholar Peter Drucker. He suggests that entrepreneurs always search for change, respond to it, and exploit it as an opportunity (Drucker, 2015). Given the notion of opportunity, it can be asked: How does opportunity itself occur?

Opportunity comes about in several different ways, caused by both exogenous shocks creating disequilibrium and by the endogenous processes moving the economy toward equilibrium. From earlier discussion, it appears that Schumpeter (1942) stressed the significance of the first reason, exogenous technical shocks, while Clark (1899) emphasized equilibrating forces.

Does an opportunity exist independently of the entrepreneur or is it a creation of the entrepreneur? In this context, it has been suggested that a look at the individual-opportunity nexus may shed light, as it focuses on 'how, by whom, and with what consequences opportunities are discovered, evaluated, and exploited' (Shane & Venkataraman, 2000, p. 218). Shane and Venkataraman believe that opportunities come from market disequilibrium caused by different expectations and beliefs. An interesting aspect of opportunities is that utilizing an entrepreneurial opportunity does not necessarily diminish the possible opportunities available to other entrepreneurs. Quite often, the exploitation of an opportunity gives rise to new opportunities for other entrepreneurs (Elkjær, 2014).

The role that entrepreneurs play in economic development follows in stages. Porter, Sachs, and McArthur (2002) describe the different roles played by entrepreneurs across three stages of economic development as exemplified by the developed economies of the world. They note that in the first stage of development, which is factor-driven, the primary sector dominates with unqualified labor force. In the second stage, which is characterized as an efficiency-driven stage, entrepreneurship drops because large firms hire most of the workforce. The third and final stage, which is defined as an innovation-driven stage, the service sector becomes more important and the start-up of new businesses, producing sophisticated products and services, increases.

It is interesting to note how entrepreneurs shape the direction of the economy in the 21st century, given the importance of services in the economy (Dimova & Pela, 2018). How the service sector has responded to the changes in the economy

Table 8.1 Comparison of the lean system with service leadership

| Lean system | Service leadership |
| --- | --- |
| Workforce engagement, in stark contrast to the previous operational approach of command and control. | Increased empowerment of employees in improving the quality of service by giving them the responsibility to decide on the spot to deliver service. |
| An increased attention to customer communications, leading to better service alignment and response to customer demand. | Regular communication between employees and management, employees to employees, and employees with customers. |
| A focus on making failure analysis a routine and normal activity. | Individuals are allowed to make one mistake but share it with all other employees of the firm. |
| Specifying activities and processes to adopt continual error reduction. | Once an error is made, it can be avoided by others when it is shared with all other employees. |
| Multi-skilling of the organization with greater training and increased functional flexibility. | Effective training through mentor–apprentice approach. |

and adopted some basic tools and strategies used in the manufacturing era is noteworthy. For example, lean manufacturing, which was introduced by Toyota in the 1950s, focused on the supply-chain side of production. Interestingly, this strategy became a common philosophical approach to supply-chain designs in the automobile industry as well as a practical approach to production excellence (Lee, Olson, Lee, Hwang, & Shin, 2008). What made lean manufacturing so popular was that it emphasized cutting waste by eliminating activities that do not add value, while emphasizing quality in the process.

Keep in mind that the process reduced supply chain bottlenecks, and the notion of demand-pull rather than supply-push was the motivating force. Furthermore, lean manufacturing emphasized other elements such as efficiency, economies of scale, and how workers – rather than executing predefined tasks over and over again – must continually improve their way of working, or 'Kaizen' (Ohno, 1988). This particular emphasis on how workers in service firms need to meet the specific requirements of each and every customer is critical to staying ahead of their competitors.

In the context of service leadership, the parallel between Ohno's 'Kaizen' and the concept of allowing workers in the service economy to continually improve their way of working to meet the needs of the customers is noteworthy. A comparison of the lean system with the service leadership system is shown in Table 8.1.

Another concept that has application to service organization is 'Agile' manufacturing systems, which focus on providing value to customers at the retail end of the supply chain. Agility is characterized by a strategic vision that enables a firm to create and deliver customer-valued, high-quality, and mass-customized goods and services. How they do this is by nimble organizational structures of a knowledgeable and empowered workforce, facilitated by an information infrastructure that links constituent partners in a united electronic network (Sanchez & Nagi, 2010). This system suggests on-time delivery and developing systems capable of rapid response to market and technology changes, where a firm gains competitive advantage in turbulent markets (Helo, 2004).

As in every other human activity, entrepreneurship thrives only if there is the right kind of habitat or environment that both fosters and links it to the socio-cultural dynamics that is part of the larger society and the economy. Undoubt-edly, entrepreneurship is at the core of innovation and consequently part of the economic growth of nations. Its impact is on improving enterprise competitive position and obtaining enterprise competitive advantage, even when it is a newly created entrepreneurial venture (Devece, Palacio-Margues, & Rocio Fernandez, 2011). Keep in mind that in the service industries, competitiveness does not depend strongly on economies of scale, but more on innovation and the flexibil-ity that are characteristics of small-to-medium enterprises, and, hence, an ideal context for entrepreneurs.

With considerable growth in the service industry, the applicability of new approaches, including lean and Agile processes, has found its way into the ser-vice sector (Hines & McGowan, 2005; Nooteboom, 2007). A case study by Apte and Goh (2004) shows how the lean manufacturing system can be applied to information-intensive services. Gray (2007) studied the service redesign and service improvement initiatives in the fields of social and health care. The study by Ritchie and Angelis (2010) in the energy services sector showed that the core elements of lean manufacturing such as removal of waste, responding to customer demand, and increased breadth of communications in the firm were highly applicable.

Walmart, Amazon, and other retailers are using electronic data, a creation of technological entrepreneurs, to allow them to track the physical location of the product in real-time. These service-industry giants have understood how to be customer-oriented by delivering quality service by using the latest technologi-cal innovations. Similar to these large service-sector providers, small-company entrepreneurs can also take advantage of these tools in their own service-delivery systems (Vignesh, Suresh, & Aramvalarthan, 2016).

As can be seen in the previous examples, improvements in the quality of entre-preneurial services can make a substantial contribution to economic growth by means of more effective management function performance (Salas & Sanchez-Asín, 2006).

Recognizing the role that services play in the economy as was discussed in Chapter 2, there are substantial entrepreneurial opportunities in services than any other sector of the economy. Interestingly, it has been found that the entre-preneurial approach that combines the individual value systems and the cogni-tive mechanisms with the social context leads to successful entrepreneurship.

This perspective uses theories from the planned behavior and propounds the idea of self-efficacy, based on the concept that individuals are more prone to fol-low the entrepreneurial path if they believe that they have the necessary abilities to succeed (Devece et al., 2011). Following this reasoning, individuals who are engaged in small and medium enterprises (SMEs) rather than in the larger enti-ties that are more capital intensive are more likely to engage in entrepreneurial activities. This is simply because small firms are more flexible to deliver the ser-vice due to their proximity to customers and the intangible nature of services that allow these smaller firms to be more attentive to the needs of their customers.

Popular approaches to entrepreneurial activities around the world have been either based on entrepreneurial orientation (EO) or business development services (BDS) (Hughes & Morgan, 2007). Since EO is a firm-level behavior, it emphasizes the tendency to innovate, take risks, and become proactive (Callaghan & Vente, 2011). Yusof, Sandhu, and Jani (2007) refer to EO as 'the set of psychological traits, values, attributes, and attitudes strongly associated with a motivation to engage in entrepreneurial activities.' These elements of EO are similar to the concept of *character* and *care* (3Cs) that are the pillars of service leadership.

On the other hand, the BDS approach is said to enable firms to deploy their resources optimally. Okeyo (2015, p. 168), citing McVay (2003), refers to BDS as a variety of activities that firms use to manage their operations and enhance efficiency, effectiveness, and improve their performance and competitiveness. BDS stimulates product development through the application of technology, while it enables firms to be located near their markets, acquire relevant infrastructure, and adopt pragmatic procurement practices (Okeyo, Gathungu, & K'Obonyo, 2016). In service leadership, the emphasis is on both of these approaches as was noted in the entrepreneurial cycle for EO, and how DHL, a service provider, used stimulation of service development by setting up operations in the markets they served (Chung, 2019).

Whatever approach is adopted in the entrepreneurial process, the entrepreneur's self-efficacy is important. Similar to the notion of self-development and self-efficacy, McGee, Peterson, Mueller, and Sequeira (2009) have conceptualized self-efficacy by dividing the construct into four phases:

1 Searching.
2 Planning.
3 Marshaling.
4 Implementing.

This perspective allows incorporating some basic ideas in the phases of searching and planning, such as the entrepreneur's educational background, the job experience, and the social context. Chung and Elfassy (2016) had suggested a similar path for entrepreneurial development that will be discussed in the next section.

## 8.2 Ways and means of entrepreneurial path

As was stated in the previous section, entrepreneurship is more than just an economic term – it is a way of thinking. Entrepreneurs create jobs, empower people, and provide individuals with the opportunity to create better lives for themselves and those who work with them. Entrepreneurship is a way of inspiring creative individuals to pursue opportunities despite the risks involved.

Approaches to entrepreneurial endeavors vary depending on the environment (habitat) of business. It should be stated that all enterprises operate within a political, social, and economic context. As such, entrepreneurs must recognize the regulatory and institutional constraints that will affect them. As services have become the major economic activity around the world, they demands a process that has to be followed to become the crucible for the development of new ideas (innovations). This process involves more than just problem-solving. Entrepreneurs, be they private, corporate, or social, must find, evaluate, and develop an opportunity by overcoming the forces that resist the creation of something new.

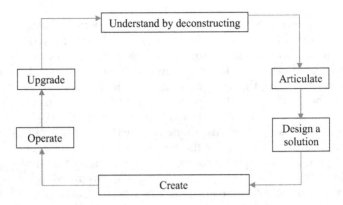

*Figure 8.1* The entrepreneurial cycle

It has been suggested that the concept of 'flow' would help in the entrepreneurial process just as in any other activity in life (Kotler, 2015). Csikszentmihalyi (1975, 2011) suggested that to achieve the state of 'flow,' one has to be completely involved in an activity for its own sake. This dampens the place of one's ego and in a state of flow, time seems to pass by below conscious awareness. Actions, movements, and thoughts inevitably follow or flow from the previous one, allowing one to use one's skills to the utmost. From a service leadership point of view, it can be stated that the concept of flow simply relies on the intrinsic motivation of an individual. This reflects the person's *competence, character*, and *care*.

Those who are intrinsically motivated feel that they 'own' their behavior and enjoy their work a great deal even though there is no outside recognition. Service leadership's concept of self-development, discussed in earlier chapters, is critical in developing the intrinsic motivation in entrepreneurs.

The approach suggested in service leadership is to take a holistic view of the role that leadership plays in what is called the entrepreneurial cycle given the intrinsic motivation of the leader. This approach has several steps that are highlighted in Figure 8.1.

### Understand by deconstructing

An important task of an entrepreneurial leader is to create an innovative and productive service environment (habitat). The entrepreneurial process is not about making small changes to your system to keep your service organization successful and viable. It is about identifying the needs of the customer, deconstructing the process of meeting the needs, and recognizing the elements that will contribute to the entrepreneurial endeavor. The ability to rebuild processes from the ground up and change the work environment (habitat) for the entire industry is what an entrepreneurial cycle is all about.

Don't limit goals to only those you believe are possible or familiar. Allowing oneself to think out of the box leads to some creative possibilities. It is the time when the entrepreneur generates the innovative idea, identifies the market opportunity, and looks for information. Recent examples of service companies who are bringing revolutionary changes in the way they operate are Uber and

Airbnb. These service entrepreneurs are practicing 'disintermediation,' which means removing a layer between the producer and the customer.

Another way of stating it is by removing the middleman in a transaction. Entrepreneurs have transformed the transportation and hospitality industries in a very short time in drastic ways. Similarly, FinTech – financial technology – companies have begun the process of making the big banks rethink how they engage customers. By deconstructing and reconstructing a single process using technology, these companies have been able to streamline, automate, and simplify a business requirement, while driving accuracy and reducing risk (Angeles, Clara, & de Guzman, 2019). It took courage and the willingness of an entrepreneur to take risks, with the opportunity to bring about major changes in the industry.

## Articulate

No idea or plan can move forward without a clear articulation of the goals and objectives of the entrepreneurial activity to self and members of the service organization. It is important that the leadership articulate the goals in a written statement that clearly defines what is to be achieved and that the statement has an appropriate level of detail, stated as current desired conditions.

The need to articulate the strategies that will be used in the service enterprise helps members of the team to understand their role in the organization and how they can bring their talents to accomplish the goals of the service entity. The rationale for articulation of the entrepreneurial activity is to enable the stakeholder such as management executives and employees to conceive what the service firm aims to achieve, and how such achievements will be sought. Madu (2013) states that articulation of strategy of the service firm should entail executives defining how the firm's leadership intends to position the firm beyond its current situation. Furthermore, he observes that a well-worded and articulated statement should be graphic, directional, focused, flexible, feasible, durable, and easy to communicate.

As a summary statement, the rationale for articulation of entrepreneurial activity is to enable the stakeholder such as management executives and employees to conceive what the service firm aims to achieve, and how such achievements will be sought.

## Design a solution

The previous two steps set the stage for designing a specific solution that addresses issues in the entrepreneurial quest. But how does one start this process? Engaging the team members in the process has more value than doing it alone. This is the stage where brainstorming ideas to find a solution becomes critical. Keep in mind that embedded cultural conditioning often limits the questions to be asked and the sense of available possibilities. Be creative. Don't wed yourself to one solution or one approach but think about the types of solutions that could work. It is important to narrow the parameters a little; otherwise, you can end up comparing apples to oranges. One way of ensuring to keep users' needs at the fore throughout this entire process is to set up a selection of possible scenarios that a user might think of using to address the challenge.

In designing a solution, it is imperative to pay attention to human capital in the service organization, the environment or habitat within the service entity, the need for resources, and the competitive environment that the service entity would operate. Attention to the details of these factors will minimize unnecessary delays in coming up with a design that addresses the challenge.

## Create

Having taken those factors in the design of a service solution, it is now time to create a prototype of the solution to a service problem.

Service design includes all the intangible aspects of how a service firm seeks to build a relationship over time with its customers. And one goal of prototyping these service design experiences is to bring tangibility to these intangible experiences. As a tool, prototyping allows you to organize your service around the needs of the end consumer. By following this process, you are determining how customers relate to your service and what's missing in your design. It's a way to depict how the experience might play out over time. Spending time to understand what excites and irritates a customer about the service paves the way for the entrepreneur to modify elements of its service for the customer. Asking the customer for feedback when modifications are made so that further improvements can take place is essential.

## Operate

This is the stage where the entrepreneur tests solutions to a service endeavor in real-time. At this stage of the entrepreneurial service activity, incorporation of resources has taken place where financial, human resources, and the habitat are in place to launch the new business to the market. The strategy and business plan begin to develop day by day, and the use of resources are invested in favor of building a successful company. It is highly desirable to continuously assess the service by means of stakeholder surveys.

## Upgrade

This is the final stage in the entrepreneurial process, where a review of surveys has taken place and further modifications are made to the plan. This stage is also called the growth stage as the business should now be generating a consistent source of income and regularly taking on new customers. The biggest challenge for entrepreneurs in this stage is dividing time between a whole new range of demands requiring attention – managing increasing levels of revenue, attending to customers, dealing with the competition, and accommodating an expanding workforce, etc.

At this stage of the entrepreneurial process, the leader should consider recruiting more talented people with complementary skillsets to achieve the goals of the service firm. As is suggested earlier, hire for *character* and *care*, and teach the skills needed for the service firm. It is at this stage that the entrepreneur will be recognized as the leader of the firm. It is understandable that the leader will still be on the front lines but needs to be aware of how his or her expanding and highly qualified team is going to be taking over a great deal of the responsibilities that were previously tightly under the leader's control. It is the leader's job now to start establishing real order and cohesion among the team according to the clearly defined and communicated goals.

It cannot be overstated that delivering a service is simply based on the reputation and professionalism of the service provider. Developing a successful reputation depends on the *character* and *care* of the service leader who in turn is vigilant that each member of the team understands how to respond to customer needs with care. Getting referrals and testimonials from business clients will help this process immensely. Needless to say, professionalism in the delivery of service is crucial in developing the reputation for a successful business.

In summary, entrepreneurship as a skill is applicable to all walks of life, which is why it can be categorized as transversal.

> It enables citizens to nurture their personal development, to actively contribute to social development, to enter the job market as an employee or as self-employed, and to start-up or scale-up ventures which may have a cultural, social or commercial motive.
>
> (Bacigalupo, Kampylis, Punie, & Van den Brande, 2016, p. 10)

Keep in mind that the entrepreneurial skills are interlinked with personal characteristics, aspirations, and motivations of an individual who possesses them.

## Key points to remember

- Economic theory of the firm suggests that in addition to land, labor, capital being the primary forces in the economy, entrepreneurship must also be considered. While land, labor, and capital can be quantified, the difficulty lies in how the efforts of an entrepreneur be measured.
- Cantillon (1755) posited that in contrast to hired labor with individuals who negotiate a price for their contribution, the entrepreneur has to pay costs for an insecure income.
- Jean-Baptiste Say (1971) defined the entrepreneur as a self-employed individual who engages in risky and profitable activities that create value.
- Schumpeter (1942) suggested that the entrepreneur is a factor in explaining economic growth and explained the role an entrepreneur plays in the business cycle. His main contention was that innovation is the core element of economic change.
- Schumpeter suggested that economic growth results not from capital accumulation, but from innovations and a new combination of resources.
- Coase (1937) stated that entrepreneurship is a vital source of endogenous change in the economy.
- Some see entrepreneurs as promoters of economic development, while others focus on the role they play in the process of structural transformation.
- The missing awareness of the entrepreneur in economics is that psychological interest in the entrepreneur often does not fit with mainstream economic theory.
- Baumol (1968) held that the neoclassical conception of the entrepreneur should be looked upon as a functionary and as another factor of production separate from the standard triumvirate: Land, labor, and capital.

- Baumol (1990) argued that most entrepreneurial activity benefits society, but not all of it, when ethical, legal, and social responsibilities are not in the mix.
- Peter Drucker (2015) suggested that entrepreneurs always search for change, respond to it, and exploit it as an opportunity. Such opportunities arise either from exogenous shocks (disequilibria) or endogenous processes moving toward equilibrium.
- Porter et al. (2002) defined the stages of entrepreneurial development. His third stage is the innovation-driven stage, where the service sector becomes more important and hence leads to the start-up of new businesses.
- The concept of lean manufacturing can easily be applied to service-sector entrepreneurship, which emphasizes eliminating activities that do not add value, and at the same time emphasizes quality in the process.
- Services aim at reducing supply chain bottlenecks (emphasized by Agile manufacturing) to provide value to customers at retail.
- Disintermediation is a process of removing a layer between the producer and receiver of the service (customers).
- Entrepreneurial orientation (EO) is considered a firm-level behavior that emphasizes the propensity to innovate, take risks, and become proactive.
- The business development services (BDS) concept deals with enhancing efficiency, effectiveness, and improving the performance and competitiveness of a firm.
- BDS stimulates product development through the application of technology, while it enables firms to be located near their markets, acquire relevant infrastructure, and adopt pragmatic procurement practices.
- The six steps of the entrepreneurial cycle are identifying the need, articulating the vision, designing a solution, creating the service, operating or implementing the service, and then upgrading the service.
- Entrepreneurship, as a skill, is applicable to all walks of life, which is why it can be categorized as transversal.
- Transversal means a skill that enables individuals to nurture their personal development, to actively contribute to social development, to enter the job market as an employee or as self-employed, and to start-up or scale-up ventures that may have a cultural, social, or commercial motive.

## Case study

### An entrepreneurial journey into cosmetics by Sa Sa

Sa Sa International Holdings Limited together with its subsidiaries (the 'Group') is a leading cosmetics retailing group in Asia. Listed on the Stock Exchange of Hong Kong Limited (the Stock Exchange) in 1997, it has over 260 retail stores in Asia selling over 700 brands of skincare, fragrance, make-up and hair care, body care products, and health and beauty supplements, including own brands and exclusive products. The Group employs about 4,300 staff in markets across the region, covering Hong Kong and Macau SARs, Mainland China, Singapore, and Malaysia.

Established in 1978, Sa Sa has grown from a 40 sq. ft. retail space to become today's regional 'beauty' enterprise and is now the leading cosmetics retail chain in Asia, according to the 'Retail Asia-Pacific Top 500' ranking of *Retail Asia* magazine and Euromonitor in 2017. As one of the largest sole agents in cosmetics in Hong Kong, Sa Sa represents over 180 international beauty brands in Asia. Sa Sa prospers on its successful and proven 'one-stop cosmetics specialty store' concept, offering customers a wide range of quality products. Its e-commerce arm, sasa.com and their mobile app, provides online shopping service to customers as well as a strong marketing tool for the Group (Sa Sa Corporation, 2020).

The entrepreneurial vision was to start Sa Sa mainly as a discount store for parallel imports. Added to this vision was to continue to strive its best to provide 'Quality Products, Best Value and Professional Service' for its customers to meet their ever-increasing needs.

To achieve this goal, Sa Sa invested heavily to upgrade all its stores for a more professional-looking format. Sa Sa wanted to introduce local suppliers and acted as sole agents for new overseas brands. Siu-ming Kwok, the current Executive Chairman and CEO of the Group, recalled how he needed to adapt to the new environment: 'Before a local supplier gives us any product, he wants to know how Sa Sa will display them. When I went to Europe to try to be the sole agent for a new brand, they asked about how Sa Sa would make their brand stand out.' So, Sa Sa recently introduced independent five-to-six-foot wide counters for their own brands. Sa Sa completely revamps its store format every seven to eight years to keep the Sa Sa brand young and trendy. The current format is the fifth-generation design.

Every detail in a store format is critical for a retailer. A top retailer like Sa Sa trains its staff in every minute detail on how to deal with its customers. When Sa Sa began its operation, it had only one store. When Siu-ming was traveling around Europe sourcing new products, Eleanor (his wife) stayed in the store and managed the entire customer experience. She subsequently put all the detailed best practices into a manual literally two inches thick. It became the 'bible for cosmetics' for all the beauty consultants. It deals with all detailed procedures at the storefront, such as how to avoid theft.

A particularly important detail is how a Sa Sa beauty consultant engages a customer who just walks into the store. The beauty consultant approaches the customer proactively and says hello. A customer can seek help immediately if she needs it. But beauty consultants are then strictly forbidden to follow the customer when she walks around the store. This is to ensure that customers feel that they are completely free to walk around and browse. Customers are free to approach any beauty consultant in the store. The 'this is my customer' mindset is not allowed in Sa Sa.

Sa Sa has understood the basic principles of service leadership. All members of the team from the top leadership to frontline employees recognize the importance of *character* and *care*. Mr. Kwok and his wife attribute their success in having a service mindset.

*Source*: Adapted from Chung, P., & Ip, S. (2018). *Pillars of a service hub: Lessons from world-class service companies based in Hong Kong*. New York, NY: Lexingford Publishing, and Sa Sa corporate relations.

## Questions related to the case

1  What factors played a role in the success of Sa Sa?
2  What particular elements of service leadership are apparent in this case study?

## End of chapter questions

1  Discuss what is meant by entrepreneurship.
2  Discuss the relationship between opportunity and entrepreneurship.
3  Understand the key factors affecting entrepreneurial viability.
4  Explain the different motivations for entrepreneurs.
5  What is the difference between the entrepreneurial concept as a function and as a factor of production?
6  Why was there a lack of interest on the part of economists to address the concept of entrepreneurship?
7  How did the economists of the 20th century view the entrepreneurial contributions to economic growth?
8  Why did economists understate the contribution of entrepreneurs?
9  Discuss the role of entrepreneurial orientation and business development services in the process of an entrepreneurial activity.

## References

Acs, Z., & Storey, D. (2004). Introduction: Entrepreneurship and economic development. *Regional Studies*, 38, 871–877.

Angeles, I., Clara, M., & de Guzman, A. (2019). The mediating effect of microfinancing on access to finance and growth of microenterprises: Evidence from the Philippines. *Journal of Global Entrepreneurship Research*, 9(24), 1–16.

Apte, U. M., & Goh, C. (2004). Applying lean manufacturing principles to information intensive services. *International Journal of Services Technology and Management*, 5(5–6), 488–506.

Bacigalupo, M., Kampylis, P., Punie, Y., & Van den Brande, G. (2016). *EntreComp: The entrepreneurship competence framework*. Luxembourg: Publication Office of the European Union.

Baumol, W. (1968). Entrepreneurship in economic theory. *American Economic Review*, 58(2), 64–71.

Baumol, W. (1990). Entrepreneurship: Productive, unproductive, and destructive. *The Journal of Political Economy*, 98(5), 893–921.

Baumol, W. (1993). *Entrepreneurship, management and the structure of payoffs*. Cambridge, MA and London: MIT Press.

Baumol, W. (2010). *The microtheory of innovative entrepreneurship*. Princeton, NJ: Princeton University Press.

Callaghan, C., & Vente, R. (2011). An investigation of the entrepreneurial orientation, context and entrepreneurial performance of inner-city Johannesburg street traders. *Southern African Business Review*, 15(1), 28–48.

Cantillon, R. (1755). *Essai sur la Nature du Commerce en Général* (H. Higgs, Ed. with an English Translation and other material, 1st ed. in 1931). New York, NY: Augustus M. Kelley (Reprinted 1964).

Chung, P. (2019). *Designed to win: What every business needs to know to go truly global.* New York, NY: Leaders Press.

Chung, P., & Elfassy, R. (2016). The 12 dimensions of a service leader: Manage your personal brand for a service age. New York, NY: Lexingford Publishing.

Chung, P., & Ip, S. (2018). *Pillars of a service hub: Lessons from world-class service companies based in Hong Kong.* New York, NY: Lexingford Publishing.

Clark, J. (1899). *The distribution of wealth: A theory of wages, interest, and profits.* London: Palgrave Macmillan.

Coase, R. (1937). The nature of the firm. *Economica N.S., 4,* 386–405.

Csikszentmihalyi, H. (2011). *Flow: The psychology of optimal experience.* New York, NY: HarperCollins Publishers.

Csikszentmihalyi, M. (1975). *Beyond boredom and anxiety: Experiencing flow in work and play.* San Francisco, CA: Jossey-Bass.

Devece, C., Palacio-Margues, D., & Fernandez, R. (2011). Entrepreneurship, research in service industries: A literature classification and trend analysis. *International Entrepreneurship and Management Journal, 7*(4), 479–493.

Dimova, R., & Pela, K. (2018). Entrepreneurship: Structural transformation, skills and constraints. *Small Business Economics, 51,* 203–220.

Drucker, P. (2015). *Innovation and entrepreneurship.* London: Routledge.

Elkjær, J. (2014, October 16–17). *Entrepreneurship in the service sector as a product of alertness and judgment.* Paper presented at the 9th Regional Innovation Policies Conference, University of Stavanger, Norway.

Eliasson, G., & Henrekson, M. (2004). William J. Baumol: An entrepreneurial economist on the economics of entrepreneurship. *Small Business Economics, 23*(1), 1–7.

Gray, J. (2007). A lean towards service improvement. *Journal of Integrated Care Pathways, 11*(1), 1–10.

Helo, P. (2004). Managing agility and productivity in the electronics industry. *Industrial Management and Data Systems, 104*(7), 567–577.

Hines, T., & McGowan, P. (2005). Supply chain strategies in the UK fashion industry. *International Entrepreneurship and Management Journal, 1*(4), 519–537.

Hughes, M., & Morgan, R. (2007). Deconstructing the relationship between entrepreneurial orientation and business performance at the embryonic stage of firm growth. *Industrial Marketing Management, 36,* 651–661.

Kirzner, I. (1971, September 29). Entrepreneurship and the market approach to development. In F. Hayek, H. Hazlitt, L. R. Read, G. Velasco, & F. A. Harper (Eds.), *Toward liberty: Essays in honor of Ludwig von Mises on the occasion of his 90th birthday* (pp. 194–208). Menlo Park: Institute for Humane Studies.

Knight, F. (1921). *Risk uncertainty and profit.* New York, NY: Houghton-Mifflin.

Kotler, S. (2015). *The rise of superman: Decoding the science of ultimate human performance.* London: Quercus Publishing.

Landström, H. (2005). Pioneers in entrepreneurship and small business research. In *International studies in entrepreneurship series* (Vol. 8). Boston: Springer.

Langlois, R. (2005). *The entrepreneurial theory of the firm and the theory of the entrepreneurial firm* (Economics Working Paper No. 200527). Storrs, CT: Department of Economics, University of Connecticut.

Lee, S., Olson, D., Lee, S., Hwang, T., & Shin, M. (2008). Entrepreneurial applications of the lean approach to service industries. *The Service Industries Journal,* 1–14.

Madu, B. (2013). Vision: The relationship between a firm's strategy and business model. *Journal of Behavioral Studies in Business, 6,* 1–9.

McGee, J., Peterson, M., Mueller, S., & Sequeira, J. (2009). Entrepreneurial self-efficacy: Refining the measure. *Entrepreneurship Theory and Practice, 33*(4), 965–988.

McVay, M. (2003). *BDS on the margins: A proposal for action research.* Arlington, VA: The SEEP Network, MEDA, Interviews.

Nooteboom, B. (2007). Service value chains and efforts of scale. *Service Business: An International Journal, 1*(2), 119–139.

Ohno, T. (1988). *Toyota production system: Beyond large-scale production.* New York, NY: Productivity Press.

Okeyo, W. (2015). The interactive nature of business development services in the relationship between external business environment and firm performance. *Advances in Social Science Research Journal, 2*(2), 164–177.

Okeyo, W., Gathungu, J., & K'Obonyo, P. (2016). Entrepreneurial orientation, business development services, business environment, and performance: A critical literature review. *European Scientific Journal, 12*(28), 188–218.

Porter, M. E., Sachs, J. D., & McArthur, J. W. (2002). Competitiveness and stages of economic development. In M. E. Porter, J. D. Sachs, P. K. Cornelius, J. W. McArthur, & K. Schwab (Eds.), *The global competitiveness report 2001–2002* (pp. 16–25). New York, NY: Oxford University Press.

Ritchie, R., & Angelis, J. (2010). Implementing lean into a servicing environment. In *Advances in production management systems: New challenges, new approaches, of the series IFIP advances* (Vol. 338, pp. 587–594). Paris: Information and Communication Technology.

Rocha, V. (2012). *The entrepreneur in economic theory: From an invisible man toward a new research field* (FEP Working Paper School of Economics and Management). Portugal: University of Porto. Retrieved December 28, 2019, from www.researchgate.net/publication/230676107

Salas, V., & Sanchez-Asín, J. (2006). Entrepreneurship, management services and economic growth. *SSRN Electronic Journal.* doi:10.2139/ssrn.878620.

Sanchez, L., & Nagi, R. (2010). A review of agile manufacturing systems. *International Journal of Production Research, 39*(16), 3561–3600.

Sa Sa Corporation. (2020). *Company profile.* Retrieved January 13, 2020, from http://corp.sasa.com/en/company-overview/company-profile

Say, Jean-Baptiste. (1971). *A treaties on the political economy of the production, distribution and consumption of wealth.* New York, NY: Augustus M. Kelly Publisher.

Schumpeter, J. (1942 [1976]). *Capitalism, socialism and democracy* (3rd ed.). London: George Allen and Unwin.

Shane, S., & Venkataraman, S. (2000). The promise of entrepreneurship as a field of research. *The Academy of Management Review, 25*(1), 217–226.

Vignesh, V., Suresh, M., & Aramvalarthan, S. (2016). Lean in service industries: A literature review. *Materials Science and Engineering, 149.*

Yusof, M., Sandhu, M., & Jani, K. (2007). Relationship between psychological characteristics and entrepreneurial inclination: A case study of students at University Tun Abdul Razak. *Journal of Asia Entrepreneurship and Sustainability, 3*(2), 1–19.

# 9 Organic vs. mechanistic structure for leadership

## 9.1 Mechanistic vs. organic organizations

In the discussion in Chapter 3 on leadership approaches, it was mentioned how leadership theories had served mechanistic organizations in the manufacturing era, and how some of those leadership strategies had been applied in some organic organizations. Given that the service era is here, it is important to understand the relevance of organic leadership in the 21st century. For this reason, this section will define the nature of mechanistic and organic organizations and then elaborate on the leadership approach that applies to each. It should be understood at the outset that organic leadership, as well as its complement – service leadership, is an outgrowth of the larger social constructions of organizations in general. Service leadership creates a network within and outside the organization so it can be creative in moving forward. As stated by Ferguson (2017), 'it is networks that tend to innovate. And it is through networks that revolutionary ideas can contagiously spread.'

Mechanistic organizations are often seen in hierarchical and bureaucratic organizations. This form of organization is characterized by its highly centralized authority, formalized procedures and practices, and specialized functions. Because of the nature of mechanistic organization, it is relatively easier and simpler to organize, but in contrast to the organic organizations, there are more rapid change. The issue of change will be discussed later.

What differentiates mechanistic organizations from organic ones is that employees in these firms work separately and on their own assigned tasks. Specifically, there is a definite chain of command, and decisions are kept as high up the chain as possible. Furthermore, regular communication does not occur between the members of the organization, and minimal interaction takes place with employees. Procedurally, there are strict company policies or operating standards with an abundance of documentation. This structural organization has had its appeal in the manufacturing sector.

In contrast to mechanistic organizations, organic organizations have the following characteristics:

1   Lack of hierarchy in the organization that allows for communications and interactions to be horizontal. Employees are often found working in groups and share input on tasks. Communication is open between employees, managers, and executives. As such, greater participation among employees and managers is noted.
2   Low specialization of tasks, as it is understood that knowledge resides wherever it is most useful. This creates an environment that is more adaptable and flexible to changes.
3   Decentralization provides a great deal of formal and informal participation in decision making. Given that service organizations are changing rapidly, and the environment is unpredictable, the freedom afforded the employees and management contributes to a happy workplace. This in turn makes for happy employees. Good examples of this type of structure would be Google and the coveted positions within the Facebook Corporation.

With the distinction made between the mechanistic and organic organizations, it is essential to discuss how each responds to changes in the environment, or service habitat.

The focus throughout this text has been on:

1   Changing the mindset from a manufacturing organizational system thinking to a service organizational system that attends to client system needs (Chung, 2012).
2   How to go about a planned changing of the system, using various strategies whether the system is at the individual, group, or organizational level (Wheeler, 2013; Bowditch, Buono & Stewart, 2008; Cummings & Worley, 2005; Burke & Bradford, 2005).
3   How open systems theory is most appropriate for service organizations that are organic in nature. This theory views organizations as an open social system that interacts with their environments to survive. Organizations depend on their environments (habitat) for several essential resources: Customers who purchase the product or service, suppliers who provide materials, employees who provide labor or management, shareholders who invest, and governments that regulate (Cutlip, Center, & Broom, 2006).

Earlier chapters elaborated that firms that seek to become innovative and responsive to the demands of the global market have recognized that the work culture and the system within the organization (the service ecosystem in the context of service leadership) play a critical role in the service they provide. Unfortunately, in organizations in which a hierarchical leadership system is in place, as opposed to organic leadership, the work culture and environment are driven by leaders who dictate direction and deliberately decide any planned change. As was noted by Cox (2005), this approach stifles creativity and breeds mediocrity.

Any change in the work culture or system requires a leadership that is aware of the intricacies of human interactions and how such system operates. Therefore, work culture will affect how leaders manage and implement changes. If the culture is top-down, conservative, risk-averse, and compliant, then leaders will state all the change details and may choose to hand-hold employees through the change. As can be imagined, any system change that has not included all members of the organization is bound to face resistance. Resistance to change often comes either with employees not liking the change or finding it hard to adjust well to the changes (Hoshmand, 2012, p. 3).

The key challenge to changes in the organization system comes from those who are working in the organization. Humans are a complex system in which one would have to consider psychological, emotional, and physiological factors of people before any change can take place (Wheeler, 2013). What is emphasized throughout this book is that service leadership, being an organic system, easily manages system changes through its collaborative and collective systems thinking.

In organic systems, communication about change is bidirectional. This implies that change can be initiated from the frontline employees or the leadership of the organization. Organic systems also require that the implementation of the system changes be implemented collaboratively.

Burns and Stalker (1961) theorized that companies facing a changing environment may have to use an organic organizational structure in order to quickly adapt to changes. In adopting organic leadership as a strategy for change, the leader must recognize the cyclical pattern that drives the organic systems, namely, that the inputs from the external environment is going into the system that affects the processes within the system, and hence the outputs coming of the system will find its way back into the environment (Wheeler, 2013; Bowditch et al., 2008; Burke & Bradford, 2005; Cummings & Worley, 2005; Bastedo, 2004). This concept was highlighted in the entrepreneurial cycle discussed in Chapter 8.

The value and contribution of organic leadership have also been recognized by voluntary community organizations. In the past two decades, there has been a shift away from a top-down and hierarchical command-and-control approach to risk reduction in various community service organizations. They have recognized that the people-centered or participatory action is crucial to strengthening resilience in the community (Scolobig, Prior, Schroter, Joren, & Patt, 2015). The ability to self-organize when the community faces shocks and adapts to them is an element of resilience. What is to be noted in this decentralized approach is recognition of the value of leadership emerging from a wide spectrum of disempowered stakeholders. Additionally, organic leadership in the community organizations depends upon regular and repeat interactions of trust-based reciprocal exchanges between people (Woodward & Shaffakat, 2017; Bailey, Bellandi, Caloffi, & De Popris, 2013).

Adopting an organic approach to bring about changes in the service environment requires some basic steps that will facilitate the process. The following steps should be considered by the leader of an organic organization when contemplating changes in the system.

### Team development

*Step 1*: State the ground rules, shared vision, collaborative process, and approach to conflict resolution to the group or teams.

*Step 2*: Adopt Tuckman's model (1965) of group process (i.e., forming, storming, norming, performing, and adjourning).

*Step 3*: Encourage members of the group to look at new approaches for personal as well as organizational growth as changes are being discussed.

*Step 4*: Recognize the importance of emotional commitment of the team in the process (Gifford, 2018). This includes the ability and willingness of individuals to reflect on their needs, conflicts, and how to share their ideas with the team (Spritzer & Kurland, 2004, p. 19).

### The process

The leader or organizer of the group may wish to approach the discussion about change by adopting an open system thinking. In the context of service leadership, this suggests that the group consider taking in from their environment (service habitat) ideas that can be integrated creatively and freely with their own thinking so that a collaborative process for change can be found (Mullen & Kochan, 2000).

Opportunity for self- or group reflection should be provided to allow individuals to interact with their environment and be inspired by interactions. At the end of the process, the leader or organizer may ask the participants the following:

1  What excited them about this process?
2  What are their goals for personal growth with the change and how can the change be achieved?
3  How will they make their goals a reality for themselves and for the firm?

### The outcome

Whatever the content is for engaging the members of the firm (changing the work environment, professional development, etc.), in a discussion, it should be kept in mind that the goals of the process have to be in the forefront. As an outcome, questions to be asked of the participants are the following:

1  Did you achieve the goals set at the beginning?
2  What approach did you take to make your goals a reality?
3  What was it about the participation that made your experience distinctive?
4  If you were to identify four to five essential elements of the discussion for your personal and professional growth to bring about the change, what are they?

The steps outlined previously for bringing about change in an organization are essential in creating an environment for collaboration and achieving organizational goals.

Earlier, it was pointed out that to bring about change in a system, leaders must consider the open systems theory. This theory and the concept of service leadership go hand in hand. The theory views organizations as an open social system that interacts with their environments, whether they are economic, political, or social in nature.

When viewed broadly, most leadership theories of organization apply the open system perspective. However, depending on the nature of the leadership theory, the open system takes different forms. For instance, institutional theorists see organizations as a means by which the societal values and beliefs are embedded in organizational structure, and they are expressed when there are organizational changes. The contingency theorists view that organizations are organized in ways that best fit the environment in which they are embedded. Similarly, resource dependency theorists argue that an organization adapts to the environment as dictated by its resource providers. Although there is variation in the perspectives provided by open systems theories, they all view that an organization's survival is dependent upon its relationship with the environment (Bastedo, 2004).

The fact that organic organizations and their leaders are able to incorporate a broader system thinking just as service leadership does with its *3Cs* (*competence*, *character*, and *care*) differentiates them from the mechanistic organization.

## 9.2 Organic leadership

What is organic leadership and how is it related to service leadership? To answer this question, let's take a look once again at how organic leadership was defined and then try to understand the parallels between organic leadership and service leadership.

Organic leadership is dramatically different from mechanistic leadership. Mechanistic leadership relies heavily on authoritative management practices that covet control, consistency, and predictability. This form of leadership breeds compliance, dependency, dominance, parenting, and care taking – all of which are responsible for stifling creativity, restricting democracy, and breeding mediocrity (Cox, 2005; Bailey et al., 2013).

Organic leadership is defined as a series of dynamic, open, complex relational and dialogic processes focused on facilitating the emergence of high-performance environments that organize human experience around social change agendas (Cox, 2005, p. ii).

An organic organization is a fluid and flexible network of multitalented individuals who perform a variety of tasks, knowing that their contributions would drive the firm's success (Morand, 1995). What needs to be understood is that organic leadership can emerge during a brainstorming session when unplanned, spontaneous, and unexpected discussions take place. This is the essence of what it means to be organic.

Another perspective offered on organic leadership by McCrimmon (2005) is that an organic organization thrives on the power of personalities and relationships, lacks rigid procedures and communication, and can react quickly and easily to changes in the environment. Thus, it is said to be the most adaptive form of organization. Decisions arise from the needs felt by individuals in the group, who propose changes to the group either by discussion or by changing behavior or operations without discussion.

Another way of describing organic leadership is that it challenges the linear, structural-functionalist view of organizations; the individualistic focus on the leader; and the ethical perspectives of its day and suggests novel ideas and alternatives on executives and the functioning of organizations.

Leaders of organic organizations, similar to service leadership organizations, pay special attention to the ideas of the employees. This attitude opens the doors to teamwork among employees as well as the leadership, instead of competition or a feeling of powerlessness. As was pointed out in Chapter 1, service leaders and followers engage with each other such that they raise one another to higher levels of motivation and morality. This is why emphasis was placed on the importance of the follower in the interaction process. The arguments throughout this text have been that a flat structure is good for self-actualization of individuals and prosperity of the firm. For self-actualization to occur, there must be a fit between the personality of the members and the organizational structure.

Follower's personality, just as the leader's personality, matters in achieving success in organic organizations. Personalities who are high on openness to experience enjoy anything out of the ordinary. Anything new excites and stimulates them, and they enjoy doing things never done before. A study found that open-mindedness contributes significantly to creating an internal and external social network, thereby contributing to innovations in organizations (Perin, Sampaio, Jiménez-Jiménez, & Cegarra-Navarro, 2016, p. 6). Furthermore, those who are open-minded find that challenges are easy for them to overcome; they have a vivid imagination and a very broad perspective about most things. They enjoy discovering new things and try to understand them (Kandalla & Krishnan, 2004).

Some studies have also shown that behaviors like articulating vision and high-performance expectations result in followers trusting in the leader, which in turn has an effect on their organizational citizenship behavior (Podsakoff, MacKenzie, Moorman, & Fetter, 1990). Service leadership recognizes the concept of psychic income as an incentive for being a part of a firm that cares enough that employees want to work for this firm than any other. Caring about the needs of employees creates an environment of collegiality and cooperation that is called citizenship behavior. This idea has also been effectively used by leaders of organic organizations to provide an incentive to employees to cooperate and perform to the best of their abilities. Other studies have shown that charismatic leadership is found more in organic organizations in which such leadership appears when radical change is needed. Pillai and Meindl (1998) believe that organic organizations enabled and encouraged expression of individual behavior by both leaders and followers (Shamir & Howell, 1999).

In addition to followers' personality, the organizational structure of organic leadership, being flat, ensures that the motivation to work is not tied to many promotions one gets, as is the case in hierarchical structures, but rather to the work one does that receives recognition by the superiors. It has been argued that in turbulent times, a mechanistic organization cannot survive due to its rigid system and inflexibility to meet the challenges (Bass, 2000). However, organic organizations, and by association service leadership organizations, are able to better cope with the changing environments. Furthermore, a study conducted by Ivancevich and Donnelly (1975) involving 295 salesmen from three different companies observed that salesmen in flat organizations faced less pressure from their supervisors, were given more autonomy, were more satisfied, and performed better (were more efficient) than those in tall organizations who found being constantly supervised stifling. The core tenets of organic leadership and those of service leadership are to bring about empowerment, accountability, service, humility, spirituality, and profitability into an organization (Chung & Bell, 2015). This form of leadership builds a strong relationship between individuals within and outside of the organization. The ultimate goal is to unleash human potential to be focused on delivery of excellent service to customer and as a consequence help the firm reach its goals (Karp, 2006).

Interestingly, voluntary self-organization appears to be a characteristic of organic leadership. This characteristic is embedded in group and team processes with temporal rather than long-term leadership by any one individual and is place specific (Lough, 2019; Ganor & Ben-Lavy, 2003). In these environments, personal interactions and frequent communication lead to individuals taking the leadership role to respond rapidly to changing dynamics and innovative response (Woodward & Shaffakat, 2017; Rok, 2009).

It is clear from the literature that an organic, nonformalized organization with a larger span of control would be positively related to the job performance and satisfaction of employees. In this context, organic leadership adds another dimension to the field of leadership by delving into the strategic direction of leadership that leader who aspires to steer away from the traditional approaches to leadership (McCrimmon, 2006). Organic leadership fuels vision, spawns novel ideas, crafts diverse methods, and produces innovative output as an outcome of grassroots thinking. It could be stated that organic leadership serves as a catalyst to impel salutary change in the ecosystem (habitat) through the effervescence of innovative change.

Having provided a definition and a short description of organic leadership, let's now show the commonality between organic and service leadership styles. This is shown in Table 9.1. Clearly, the two approaches to leadership have commonalities between them. One can say that at the core, service leadership is organic in nature. In the same vein, a comparison of service leadership, being organic, with the concept of exemplary leadership put forward by Kouzes and Posner's (2011) popular book on leadership provides an empirical base for understanding leadership in the current environment is shown in Table 9.2.

Kouzes and Posner's model is structured around several characteristics that people look for and admire in a leader that is similar to the elements of the 3Cs that was discussed in Chapters 1 and 4. The characteristics identified by Kouzes and Posner (2011) are:

- Being honest: Truthful, ethical, principled, and worthy of trust.
- Being forward-looking: Articulating a vision and sense of direction for the organization. Having the ability to do strategic planning and forecasting.
- Competent: Having a track record to get things done with relevant experience to understand the fundamentals of the organization.
- Inspiring: Being enthusiastic, energetic, and positive about the future.

Those characteristics are very similar to those identified in the *character* and *care* of the 3Cs of service leadership in Chapter 1.

Table 9.1 Commonality between organic leadership and service leadership

| Organic leadership[1] | Service leadership[2] |
|---|---|
| Provide support and encouragement to someone with a difficult task. | Apprentice/mentoring begins on day one. |
| Express confidence that a person or group can perform a difficult task. | Use of competence, character, and care applies throughout the firm. |
| Socialize with people to build relationships. | Team building begins from the start for all employees. |
| Recognize contributions and accomplishments. | All elements of 'care ' of the 3Cs apply. |
| Provide coaching and mentoring when appropriate. | Apprentice/mentoring. |
| Consult with people on decisions affecting them. | Grassroots decision making. |
| Allow people to determine the best way to do a task. | Service employees make decisions on the spot for better service. |
| Keep people informed about actions affecting them. | Individuals allowed to make mistakes as long as they share them with the team. |
| Help resolve conflicts in a constructive way. | Constructive team discussions and open communication. |
| Use symbols, ceremonies, rituals, and stories to build team identity. | Sharing of stories (success and failures) among team members. |
| Recruit competent new members for the team or organization. | Hire for character and care and teach the skills for delivering exceptional service. |

Source (1): Yukl (2006), *Leadership in organizations* Table 3–1, p. 66.
(2): Chung and Bell (2015), *25 Principles of service leadership*.

Table 9.2 Comparison of service leadership with exemplary leadership

| Service leadership[1] | Exemplary leadership[2] |
|---|---|
| Character. | Inspire a shared vision. |
| Competence. | Challenge the process. |
| Character. | Enable others to act. |
| Care. | Encourage the heart. |

Source (1): Chung (2015). 25 principles of service leadership.
(2): Kouzes, J., & Posner, B. (2011). *The five practices of exemplary leadership* (2nd ed.). The Leadership Challenge and A Wiley Brand.

## 9.3 How to develop organic leadership in an organization

This text started with the view that leadership, with all its nuances, starts from the 'self'. Chapter 1 elaborated that to be an effective service leader in this era, one has to understand how self-development contributes to personal growth and enhances leadership abilities in an organic organization. The same concept applies to organic leadership too. In the words of Maslow, humans aim to be self-actualized. Getting to be self-actualized requires an inner development of self, and how one approaches personal growth. Figure 9.1 depicts an organic process of personal growth. This framework developed by Wheeler (2013) allows an

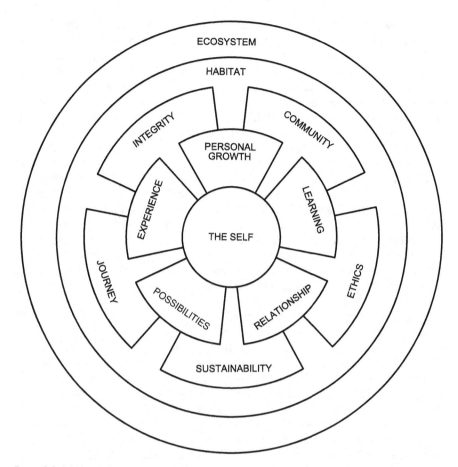

*Figure 9.1* A holistic, organic process of personal growth and leadership

*Source:* (1) Adapted from Wheeler, J. (2013). *A holistic, organic process of personal growth and leadership,* p. 41, and (2) Chung, P. and Bell, A. (2015). *25 principles of service leadership.*

individual to recognize that input from the internal (the habitat) and external environment (ecosystem) will shape the individual's behavior in an organization and at the same time the individual will affect the habitat and the ecosystem too. The process of give-and-take from the service habitat and the ecosystem is referred to as personal growth.

This organic personal growth and leadership model encompasses all areas of one's life. However, it is a mere representation of a very fluid and organic living process. Each one of us faces unique circumstances in life that either contributes to or detracts from personal growth. As part of self-development in service leadership, emphasis was placed on the centrality of open-mindedness to challenges in life. Every one of the challenges contributes to an individual's growth. Learning goes hand in hand with experience. In this model, Wheeler (2013) suggests that the process of leadership development in an organic organization begins with 'Self' and then proceeds outward through the layers, always returning back to the self. Emerging from the self is the first layer, consisting of 'Experience' (knowledge and skill that have come from life experiences). The 'Possibilities' that come our way in life are indicating potentialities that an individual can pursue. Depending on the *character* of the individual (being cautious, or risk-taker), these possibilities open the door for personal growth. 'Personal Growth' takes many forms by broadening one's capacities and understanding, becoming more sensitive to the environment, and deeper and more meaningful reflection on life. The concept of 'Learning' (knowledge or skill acquired by instruction or study) is referred to as *competence* in service leadership.

Developing competence does not mean only professional competence in technical knowledge such as being a doctor, a lawyer, or an accountant, but rather social competence, and cultural competence as well. Once achieved, it allows an individual to develop a 'Relationship' with self, family, friends, and those inside and outside of the organization. In service leadership, building a relationship is tied to the *character* and *care* of an individual. Without them, it is not possible to develop a long-term meaningful relationship. The elements of *character* and *care* appear in the second layer of the diagram where the true 'Journey' whether personal or professional permeates into the 'Community.' This is where sharing ideas and working on a common vision in the community begins with 'Integrity' and 'Ethics.'

Integrity as a virtue refers to the quality of a person's character. This attribute shows up in the professional, intellectual, or artistic work of an individual. As was mentioned in Chapter 1, integrity involves two aspects – one dealing with the relationship one has with oneself and the other is the integrity connected with acting morally with others. As for ethical issues, no matter what an individual's personal values, upbringing, and societal norms are, the process of learning to be ethical does not stop. In Chapter 7, the five fundamental codes of ethics for any business organizations organic or otherwise were stated: Integrity, objectivity, professional competence and care, confidentiality, and personal behavior. The notion of 'Sustainability' in this layer of the diagram suggests how self-development in organic leadership can perpetuate itself by remaining true to those elements just mentioned.

In the third layer of the diagram, the service habitat and ecosystem serve as a backdrop for self-development. This is where organic 'Self' acts and reacts to the conditions of the habitat and prepares itself for being a constructive member of the ecosystem or an organization.

This holistic, organic process model of personal growth and leadership provides a framework for learning about the 'Self' and how an individual's growth depends on his or her ability to respond to many factors within the habitat and the larger ecosystem.

In summary, organic leadership has been recognized as an important leadership model and is beginning to reverse the dominant trend of positional, heroic, individualistic leadership models that were prevalent in the manufacturing era. With the realization that organizations are complex, chaotic webs of human systems – social collectives of interrelatedness ebbing and flowing through time, striving to achieve a predefined yet ever-changing purpose – firms are recognizing that employees are its lifeblood as they interact, build relationships, disseminate information and knowledge, participate in decision making to build a service habitat that makes sense for the growth and sustainability of the organization.

## Key points to remember

- An organic organization is a fluid and flexible network of multitalented individuals who perform a variety of tasks, knowing that their contributions would drive the organization's success.
- Organic leadership can emerge during a brainstorming session when unplanned, spontaneous, and unexpected discussions take place.
- An organic organization thrives on the power of personalities and relationships, lacks rigid procedures and communication, and can react quickly and easily to changes in the environment; thus it is said to be the most adaptive form of organization.
- Organic organizations pay special attention to the ideas of the employees. This attitude opens the doors to teamwork among employees as well as the leadership, instead of competition or a feeling of powerlessness.
- For self-actualization to occur, there must be a fit between the personality of the members and the organizational structure.
- Follower's personality, just as the leader's personality, matters in achieving success in organic organizations.
- Charismatic leadership is found more in organic organizations in which such leadership appears when radical change is needed.
- Organizational structure of organic leadership, being flat, ensures that the motivation to work is not tied to many promotions one gets, as is the case in hierarchical structures, but rather to the work one does that receives recognition by the superiors.
- The goal of organic leadership is to unleash human potential to be focused on the delivery of service to customers.
- Organic leadership fuels vision, spawns novel ideas, crafts diverse methods, and produces innovative output as an outcome of grassroots thinking.
- System thinking allows for a holistic view of organizations and the challenges they face.

## Case study

### Organic approach of DHL: A global company

This case was developed from the material presented in Chung, P. (2019). *Designed to win: What every business needs to know to go truly global.* New York, NY: Leaders Press.

DHL was founded in a carpark after work one evening, when Larry Hillblom and Adrian Dalsey agreed to go into business. Within months of founding DHL Corporation, USA, the founders were looking into broadening their boundaries of service into the Pacific region. With a long-term vision, the leaders built a cross-cultural and international network that covers every major nation and territory in a little over 15 years – and the organization became larger than the UN and FIFA within 20 years (Chung, 2019, p. 39).

DHL believed in leadership first and foremost, and so the founders developed a leadership-centric philosophy to create, build, and operate a global network. The philosophy was rooted in natural systems, as they honored the organic insights of those people's feelings and those human relations between leader and follower (along with those between one leader and another). The best way to describe the process of DHL's success when there was no deliberate process is to follow natural laws. This case introduces those laws, the implicit trust that allowed DHL to grow for ten years without much structure, much discipline, any financial planning, and without a head office. DHL founders had recognized that there will always be aspects of one's design that emerge over time; there will always be the optimization of flow in process, ideas, and culture. Science has identified organic emergence as one of the most powerful organizing forces in nature. Any large-scale organic system achieves what it does through emergence. Think of the human central nervous system. It's made up of simple neurons, which have two basic states: Firing or at rest. They're completely deterministic: If there's the right stimulus, they fire; if there's not, they don't. On its own, a single neuron is a pretty simple unit. However, a group of these simple neurons together, allowing them to communicate in their simple way, can become human consciousness, capable of putting a rover on Mars and writing Bach's cello concertos.

Societies, economies, and political orders are examples of such organic systems. When hierarchical management systems or dictatorial regimes attempt to redesign a system from the top-down, they fail to demonstrate how important the organic aspect of leadership is. Having recognized the logic of organic systems, DHL implemented the organic laws to produce emergence. DHL leadership believed in the following four leadership tenets that moved the firm on its path to growth:

- No hierarchy push decisions to the lowest level. Give couriers responsibility.
- Everyone is encouraged to think strategically, then systematically.
- Allow people to learn from their mistakes.
- Let employees know that DHL practices family values.

Based on these tenets, the DHL networks emerged, and the firm grew exponentially. Like the neurons in the central nervous system, the basic units of DHL's network are its couriers. Like neurons, they have complete freedom to respond to situations facing them in the way they consider best. This means that when they encounter a change in their environment, they can quickly adapt to it.

The system adopted made sure that such adaptations were shared with the rest of the network. Like in the central nervous system, communication between all parts was vital. Mistakes were fine, as long as they were communicated, thus allowing the network as a whole to learn from them. This made the whole network responsive and adaptable.

On a more local, regional level, a culture was promoted of sharing stories over meals or a few beers. With couriers flying from place to place all the time, when one spent a night somewhere, they'd get a bite and a drink with the local crew and swap war stories. One initiative involved renting houses for couriers from various places to stay in, to foster such communication. For example, couriers coming into London from North America, South America, and the Middle East could all stay in the rented house in London, get to know each other, and share their experiences and insights about what was happening on the ground.

Organic systems are constantly correcting. Take the human body: It needs to be within a specific temperature range to operate, but the environment around it is changing all the time. This means the body will constantly be making small errors in its correction for temperature. When it gets hotter, it'll cool down, but if the outside temperature cools, then it'll need to correct. It is recognized that these small overcorrections are mistakes. Any organic system is constantly making mistakes because it's constantly adjusting to a changing situation. Hence, DHL adapted to the mistakes made in the firm by sharing it within the network and correcting the mistake.

The permissive culture of allowing nonmoral mistakes was huge because anyone and everyone was allowed to screw up – including the boss – and no one lost face by making mistakes. This was especially important in cultures such as in China, Japan, and Korea that heavily emphasized personal responsibility in a way that could bring too much pressure to bear and ultimately be counterproductive.

Leadership of any organization is responsible for creating the habitat. To create and run a thriving habitat, DHL knew that they had to learn everything about the courier, and how the couriers interacted with each other, and with people in the rest of the ecosystem. It was understood by the leaders of DHL that a healthy habitat creates a happy environment for the people who worked for the organization, and this leads to higher financial returns for the company. When this naturalist's model was applied to the couriers, internal habitat, customers, suppliers, regulators, and so on, the firm began to see the fruit of this approach no matter where DHL went. With success in hand, DHL adopted the following philosophy for building a global network company habitat:

1 Have rules that are simple and easy to remember.
2 Make sure the rules align with simple human needs, values, and emotions.
3 The rules must be logical, ethical, and caring.
4 The closer a company's values are to family values, the better.

The leadership of the firm believed strongly in these Four Key Tenets. They argued that the success of the firm depends on how each member of the organization internalized the following:

- Inform the behaviors using the Four Key Tenets (guidelines).
- Practice the highest level of *competence, character,* and *care.*
- Keep it simple and easy to remember.
- Use the master–apprentice method to grow the team and scale-up.

The firm simply transferred the values, behaviors, and stories from a family-habitat/context to the company's habitat and context, which then supported the individual, family, and the company.

Organic systems provide outcomes exponentially greater than their inputs. DHL's growth and progression were exponential because of network effects and designs.

## Questions related to the case

1   What contributed to the success of DHL?
2   What elements of service leadership show up in this case study?
3   Does the growth in DHL indicate adopting service leadership concepts of the 3Cs?
4   What elements of the 3Cs appears in this case more than others?
5   Does the case draw the parallel in organic leadership and service leadership? How and where?

## End of chapter questions

1   What is organic leadership and how different is it from other forms of leadership?
2   Why would organic leadership be more appropriate for the service industry?
3   Are there differences between organic leadership and service leadership?
4   Would organic leadership be appropriate for a very large service organization as compared to a microenterprise? Why or why not?
5   What is meant by systems thinking and what is its relations with organic leadership?
6   What are the elements that contribute to 'self' development in an organic organization?

## References

Bailey, D., Bellandi, M., Caloffi, A., & De Popris, L. (2013). Place-renewing leadership: Trajectories of change for mature manufacturing regions in Europe. In *Leadership and place* (pp. 107–124). Abingdon: Routledge.

Bass, B. (2000). The future of leadership in learning organizations. *Journal of Leadership Studies, 7*(3), 18–40.

Bastedo, M. (2004). Open systems theory. In *The Sage encyclopedia of educational leadership and administration*. Thousand Oaks, CA: Sage.

Bowditch, J., Buono, A., & Stewart, M. (2008). *A primer on organizational behavior* (7th ed.). San Francisco, CA: John Wiley & Sons, Inc.

Burke, W., & Bradford, D. (2005). The crisis in OD. In D. L. Bradford & W. W. Burke (Eds.), *Reinventing organizational development: New approaches to change in organizations* (pp. 7–14). San Francisco, CA: John Wiley & Sons, Inc.

Burns, T., & Stalker, G. (1961). *The management of innovation*. London: Tavistock.

Chung, P. (2012). *Service reborn*. New York, NY: Lexingford Publishing.

Chung, P. (2019). *Designed to win: What every business needs to know to go truly global (DHL's 50 years)*. New York, NY: Leaders Press.

Chung, P., & Bell, A. (2015). *25 principles of service leadership*. New York, NY: Lexingford Publishing.

Cox, K. (2005). *Organic leadership: The co-creation of good business, global prosperity, and a greener future* (PhD dissertation). UMI Microform: ProQuest Information and Learning Company, Benedictine University, Lisle, IL.

Cummings, T., & Worley, C. (2005). *Organizational development and change* (8th ed.). Mason, OH: Thomson – South-Western.

Cutlip, S. M., Center, A. H., & Broom, G. M. (2006). *Effective public relations* (9th ed.). Upper Saddle River, NJ: Pearson Prentice Hall.

Ferguson, N. (2017). *The square and the tower*. London: Penguin Books.

Ganor, M., & Ben-Lavy, Y. (2003). Community resilience: Lessons derived from Gilo under fire. *Journal of Jewish Communal Service, 79*(2–3), 105–108.

Gifford, R. (2018). *In times of change, feelings matter: Managing emotions during organizational change*. Centre of Expertise HRM&OB. Faculty of Economics and Business, University of Groningen. Retrieved March 18, 2020, from www.rug.nl/hrm-ob/bloggen/in-times-of-change-feelings-matter-managing-emotions-during-organizational-change-25-09-2018

Hoshmand, A. (2012, June 12–14). *Barriers to change: General education in Hong Kong*. Proceedings of the General Education and University Curriculum Reform: An International Conference, Hong Kong, China, pp. 37–43.

Ivancevich, J., & Donnelly, J. (1975). Relation of structure to job satisfaction, anxiety stress and performance. *Administrative Science Quarterly, 20*(2), 272–280.

Kandalla, H., & Krishnan, V. (2004). Impact of follower personality and organizational structure on transformational leadership. *Global Business Review, 5*(1), 15–25.

Karp, T. (2006). Transforming organisations for organic growth: The DNA of change leadership. *Journal of Change Management, 6*(1), 3–20.

Kouzes, J., & Posner, B. (2011). *The five practices of exemplary leadership* (2nd ed.). San Francisco, CA: The Leadership Challenge and A Wiley Brand.

Lough, B. (2019). *Voluntary "organic" leadership for community resilience*. Report prepared for the United National Volunteers (UNV) for the 2018 State of the World's Volunteerism.

McCrimmon, M. (2005). Thought leadership: A radical departure from traditional, positional leadership. *Management Decision, 43*, 1064–1070.

McCrimmon, M. (2006). *Burn! 7 leadership myths in ashes*. London: Action Publishing Technology, Ltd.

Morand, D. (1995). The role of behavioral formality and informality in the enactment of bureaucratic versus organic organizations. *Academy of Management Review, 20*, 831–872.

Mullen, C., & Kochan, F. (2000). Creating a collaborative leadership network: An organic view of change. *International Journal of Leadership in Education, 3*(3), 183–200.

Perin, M., Sampaio, C., Jiménez-Jiménez, D., & Cegarra-Navarro, J. (2016). Network effects on radical innovation and financial performance: An open-mindedness approach. *Brazilian Administration Review, 13*(4), 1–24.

Pillai, R., & Meindl, J. (1998). Context and charisma: A meso level examination of the relationship of organizational structure, collectivism, and crisis to charismatic leadership. *Journal of Management, 24*(5), 643–668.

Podsakoff, P., MacKenzie, S., Moorman, R., & Fetter, R. (1990). Transformational leader behaviours and their effects on followers. *Leadership Quarterly, 1*(2), 107–142.

Rok, B. (2009). Ethical context of the participative leadership model: Taking people into account. *Corporate Governance: The International Journal of Business in Society, 9*(4), 461–472.

Scolobig, A., Prior, T., Schroter, D., Joren, J., & Patt, A. (2015). Towards people-centred approaches for effective disaster risk management: Balancing rhetoric with reality. *International Journal of Disaster Risk Reduction, 12,* 202–212.

Shamir, B., & Howell, J. (1999). Organizational and contextual influences on the emergence and effectiveness of charismatic leadership. *Leadership Quarterly, 10,* 257–283.

Spritzer, G., & Kurland, N. (2004). What matters most for leadership and organizational development. *Journal of Management Inquiry, 13*(1), 19–20.

Tuckman, B. (1965). Developmental sequence in small groups. *Psychological Bulletin, 63,* 384–399.

Wheeler, J. (2013). A holistic, organic process of personal growth and leadership. *Organizational Development Practitioner, 45*(4), 38–42.

Woodward, I., & Shaffakat, S. (2017). Innovation, leadership, and communication intelligence. In N. Pfeffermann & J. Gould (Eds.), *Strategy and communication for innovation* (pp. 245–264). Singapore: Springer.

Yukl, G. (2006). *Leadership in organizations* (6th ed.). Upper Saddle River, NJ: Prentice Hall.

# 10 Microenterprises and service leadership

## 10.1 Microenterprises and entrepreneurship

A microenterprise is a small business enterprise that sells goods and/or services to a local area or a local market. It is the size of the enterprise that distinguishes it from other forms of business. It generally employs fewer than ten people and is geographically restricted (OECD, 2017, p. 36). Just like any other forms of business, its aim is to create income for the entrepreneur and at the same time generate employment in the local community by improving income levels and promoting commerce. These microenterprises serve as the economic backbone of many countries around the world. Small and medium enterprises (SMEs) account for the majority of businesses worldwide and are important contributors to global economic development. They represent about 90% of businesses and more than 50% of employment worldwide. Formal SMEs contribute up to 40% of national income (GDP) in emerging economies (Kumar, 2017, p. 5). If one is to look at the contribution of SMEs in the Asian context, some very impressive observations can be made. As noted by Joynal Abdin (2016), the scale of these enterprises is slightly different for different Asian countries.

SMEs account for 97.3% of enterprises in China, 97.3% of enterprises in Malaysia, 97.5% of enterprises in Kazakhstan, and 97.7% of enterprises in Vietnam. On an even higher side of the scale, SMEs account for 99% of Bangladeshi enterprises, 99.4% of enterprises in Singapore, 99.5% of Sri Lankan enterprises, 99.6% of enterprises in the Philippines, 99.7% of enterprises in Thailand, 99.7% of enterprises in Japan, and 99.9% of enterprises in the Republic of South Korea. In Hong Kong, the number of microenterprises amounted to some 302,000, representing 90% of all enterprises (Government of Hong Kong SAR, 2018). Between 2012 and 2017, around 95% of new enterprises coming into operation each year were microenterprises, probably because starting small can reduce some business risks (Government of Hong Kong SAR, 2018, p. 1).

The growth and vibrancy of these firms are also important for broader economic growth, diversification of economic base, and as a source of innovation that is exhibited by some of the start-ups. Needless to say, Apple, Microsoft, DHL, and Uber started as microenterprises. These firms followed stages in their development to survive, grow, evolve, and blossom into larger, powerful entities over time (Singh, 2018). Achieving the goal of becoming a major player means that small enterprises must operate in a habitat that is conducive for collaboration and nurtures its employees. Creation of a nurturing habitat was discussed earlier in the context of larger organizations, but it also applies to microenterprises.

As is often the case, microenterprises emerge in response to some viable business idea or hobby of an entrepreneur who recognizes potential market demand and responds to it. The viability of that market demand and a growing customer base is just as important to a start-up as is to a larger corporation. How the owner of a microenterprise manages the challenges and trends of the market requires some basic understanding of the service environment. Service leadership offers the necessary tools for growth and how to build a customer base that has been discussed in earlier chapters.

Given the sheer size of microenterprises and medium-sized firms around the world, it is imperative that every attempt be made to minimize their failure. According to the World Bank, there are approximately 35–45 million formal non-agricultural SMEs globally, comprising about 10% of the universe of both formal and informal 'micro-SMEs' (MSMEs) of 400–500 million (Kumar, 2017, p. 7). These data show that there are approximately 67%, or 25–30 million operating in developing countries, with the largest share in Asia Pacific. Recent data from the OECD show that microenterprises have been increasing in many countries. Most often, microenterprises are associated with the developing economies, but this is not always the case. In the developed nations, it appears that the services sector has been the main driver of these upward trends in recent years. In Canada, France, Germany, and the US, the trend of the growth of enterprise creations in the services sector outpaced that of the manufacturing sector (OECD, 2017).

In most developing countries, microenterprises serve as an engine of growth by overcoming unemployment and alleviating poverty (Hameed, Nawaz, Basheer, & Waseem, 2019; Hameed, Hussin, Azeem, Arif, & Basheer, 2017; Hameed, Hashmi, Ali, & Arif, 2017). As microenterprises and small firms comprise a dominant part in the market, their growth has not been evident in the way that they affect the economy (Nichter & Goldmark, 2005). A more entrepreneurial services sector may also help to continue to reduce gender inequalities, as women disproportionately engage in service sector start-ups. Over the last ten years, the gap between male and female self-employment rates has closed in nearly all countries. But significant gender gaps remain. In OECD countries, one in ten employed women is self-employed, almost half the rate of self-employed men, which is 17% (OECD, 2017).

In addition to the previously listed positive impacts of microenterprises, it should be noted that the expansion of the service sector has also led to an increased emphasis on activities whose fundamental purposes are social and civic in nature. Similar to the ideals of service leadership, the social cohesion in a microenterprise leads to better customer relations for the business. Similarly, service nongovernmental organizations (NGOs) whose mission is civic in nature have to recognize that to fulfill their mission, the element of *care* must be present.

The most important characteristics of these enterprises are the desire of the entrepreneur to keep the size and scope of their business manageable so that they can accomplish all business-related responsibilities by themselves. What also sets these enterprises apart from other business forms is that they can be started with minimal infrastructure or funding, and in most cases no business plans. The simplicity of these enterprises is appealing to entrepreneurs who are developing business skills as they run their businesses. This notion of 'learn by doing' provides the entrepreneur with the opportunity to create a niche for their business. The characteristic that is in line with the concept of service leadership is how micro-entrepreneurs measure their business's growth.

For instance, they tend to balance income generation with factors such as flexibility, business autonomy (psychic income), personal well-being (self-development), and self-reliance (self-actualization). To enhance their capabilities, microenterprise entrepreneurs can apply the core values of service leadership enshrined in the *3Cs* – high *competence*, *character*, and *care* – to their service activities. These core values are as relevant to them as they are to major corporate sector players. Given the size of these enterprises, it's the owners who need to develop the necessary skills to operate their service business and recognize that to maintain the viability of the business, character and care of the individual become critical. How to enhance their capabilities will be discussed in a later section of this chapter.

## 10.2 Factors affecting the development of microenterprises

To have a clear picture of the development of microenterprises, the factors in their growth and future sustainability will be discussed. Numerous factors such as the risk-taking attitude of the entrepreneur, market conditions, availability of capital, and government policies toward such enterprises significantly contribute to their development and growth. Gibrat (1931) argued that a firm's growth is not affected by its size but rather is a seemingly random process resulting from an interaction of several factors including political trends and the entrepreneur's relative risk aversion.

Chapter 8's analysis of the entrepreneurial process included a discussion of the notion of risk aversion as a factor in innovation. A collection of data gathered by the International Finance Corporation (Kozak, 2005) provides some illustration. Around 40% of the working-age populations of lower- and upper-middle-income countries are employed in businesses with ten or fewer employees. This percentage is indicative of the willingness of entrepreneurs to take risk with the hope of success. A recent debate in the literature involves constraints to microenterprise growth and eventually to its demise. What these studies have shown is that a lack of access to financing significantly retards growth (Angeles, Clara, & de Gusman, 2019; Beck, Lu, & Yang, 2015; Prohorovs & Beizitere, 2015; Khandker, Samad, & Ali, 2013). Krishnaswamy (2007) states that capital increases the opportunity of small firms to boost productivity. Others have argued that banks play a significant role in providing capital for micro, small, and medium enterprises. This notion suggests that bank credit is imperative in supplying reasonable and flexible capital to microenterprises Beck and Demirguc-Kunt (2006). In most developing countries, however, banking policy along with the lack of support from government makes it difficult for the microenterprises to comply with the financial requirements and discourages firms from borrowing. The reluctance of banks to support the capital needs of the small firm borrower affects their initiative to grow. Wang (2016) claimed that collateral, processing, and asymmetric information are among the challenges that borrowers have experienced with banks.

As one explores the development patterns of these enterprises, it is important to understand the factors that contribute to their growth. Economic theory suggests that in any profit-maximizing business, marginal returns to capital should equal the market interest rate (Dodlova, Göbel, Grimm, & Lay, 2015). Business growth is driven by high marginal returns to capital (Grimm, Krüger, & Lay, 2011), and such high marginal returns are observed in the developing countries around the world. This suggests that some firms are willing to pay an extremely high interest rate as the capital used in their productive businesses generate high returns (Banerje & Duflo, 2005). Some empirical evidence further supports this notion (De Mel, McKenzie, & Woodruff, 2008; McKenzie & Woodruff, 2008).

In contrast, others have argued that capabilities of the entrepreneur and opportunities in the market have a larger influence on achieving growth (Simeon & Lara, 2005). Some authors have looked at the behavioral responses of the owners when capital is given. This would suggest that the owners' partiality toward either distributing resources on productivity or not may have an effect on the growth of small firms (Demirgüc-Kunt, Beck, & Honohan, 2008).

While it is certainly plausible that a firm that can borrow may be better able to take advantage of opportunities by investing (and thereby expanding), it is also possible that a firm's growth is more strongly influenced by other factors (for example entrepreneurial zeal), with growth actually affecting a firm's probability of getting a loan rather than the other way around (McPherson, Molina, & Jewell, 2010).

In addition to the risk-taking attitude of the entrepreneur, a number of studies, including Akoten and Otsuka (2007), Akoten, Sawada, and Otsuka (2006), and Brown, Earle, and Lup (2004), have also found evidence that human capital embodied in the proprietor or its workers (usually measured as education, age, or experience) promotes firm growth.

Human capital develops on different occasions through the knowledge acquired within the family circle. This includes both formal and informal education and training, workplace training, and the knowledge accumulated during the professional life. Finally, there is the informal training or the job learning that takes place every day. The positive impact of human capital on the development of an enterprise as well as its sustainability and growth should be highlighted. First, human capital increases the ability of owners to realize the generic tasks of entrepreneurship to discover and exploit opportunities (Anis & Mohamed, 2012; Shane, 2003). For example, prior knowledge increases the entrepreneurial alertness of owners and prepares them to identify specific opportunities that are not visible to others. Second, human capital is positively related to the planning and strategy of the company, which in turn positively affects entrepreneurial success

(Frese et al., 2007). Third, knowledge is useful to acquire other utility resources such as financial and physical capital (Brush, Manolova, & Edelman, 2008).

Such evidence supports the basic premise of necessary skills in service leadership for microenterprises to be successful. What must be stated clearly is the fact that a majority of the individuals in developing countries may not have the education necessary to handle simple tasks for the survival of the business. It is here that training by the government and nongovernmental agencies for these entrepreneurs of small services following the concepts of service leadership is recommended. Such a direction in government policy, in addition to providing financial support, would have a significant impact on the sustainability of these microenterprises. Building human capital, or leadership capacity, in the proprietor or its workers is what is needed in this service era. Numerous studies have shown the positive impact of increasing human capital through formal or informal training that contributes to the success of microenterprises (Zainol, Al Mamun, Ahmad, & Simpong, 2018; Kessy, Msuya, Mushi, Stray-Pedersen, & Botten, 2016).

Studies have also found that some factors contribute to the failure of microenterprises, which include the skills of the business owner or top managers, inability to have access to capital, market conditions, and not knowing how to sell a service. If business owners or top managers lack the skills and competencies to drive their businesses forward, they are bound to fail. For instance, Tocher and Rutherford (2009) note that accumulated social competence or social skills should better prepare small business owners and entrepreneurs to deal with their management structures and systems and to address many challenges that threaten firm survival and performance. Teaching these entrepreneurs these skills is what service leadership is all about. It is essential to keep in mind that there is a competence-only bias in the literature, and it is strongly suggested that the convergence of *competence*, *character*, and *care* leads to successful leadership.

It was stated in the previous chapter that smaller firms are driven largely by the will and power of their owners or top managers, and hence their social skills play a critical role in abating failures.

Demand for a service in the local market may not be as clear to the entrepreneur as the desire to start the business. Failing to understand market conditions only adds to the many problems entrepreneurs face in many developing countries. Again, emphasis should be placed on the role that government and NGOs can play in educating entrepreneurs in the developed and developing countries to be aware of this factor when planning to start a business.

No matter what service business entrepreneurs are contemplating, the inability to sell their ideas to their client will contribute to the failure of the business at the outset. Salesmanship is a skill that is based on the character and care of the individual. Earlier chapters have stated that *character* and *care*, the two elements of service leadership 3Cs, define an individual and hence lead to the concept of trust that the community places on the entrepreneur. Lacking an honest character and failing to care for the client just to make a sale have long-term implications that must be understood.

Theoretical discussions on the growth of microenterprises make it clear that the entrepreneur's attributes along with the nature of business and environmental factors (issues related to habitat) are critical determinants of the success of the enterprise (Alom, Moha, Moten, & Azam, 2016).

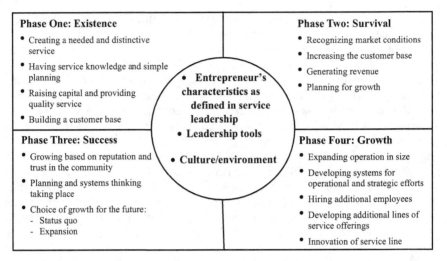

**Phase One: Existence**
- Creating a needed and distinctive service
- Having service knowledge and simple planning
- Raising capital and providing quality service
- Building a customer base

**Phase Two: Survival**
- Recognizing market conditions
- Increasing the customer base
- Generating revenue
- Planning for growth

- **Entrepreneur's characteristics as defined in service leadership**
- **Leadership tools**
- **Culture/environment**

**Phase Three: Success**
- Growing based on reputation and trust in the community
- Planning and systems thinking taking place
- Choice of growth for the future:
  - Status quo
  - Expansion

**Phase Four: Growth**
- Expanding operation in size
- Developing systems for operational and strategic efforts
- Hiring additional employees
- Developing additional lines of service offerings
- Innovation of service line

*Figure 10.1* Framework for starting and growing a microenterprise

Adapted from: Chung, P. & Ip. S. The five-dynamics of entrepreneurship: The first 10 yards, Singapore: Cengage Learning Asia Pte. Ltd. 2009. p. 7.

## 10.3 Microenterprises in the service sector

Having discussed the role that microenterprises play around the world in economic development of a community, and in the country, it is now time to take an in-depth look at how to categorize the problems and growth patterns of microenterprises in services. Even though it is recognized that microenterprises vary widely in size and growth, they are characterized by the independent action of the entrepreneur, the organizational structure of the enterprise (the habitat), and the management or leadership style of the entrepreneur. However, it appears that microenterprises face common problems (financing, market conditions, location, and other problems that most start-ups face) at similar stages in their development (Seitz, 2017). It is important to recognize these similarities and place them in a framework for a better understanding of the nature, characteristics, and problems these businesses face, whether they are a corner grocery store with one or two employees, or an IT start-up with $5 million a year that is experiencing 30% growth rate annually. A four-phase framework that will serve as a guide to an entrepreneur is offered. It has to be kept in mind that each phase is characterized by size, diversity, and complexity. As can be seen in Figure 10.1, management factors such as leadership style, organizational structure, major strategic goals, and the owner's involvement in the business play a critical role in the success of the business enterprise. At the core of this framework, shown in the center of the diagram, are service leadership elements such as characteristics of the entrepreneur, the tools for leading, and the cultural and environmental (habitat) factors in each of the phases of the microenterprise.

Each phase identifies the elements and context needed for its development. These phases are discussed next.

### Phase one: Existence

The owner does everything, including directing subordinates if employees are hired. At this phase, systems and formal planning are minimal to nonexistent.

The owner makes all the decisions in providing direction and location of the business and moves ahead with capital from his or her family and friends. This is a critical phase for a start-up. It is here that an entrepreneur's service leadership characteristics such as honesty and integrity, trust, empathy, and courage are critical in gaining a sufficient customer base to continue its operation. This is where customers have recognized the capabilities of the service firm to meet their needs.

### Phase two: Survival

This phase suggests to the entrepreneur that his or her efforts in phase one has contributed to the viability of the service enterprise. At this phase, the entrepreneur's context shifts from simply existing to larger issues of revenue generation and the cost of operation. Now, the entrepreneur has to face the question whether in the short run, the business can generate enough revenue to break even, or at a minimum generate enough cash flow to stay in business and grow it. Planning for growth requires attention to details such as whether the niche that the business has created for itself can make it stand out from the competition and generate more cash flow. It is in this phase that the owner has to decide whether to hire additional employees to carry out the day-to-day tasks. If additional employees are needed, the owner still needs to provide direction and ask employees to carry out well-defined tasks. Being a microenterprise, system development is minimal at this phase, and the major planning task for the entrepreneur is to be able to project cash flows. The strategy still is to survive, and the owner *is* the business. In many developing countries, business firms remain in this survival phase for a long time. Examples of firms in this phase are the corner grocery stores. These marginal entities depend heavily on a customer base that relies on the service they provide in the local market. Depending on the courage and future outlook of the owners, the firms may survive and move to the next phase of their development.

### Phase three: Success

The fruit of hard work in the previous phases of the business creates an environment that allows the entrepreneur to make alternative business decisions. During this phase, the owner may pursue one of these alternatives that are often noted in the business world.

- Firm as a platform for growth:

  A risk-taking entrepreneur makes a calculated and informed decision to take the revenues generated by the firm along with the established borrowing power to follow a growth path for the firm. Growth may come in the form of expanding the size of operation as was done in the case of DHL, where a small California-based firm within 15 years of its operation expanded to 120 countries (one country every five weeks, as well as 700 cities (one city every eight days) using the concept of service leadership (Chung, 2019, p. 39).

  Alternatively, a firm may choose to broaden its operation by adding new value-added elements to the business offerings for the convenience of the customers.

- Firm as a means of support for the owner:

  When the firm has attained economic health, that is, it earns average or above average profits and sufficiently penetrated the market to ensure economic success, it can stay at this phase indefinitely as long as the owner (operator) provides effective leadership to the firm to maintain its market niche.

  Some entrepreneurs may completely or partially disengage from the firm.

  If the entrepreneur decides to disengage partially, he or she must hire functional managers to take over certain duties performed by the owner. In hiring the managers, the owner should keep in mind the 3Cs of service leadership. In particular, hire for *character* and *care* and train them for the skills needed for success.

  If the entrepreneur decides to disengage fully, the business will operate with a management team that may pursue the niche that the service business has created for itself. This is often observed with service businesses that are small and growing slowly in the community they serve.

### Phase four: Growth

The precursors to this phase of business development have shed light for the entrepreneur as to which path the entrepreneur may pursue. A risk-taking entrepreneur understands that the cash generated by the business can be used effectively to expand operation of the business and, at the same time, the added revenue could serve as collateral to acquire additional funding from the capital market to meet the needs of a growing firm. What should be considered at this phase by the owner will have a major impact on the operational strategies of the firm. Often, the operational decisions will become decentralized as the system becomes more refined and extensive. The task of operational and strategic planning becomes part of the responsibility of unit managers. The owner may feel a sense of separation from the business, but the business firm is still under the owner's control.

In service leadership, it is emphasized that when a firm grows, delegating responsibility to the frontline staff becomes a necessity. When delegating, the owner should recognize that controls on performance and willingness to accept mistakes made by the subordinates is an accepted norm of effective leadership.

Having reached the success phase, the firm has to decide whether to expand by consolidating and controlling the financial gains brought on by rapid growth or to retain the advantages of small size, including flexibility of response and the entrepreneurial spirit.

### Key points to remember

- A microenterprise is distinguished from other forms of business in terms of the number of employees. According to the Organisation for Economic Co-operation and Development (OECD), a microenterprise generally employs fewer than ten people and is geographically restricted.
- Its aim is to create income for the entrepreneur and at the same time generate employment in the local community by improving income levels and promoting commerce.

- They represent about 90% of businesses and more than 50% of employment worldwide.
- Achieving the goal of becoming a major player means that small enterprises must operate in a habitat that is conducive for collaboration and nurtures its employees.
- Microenterprises emerge in response to some viable business idea or hobby of an entrepreneur who recognizes potential market demand and responds to it.
- According to the World Bank, there are approximately 35–45 million formal nonagricultural SMEs globally, comprising about 10% of the universe of both formal and informal microenterprises.
- Most often, microenterprises are associated with the developing economies, but this is not always the case. In Canada, France, Germany, and the US, the growth trend of enterprise creations in the services sector outpaced that of the manufacturing sector.
- In most developing countries, microenterprises serve as an engine of growth by overcoming unemployment, alleviating poverty, and bringing gender equality in business.
- Expansion of the service sector has also led to an increased emphasis on activities whose fundamental purposes are social and civic in nature, which are similar to the ideals of service leadership.
- Microenterprises can be started with minimal infrastructure or funding, and in most cases, no business plans.
- The simplicity of these enterprises is appealing to entrepreneurs who are developing business skills as they run their businesses.
- The microenterprise entrepreneur views income generation with factors like flexibility, business autonomy (psychic income), personal well-being (self-development), and self-reliance (self-actualization), which are at the heart of service leadership.
- The risk-taking attitude of the entrepreneur, market conditions, availability of capital, and government policies toward such enterprises significantly contribute to their growth.
- A firm's growth is driven by the entrepreneur's capabilities and high marginal returns to capital, and such high marginal returns are observed in the developing countries around the world.
- Human capital embodied in the proprietor or its workers (usually measured as education, age, or experience) contributes to the development and growth of a microenterprise.
- Factors that contribute to the failure of microenterprises include the skills of the business owner or top managers, inability to have access to capital, market conditions, and not knowing how to sell a service.
- Salesmanship is a skill that is based on the *character* and *care* of the individual.
- To minimize failures in these microenterprises, training especially in developing countries by the government and NGOs is critical.
- The four-phased microenterprise development is characterized by size, diversity, and complexity.
- The four phases that microenterprises go through are existence, survival, success, and growth.

## Case study

### Er-Ji-Shuan – a food service microenterprise in Taiwan

This case study was adapted from a study done by Yeh and Chang (2018).

Microenterprises have played a significant role in Taiwan's economic development and carried much weight. According to the *White Paper on Small Medium Enterprises (SMEs)* published by the Ministry of Economic Affairs (Wu, 2014), the microenterprises that employ fewer than five individuals in Taiwan accounted for 70% of all its enterprises. The contribution of microenterprises to Taiwan's economic development of microenterprises with fewer than five people is considerable in the sector of food and retail sales.

Unlike the microenterprises in any general developing countries, the microenterprises in Taiwan are not running as the only means of making a living for the class of the poor as in most developing countries; instead, many of them are the result of entrepreneurship by individuals after having amassed certain capitals for a higher career development.

Their capitals by far exceed US$1,000 for those in developing countries, and their growth is considerable, too. As such, many microenterprises in Taiwan are start-up ventures. With a view to create a good environment that helps entrepreneurship, the government is planning on a start-up platform to simplify the procedure of start-up ventures establishment. Meantime, the government has knowledge and information centers and consulting windows on entrepreneurship in place for those who are keen to start up an enterprise; it also holds expos of start-up, providing ways of starting up for entrepreneurs.

In addition, to strengthen the functions of such a start-up platform, the government will also assist the new enterprises in financing and help reduce administrative obstacles to the establishment of new enterprises.

With a start-up fund of NT$15,000, Er-Ji-Shuan enterprise was founded by the owner and his wife in 1988. In the beginning, they did business as street vendors, but considering the difficulty of controlling hygiene and quality, they converted to a physical shop a year later. This let them control business hours freely and on a larger scale. The shop in Douliu City where it began its operation had only one competitor. Together, they had a monopoly market. In the beginning, the products and flavors were identical to those of the competitor, but the owner constantly developed new items to have more customers. In terms of price competition, they both offered similar prices.

Er-Ji-Shuan constantly revealed new merchandise to cater to consumers' curiosity for new flavors. The owner also kept improving and developing to produce the pocket pancake and deep-fried dough stick that consumers wanted. By doing so, the company not only increased its customer base but also made Er-Ji-Shuan a known brand that marched toward a successful operation for franchising the chain.

The owner of Er-Ji-Shuan controlled the product quality rigorously and often adjusted his range of items appropriately following customers' opinions. He and his wife started with four employees, but he handled all the products sold at the shop by himself. He had run a snack cart for years before he started this shop, so his acquired experience over the years added to his skills as an entrepreneur. For example, egg pancake sheets and fried dumplings both were developed by him. The couple were also the sole contributors to the start-up's capital. In purchasing, their suppliers were mainly from Douliu City, where the shop is located, and with whom the entrepreneur has maintained good relationships. Financially, they operated solely on a cash basis and the owner was able to review the bookkeeping by himself.

Er-Ji-Shuan adopted a strategy of cost advantage when starting up. The operation of the enterprise began in the building that was owned by the operator. Hence, rental cost was eliminated. In the meantime, in product pricing, the business owner practiced differentiation, where despite the competitors increased prices, he was able to maintain his price because he was capable of absorbing cost increases. To promote the business at its inception, he held a three-day promotion sale with a buy-10-get-1-free incentive program, and an all-you-can-eat contest, which successfully attracted massive consumers and students.

With respect to the demand of customers wanting healthier items, the founder took time to refine the dietary content of his products and their nutritional value. He practiced the core elements of service leadership by treating his employees as members of his family and is a hands-on leader who wants to create a kind and warm atmosphere in his shop. He asked every employee to smile warmly with their heart at all times and greet each customer. In addition, he applied the philosophy of 'customer first' as his motto.

Er-Ji-Shuan's relationship competencies showed that paying attention to innovation on product taste, product quality, and the owner's service leadership attitude to cater to customer demand contributed to the company's success. A key factor in the company's success came from the cooperative nature between suppliers and customers. At the heart of this success was the deeply established trust among everyone. As for interpersonal connections, employees maintained strong connections and an increasing network through friends and relatives, relying on good communication skills and competencies.

## Questions related to the case

1  What factors played a role in the success of Er-Ji-Shuan?
2  What particular elements of service leadership is apparent in this case study?

## End of chapter questions

1  What role do microenterprises play in the economy?
2  How is a microenterprise defined?
3  What is needed to start a microenterprise?
4  What are the major barriers to entry into the market for a microenterprise?

5  Are there any differences between microenterprises and those of a medium to larger size firms?
6  Does the government have a role to play in support of microenterprises?
7  What should be the government policy in supporting microenterprises?
8  What lessons could a microenterprise entrepreneur learn from using the service leadership framework?
9  What are the steps in nurturing a successful microenterprise?
10 A microenterprise goes through phases defined by size, diversity, and complexity. If you were to start your microenterprise, what phase would you consider to be critical and why?

## References

Akoten, J., & Otsuka, K. (2007). From tailors to mini manufacturers: The role of traders on the performance of garment enterprises in Kenya. *Journal of African Economies*, 16, 564–595.

Akoten, J., Sawada, Y., & Otsuka, K. (2006). The determinants of credit access and its impacts on micro and small enterprises: The case of garment producers in Kenya. *Economic Development and Cultural Change*, 54(4), 927–944.

Alom, F., Moha, A., Moten, A., & Azam, S. (2016). Success factors of overall improvement of microenterprises in Malaysia: An empirical study. *Journal of Global Entrepreneurship Research*, 6(7).

Angeles, I., Clara, M., & de Gusman, A. (2019). The mediating effect of microfinancing on access to finance and growth of microenterprises: Evidence from the Philippines. *Journal of Global Entrepreneurship Research*, 9(24), 1–16.

Anis, O., & Mohamed, F. (2012). How entrepreneurs identify opportunities and access to external financing in Tunisian's micro-enterprises? *African Journal of Business Management*, 6(12), 4635–4647.

Banerjee, A., & Duflo, E. (2005). Growth theory through the lens of development economics. In P. Aghion & S. Durlauf (Eds.), *Handbook of economic growth* (Part A, Vol. 1, pp. 473–552). Amsterdam: Elsevier.

Beck, T., & Demirguc-Kunt, A. (2006). Small and medium-size enterprises: Access to finance as a growth constraint. *Journal of Banking and Finance*, 30(11), 2931–2943.

Beck, T., Lu, L., & Yang, R. (2015). Finance and growth for microenterprises: Evidence from rural China. *World Development*, 67(4), 38–56.

Boin, A., & 't Hart, P. (2003). Public leadership in times of crisis: Mission impossible? *Public Administration Review*, 63(5), 544–553.

Brown, J., Earle, J., & Lup, D. (2004). *What makes small firms grow? Finance, human capital, technical assistance and the business environment in Romania* (William Davidson Institute Working Paper No. 702). University of Michigan, Ann Arbor, MI.

Brush, C., Manolova, T., & Edelman, L. (2008). Properties of emerging organizations: An empirical test. *Journal of Business Venturing*, 23(5), 547–566.

Chung, P. (2019). *Designed to win: What every business needs to know to go truly global (DHL's 50 years)*. New York, NY: Leaders Press.

De Mel, S., McKenzie, D., & Woodruff, C. (2008). Returns to capital in microenterprises: Evidence from a field experiment. *The Quarterly Journal of Economics*, 123(4), 1329–1372.

Demirgüç-Kunt, A., Beck, T., & Honohan, P. (2008). *Finance for all? Policies and pitfalls in expanding access.* Tilburg: Tilburg University, School of Economics and Management publication TiSEM.

Dodlova, M., Göbel, K., Grimm, M., & Lay, J. (2015). Constrained firms, not subsistence activities: Evidence on capital returns and accumulation in Peruvian microenterprises. *Labour Economics, 33,* 94–110.

Frese, M., Krauss, S., Keith, N., Escher, S., Grabarkiewicz, R., Luneng, S., . . . Friedrich, C. (2007). Business owners' action planning and its relationship to business success in three African countries. *Journal of Applied Psychology, 92*(6), 1481–1498.

Gibrat, R. (1931). *Les Inégalités économiques.* Paris, France: Recueil Sirey.

Government of Hong Kong SAR. (2018). A snapshot of micro enterprises in Hong Kong. *First Quarter Economic Report,* 1–3.

Grimm, M., Krüger, J., & Lay, J. (2011). Barriers to entry and returns to capital in informal activities: Evidence from Sub-Saharan Africa. *Review of Income and Wealth, 57*(1), 27–53.

Hameed, W., Hashmi, F., Ali, M., & Arif, M. (2017). Enterprise risk management (ERM) system: Implementation problem and role of audit effectiveness in Malaysian firms. *Asian Journal of Multidisciplinary Studies, 5*(11).

Hameed, W., Hussin, T., Azeem, M., Arif, M., & Basheer, M. (2017). Combination of microcredit and micro-training with mediating role of formal education: A micro-enterprise success formula. *Journal of Business and Social Review in Emerging Economies, 3*(2), 319–325.

Hameed, W., Nawaz, M., Basheer, M., & Waseem, M. (2019). The effect of Amanah Ikhtiar Malaysia (AIM) on microenterprise success in Sabah State Malaysia. *The Dialogue, 14*(2), 223–238.

Joynal Abdin, M. (2016). *Role of SMEs in Asian economies* (pp. 1–3). Dhaka, Bangladesh: SME Foundation.

Kessy, J., Msuya, S., Mushi, D., Stray-Pedersen, B., & Botten, G. (2016). Integration of microfinance institutions and health programs in northern Tanzania. *Indian Journal of Research, 5,* 87–91.

Khandker, S., Samad, H., & Ali, R. (2013). Does access to finance matter in microenterprise growth? Evidence from Bangladesh. *Institute of Microfinance Working Paper, 15,* 1–49.

Kozak, M. (2005). *Micro, small, and medium enterprises: A collection of published data.* Washington, DC: International Finance Corporation.

Krishnaswamy, K. (2007). *Competition and multiple borrowing in the Indian microfinance sector* (Institute for Financial Management and Research Centre for Micro Finance Working Paper No. 1–60), Andhra Pradesh, India.

Kumar, R. (2017). *Targeted SME financing and employment effects: What do we know and what could be done differently?* Washington, DC: World Bank Group, Jobs.

McKenzie, D., & Woodruff, C. (2008). Experimental evidence on returns to capital and access to finance in Mexico. *The World Bank Economic Review, 22*(3), 457–482.

McPherson, M., Molina, D., & Jewell, R. (2010). The determinants of the growth of microenterprises in Central Mexico: Evidence from a survey in Toluca. *Canadian Journal of Development Studies, 31*(1–2), 223–252.

Nichter, S., & Goldmark, L. (2005). Understanding micro and small enterprises growth. *United State Agency for International Development Micro-Report, #36*, 19–25.

OECD. (2017). *Entrepreneurship at a glance 2017*. Paris: OECD Publishing.

Prohorovs, A., & Beizitere, I. (2015). Trends, sources and amounts of financing for micro-enterprises in Latvia. *Procedia – Social and Behavioral Sciences, 213*(66), 404–410.

Seitz, H. (2017). *Microenterprises in developing countries: Is there growth potential?* Berlin: Department of International Economics at Deutsches Institut für Wirtschaftsforschung. DIW.

Shane, S. (2003). *A general theory of entrepreneurship: The individual-opportunity nexus*. Cheltenham, UK: Edward Elgar.

Simeon, N., & Lara, G. (2005). Understanding micro and small enterprises growth. *United States Agency for International Development*, 19–25.

Singh, R. (2018). Small enterprises development: Challenges and opportunities. In A. Farazmand (Ed.), *Encyclopedia of public administration, public policy, and governance* (pp. 1–6). Singapore: Springer International Publishing AG, part of Springer Nature 2018 Global.

Tocher, N., & Rutherford, M. (2009). Perceived acute human resource management problems in small and medium firms: An empirical examination. *Entrepreneurship Theory Practice, 33*(2), 455–479.

Wang, Y. (2016). What are the biggest obstacles to growth of SMEs in developing countries? – An empirical evidence from an enterprise survey. *Borsa Istanbul Review, 16*(3), 167–176.

Wu, H. (2014). *2014 the white paper on SMEs* (pp. 38–42). Taipei: Small Medium Enterprise Administration.

Yeh, T., & Chang, H. (2018). A multi-case study of entrepreneurial competencies in microenterprises. *International Journal of Management, Economics and Social Sciences, 7*(4), 321–346.

Zainol, N., Al Mamun, A., Ahmad, G., & Simpong, D. (2018). Human capital and entrepreneurial competencies towards performance of informal microenterprises in Kelantan, Malaysia. *Economics and Sociology, 11*(4), 31–50.

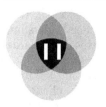

# Service leadership in times of crisis

## 11.1 Why service leadership matters in times of crisis

The title of this book is *Service Leadership: Leading with Competence, Character and Care in the Service Economy*. When transformation takes place in societies, organizations, or individuals, how do these groups respond to events that have caused the transformation? The change may come from the dynamic changes in the organization, or it could have been caused by natural or man-made disasters. What tools are necessary to accommodate such transformation with ease, and simultaneously inspire people to look into the future with possibilities and optimism? The service leadership model presented in this text is a multidimensional model that considers all the different aspects of leadership: Functional, relational, and attributional. This chapter discusses the *3Cs* of service leadership's role in developing cooperation networks, maintaining high ethical standards, and showing the contextual intelligence needed to deal in times of crisis.

One of the critical aspects of service leadership is how leaders and followers work together to attend to the needs of those who are affected by the changes in their communities, organizations, or nation. Those leaders who have high *competence, character,* and *care* – the *3Cs* – are able to engage everyone in their service ecosystem to respond and deliver service in an effective and a caring manner. Having high *3Cs* is so critical in effectively handling threats, challenges, or setbacks, especially at a time of crisis. A review of historical events can highlight how leadership that depends only on the perceived competence of the leader can fall short when handling a crisis.

Broadly speaking and just to name a few, an organizational or a national crisis includes natural disasters, terrorist attacks, hostile takeovers, product recalls, environmental spills, and financial scandals (James, Wooten, & Dushek, 2011; Greyser, 2009; James & Wooten, 2005). According to Boin and 't Hart (2010), the modern crisis is highly complex because it is not confined to local borders. A crisis quickly becomes entangled with other major problems due to processes such as globalization, deregulation, and developments in communication technologies.

The litmus test for leadership in a time of crisis is revealed by how a leader responds. A leader can make a crisis worse by ignoring impending threats, making unwise decisions, or by acting in ways that suggest that he or she does not care (Boin & 't Hart, 2010). In the words of the former UN Secretary-General Ban Ki-moon, 'we need a new understanding of business ethics and governance which will be more open to empathy and less uncritical to the magic of the market' (as cited by Wanat & Potkański, 2011).

Service leadership defines leadership in times of crisis as the sum of activities that conveys the leader's *competence, character,* and *care.* The leader's performance should minimize the impact of the crisis, whereby the impact is measured in terms of damage to people, critical infrastructure, and private and public institutions. Effective crisis leadership saves lives, protects infrastructure, and – most importantly – restores trust in public institutions (Boin, Kuipers, & Overdijk, 2013).

Examples of negative outcomes around the globe show that they are tied to a lack of leadership in times of crisis. The emergence and global outbreak of COVID-19 in China – or Ebola in West Africa (2013–16), the nuclear disaster in Fukushima, Japan (2011), and the financial crisis of 2008 provide ample opportunity to assess the failure of leadership in times of crisis.

Applying service leadership concepts, especially in times of crisis, can have a positive impact on the outcomes. All leaders in a time of crisis must make decisions. Service leadership offers a broader platform from which leaders can set their vision to reach the best outcome for the long term.

Chapter 1 elaborated on the concept of *competence* as one of the core elements of service leadership. Competence was defined broadly to include the knowledge one gains from education or experiential training in a field of study, as well as behaviors in any professional, social, or cultural capacity. Then, the ability of any leader to navigate through a crisis by organizing, directing, and implementing the right actions will minimize the impact of the threat. To assess the effectiveness of that leader in a crisis, the framework suggested by Boin et al. (2013) is adopted. This framework has the following dimensions that when used with the 3Cs of service leadership can serve as a guideline in times of crisis.

### Early recognition of a crisis

Service leadership recognizes that to effectively manage any crisis within an organization, the leader must begin with a shared recognition that a threat has emerged and that it requires immediate attention. The difficulty lies in knowing how to predict a crisis when there are so many unknown factors. However, some researchers have identified factors that can help in predicting possible threats in the early stages.

The first factor relates to past experience of the leader or the organization with crisis and its dynamics. This relates to the notion of competence through experience in which a leader has developed an ability to recognize deviations from complex but unknown processes (Roe & Schulman, 2008). The second factor is tied to the organizational culture. This too depends on the cultural competence of the organization that has been emphasized. Some organizations have a culture that facilitates rapid collective awareness of possible threats (Weick & Sutcliffe, 2002). A tenet of service leadership is to share experiences and be vigilant to deliver quality service under any circumstances including times of crisis. Tolerance for mistakes and admission of error is an accepted norm in service leadership as long as the mistakes are shared with others in the service habitat. It is only through such admission and sharing that the quality of service can be improved.

### Making sense of a crisis

During a time of crisis, arriving at a collective understanding of the nature, characteristics, consequences, and potential scope of an evolving threat is clearly a major challenge. Several studies have shown why most people find it hard to process and share information under the conditions of uncertainty and stress (Coates, 2012; Kahneman, 2011). One study suggested that by creating a 'knowledge commons', it will assist leaders in times of extreme crisis (Comfort & Okada, 2013). The idea of a knowledge commons is to create a repository of information that organizations and other groups can access in times of crisis. For example, in the environment dealing with the COVID-19 pandemic, the United Nations World Health Organization (WHO) has been serving as the 'knowledge commons' by receiving information from various sources and countries and sharing it with nations around the world. In organizations that are flat in structure, as the best service organizations tend to be, the challenge of sharing information is minimized because these organizations depend on broad participation from employees. The channels of communication help members understand the nature of emerging threats, and they quickly offer potential solutions so the service leader can make a better informed decision.

A leader who better understands threats and their impacts on the organization will find it easier to communicate in a way that helps members in the group deal with the threat. As Stephen Covey (2012) wrote, 'first seek to understand, then to be understood.' The more understanding a leader has, the more empathy and compassion he or she will show.

When organizations or a community is hit by a crisis, group members will look to their leaders for an assessment of the situation and how to deploy strategies that restore a state of normalcy. To put it differently, leaders are expected to provide 'authentic hope and confidence' (Leonard & Howitt, 2009). The process of understanding the crisis is crucial to the long-term legitimacy of a public institution (Rosenthal, Boin, & Bos, 2001), and this sheds light on the group's core values. One of service leadership's 3Cs is *care*, and this emphasizes why empathy and compassion are crucial in time of crisis.

## Making decisions

With greater member participation, a leader can make better critical decisions when dealing with threats. Service leadership emphasizes that such decisions are informed by the values that drive the organization and that this is based on sound processes (George, 1980). Additionally, the decisions must consider not only organizational values but also societal values when responding to the threat (Leonard & Howitt, 2009). An interesting suggestion is that effective crisis leaders orchestrate a process of adaptation, not a search for technical fixes (Heifetz, 1994, 2003).

It is important to keep in mind that leaders and bureaucracies produce decisions within crisis contexts (Allison, 1971), and some researchers have suggested that leaders might bend informational ambiguity or situational uncertainty to their ends (Bailey, 1988; Edelman, 1988). This is a less accusatory way of saying that some leaders at times of crisis will pick the means to reach whatever ends they want. This can mean making decisions that are immoral or offensive to reach desired outcomes, which from a service leadership point of view runs counter to having high levels of character. These are times when a leader of high 3Cs who has integrity and honesty would try to remain transparent, honest, and upfront and not be tempted to bend the facts in order to reach his or her goals.

In the process of making decisions, a leader must show confidence in dealing with a threat. This can be done by showing faith in the experts and people around the leader who will move the process forward. To balance things out, a leader must recognize that being overconfident can have the opposite effect and lead to a decline in confidence in the leader. Again, going back to the COVID-19 pandemic, many examples of negative outcomes when a leader is overconfident and assumes the crisis can be handled or dismissed simply on the basis of his or her unshaken confidence has been observed.

## Communicating

Chapter 4 discussed the importance of a leader's ability to communicate well. The guiding principle of communication when it comes to service leadership is to follow a process of listening to different voices, noting and accommodating what is demanded, reflecting, analyzing, and then communicating messages in both caring and persuasive channels that reach everyone. Communication is critical when it comes to change management or dealing with threats, as it profoundly influences the motivation for and interpretation and consequences of change and the threat (Duncan, Mouly, & Nilakant, 2001).

In times of crisis, the leader must pay special attention to how a message is communicated. Members of an organization and the citizens of a country want to hear the specifics of the threat and how the leader plans to face challenges from it. Communicating with facts is incredibly important (Palttala, Boano, Lund, & Vos, 2012; Frandsen & Johansen, 2011). Vague and inconsistent communication can only lead to confusion and can have severe repercussions for the safety of people. For example, contrasting the styles of communication during the COVID-19 pandemic between various American state governors and the federal government provides a view of how critical communication is in dealing with a crisis. New York Governor Andrew Cuomo communicated with citizens daily to inform the populace of threats and measures taken to handle how infection rates and groups were unfolding. Consistent and clear message from the governor helped minimize the severity of the threat.

On the other hand, there were inconsistent communication coming from the federal level, with lacking information that resulted in confusion and panic. This led to significant loss of life in the country and a tremendous damage to the economy.

One must remember that there are clear differences between routine communications and crisis communications (Goidel & Miller, 2009). Since the context of crisis is different from routine situations, communication techniques must be adapted to the unpredictable pace and persistent difficulties in verifying information that arise from a crisis. Communication skills are competencies that were discussed in Chapters 1 and 4. The point to highlight is that once the competencies are learned, the leader's *character* and *care* are crucial for how well the message will be received by those who are affected by the threat. It is this combination of the *3Cs* that provides a meaningful approach in communicating with the public during a crisis.

### Implementing

Once a collective decision has been made, implementation of the plan to deal with the threat requires cooperation of units within and outside the organization. Internal implementation in a flat organization is more effective and easier than in more hierarchical structures. External implementation demands significant cooperation by those affected by the threat. The ability of the leader to solicit cooperation depends on the level of trust given to the leader, captured by the *character* part of the *3Cs*. Orchestrating cooperation lies somewhere on a continuum between the extremes of persuasion and command and control, as persuasion alone is not enough to bring all parties to a state of optimal cooperation. Command and control, on the other hand, tends to backfire (Boin et al., 2013). In this context, being open and honest is the best strategy. That doesn't mean that everything needs to be shared, but it does mean that the leader should not deny what people can clearly see. A humble service leader knows not to fabricate information or deliberately mislead people. The recent threat from the COVID-19 pandemic shows how leaders around the world have dealt in making decisions. Some have shared the truth, trusted the judgment of the advisers, and have made decisions that prevented catastrophes. Others, on the other hand, have increased risks, were ill-prepared to deal with the threat, and placed the blame on others without realizing that the consequence of their decision have caused significant loss of lives or economic repercussions. A service leader who has internalized the 3Cs will likely move forward with confidence in leading the organization.

It must be emphasized that in times of crisis, it is crucial that the leader provides clear directions that are concise, consistent, and informed by rationality. Directions should also be aligned with the organization's values. Leading in a time of crisis is one of the most significant challenges for a leader, and a leader who can demonstrate understanding, calmness, confidence, honesty, and direction will be able to effectively deal with the threat.

Other examples from the current environment of dealing with COVID-19 are New Zealand, Taiwan, and South Korea, which became models of crisis leadership. The leaders in these countries recognized the problem; handled the challenges with calm, confidence, and honesty; and provided effective direction. Once again, applying the 3Cs of service leadership is an effective approach for understanding how an organization or country coped during the crisis. In sum, organizational leaders can be seen as catalysts of success or failure. When a crisis sparks uncertainty and fear, effective leadership can counter with anticipation, vision, flexibility, and empowerment to minimize the economic and social costs.

### Being accountable

Accountability in a leader is critical in the final outcome of a crisis. When a crisis occurs, its impact is felt not only at the moment but also across the long term. Sometimes, consequences can affect the future well-being of the whole society. Hence, the leader must explain what actions were taken and why, and this should happen before, during, and even after the crisis has passed. Details as to what worked and went wrong must be explained. Being accountable satisfies many obligations, some being legal, and also one being the organization's moral commitment. Restoration of trust in the leader and the service organizations is critical once a threat is gone. Often during a crisis, many leaders react defensively, try to justify their actions, and even deflect blame. This is due to uncertainties that surround a crisis, and some leaders can feel their actions were misunderstood or misperceived by members of the organization or the public. This is the kind of situation in which a blame game begins, along with all its dynamics (Sulitzeanu-Kenan, 2010). A strong service leader with the inner resilience and compassion for others tends to react differently to criticism, isn't fearful of taking responsibility for his or her actions, and doesn't blame others. Now that the COVID-19 pandemic has gripped the world, the actions of strong and weak leaders have been amplified. It can be easily seen that when a crisis is politicized, accountability gets affected and group cohesion is eroded.

### Learning from a crisis

It was mentioned earlier that a service-network leader is sure to face tough challenges when a crisis occurs. These times, however, can also be seen as opportunities for learning. With crisis comes success and failures, and an organizational culture that focuses solely on past successes can prevent future success by blinding the organization to potential failures. Taking the failures as an opportunity to learn ensures the same mistakes won't be repeated. In the literature, authors like Sitkin (1996) stress that without failure, one cannot learn. He wrote, 'Failure is an essential prerequisite for effective organizational learning and adaptation' (p. 541), and 'the absence of failure experiences can result in decreased organizational resilience' (p. 542).

Effective leadership demands of everyone to discover, improvise, and experiment with approaches that lead to a more effective response to a threat. The capacity to learn from mistakes and to acknowledge an effective response to the threat is important during and after the crisis. Hence, learning is a prerequisite for adaptation, which in turn, can help correct dysfunctional processes and facilitate freshly discovered solutions (Boin et al., 2013). Organizational learning is a process of detecting and correcting error (Argyris, 1982), and learning occurs when errors are shared and analyzed and the experience is distributed as a lesson learned by the organization to enact changes in the routine process (Popper & Lipshitz, 2000). In service leadership, emphasis is placed on the notion that anyone can make mistakes, so long as it is shared with all. Chung (2019) points out how this philosophy of accepting mistakes as long as the experience was shared with the collective contributed to the phenomenal success of the international courier, DHL.

One key element of learning in this context is how to plan for future threats. The planning process should recognize the success and failure of strategies in the past. It should answer questions on how well the organization adapted to unexpected threats and what changes, if any, in the organization's structure and policies would enhance the sensitivity and responsiveness to crisis situations. Since crisis events have a dramatic impact on an organization's ability to survive, good planning is crucial. Penrose (2000) noted that about 40% of Fortune 1000 industrial companies do not have an operational crisis plan and fully 80% of companies without a comprehensive crisis plan vanish within two years of suffering a major disaster.

### Enhancing resilience

A common maxim advises that facing difficulties makes one stronger. Thus, organizations that show resilience will cope better with threats. It was mentioned earlier that it is difficult to predict threats since there are many factors in running an organization. A resilient organization shows flexibility and a capacity to rapidly adapt in the face of a crisis. Comfort and colleagues have suggested that knowing how to create such resilient organizations isn't clear (Comfort, Boin, & Demchak, 2010), and they noted that one key factor in building a well-prepared resilient organization is to engage constantly in preparatory practices, such as vulnerability analyses, drills, scenario exploration, and network exercises.

Organizations that internalize and practice the principles advocated in service leadership are better shaped to build resilience through mindful learning (Veil, 2011). The organizational culture that service leadership promotes creates awareness and a shared belief that the team will be ready to cope in a crisis.

This framework applies across sectors and organizational design, notably in the private and public sectors. The next section discusses regional and global application of the framework, given that the world has become highly interconnected. Nations and communities are no longer isolated and what happens in one corner of the world affects others far away. Hence, it is crucial for leaders in regions or nations around the world to collaborate and build trust before a crisis takes hold and expands. Predicting a crisis may not be easy, but scenario planning for disasters that erode any of Abraham Maslow's basic needs can greatly help minimize human suffering and create a better world for all.

## 11.2 Global leadership in times of crisis

In the last few decades, the world has seen crises of unprecedented proportions. These disasters offer concrete examples of how leaders from different parts of the world, philosophical and political models, and other ideologies have come to respond to challenges of all kinds. Some of these crises were man-made and others are natural disasters that have had global impact. It would be worthwhile to look at a few examples to showcase what having a high level of the 3Cs could mean and what lessons could be learned from each.

### 11.2.1 *Global financial crisis (GFC) of 2008*

The GFC of 2008 is often referred to as the financial tsunami that began in the summer of 2007. This event had a massive impact in the economies and societies around the world, hinged on the trust that was placed on the banking and market system that quickly eroded and collapsed. Government intervention was needed to stop the spread of the contagion in the economy and to prevent another economic depression.

Arguably, that intervention prevented a second Great Depression, although the inhabitants of nations including Greece and Spain would beg to differ. The economic downturn was definitely worse than any other since the Great Depression, and the world economy continued to struggle for years to recover (Fox, 2013).

The causes of this crisis are numerous and have their roots in economics, management, business, sociology, and psychology. A crisis of this nature was generated by ill-designed institutions or regulations that worsened asymmetric information and moral hazard by encouraging risk-taking behavior. It has been pointed out that the warning signals of an impending financial crisis was ignored by political elites, treasury officials, and financial regulators (Hindmoor & McConnell, 2013, 2015).

World Bank researchers have argued that the root cause of the GFC was the partnership created between the state, GSEs (government-sponsored enterprises), and lobbies that had developed the National Homeownership Strategy of 1994. This strategy was to give an opportunity of 'affordable housing' to all Americans by the end of the century. In this process, two different institutions were created to facilitate the effort. The Federal Housing Administration (FHA) and the GSEs came into existence. As part of the GSEs, Fannie Mae and Freddie Mac were set up to provide home mortgage funds to low- and moderate-income families (Furceri & Mourougane, 2009). Such an elaborate system that included the federal and state governments, along with the private sector and the vested interest of the lobbyists, created an environment that became susceptible to mismanagement and unethical behavior that led to the crisis.

Among the other explanations for the causes of the financial crisis that wreaked havoc in the global economies are economic deregulation, subprime mortgages, securitized loans, complex derivatives, consumer indebtedness, inadequate regulations, economic dependence on financial services, undue faith in the property boom, short-termism, bonus culture, greedy bankers, contagion of optimism, irrational hubris, neoliberal consensus, and government complacency – none seemed to problematize leadership and its ethical failures (Knights, 2016). Sadly, lack of *character* and *care* (the pillars of service leadership) among the players exacerbated the problem.

Other researchers have stated that there was not an adequate foresight strategy mainly in the monitoring and management of risk and also that the incentives toward systems remuneration and bonuses instigated the risky activities taken especially by senior managements (Kirkpatrick, 2009). There are many arguments that support the claim that a lot of leaders from the private and public finance sectors failed the prudence test. Besides this, it is argued that financial leaders lacked foresight, reason, and self-control to accept, learn, and correct their mistakes (Hamilton, 2008). All these factors and a belief that heroic leaders are the panacea for all the ills of society led to such disaster.

The GFC that began in 2007 eventually brought the collapse of the US mortgage market, along with sharp international declines in real estate valuation, firm failures, runs on banks and intervention by the International Monetary Fund (IMF). Oliver Blanchard, an IMF economist, estimated that the total losses caused by the GFC exceeded $4,700 billion (Hindmoor & McConnell, 2013, p. 543). Given how severe the impact of this crisis was throughout the world, what lessons did the world learn?

### Lessons learned

Since this problem began in the US, a number of policy decisions were made by the US policymakers to prevent such occurrences again. As a first step, the US Congress introduced the Dodd-Frank legislation of 2010 to strengthen the weaknesses in the banking and financial systems that led to the crisis. The extensive list of initiatives includes more stringent regulatory capital requirements, stricter consumer protections when accessing credit, a new office to monitor and address risks to financial stability, a new resolution process for troubled financial firms whose collapse might cause widespread damage, the prohibition of proprietary trading by banks, greater transparency for derivative instruments, the provision for shareholders of a nonbinding vote on executive compensation, more regulatory enforcement power over credit ratings agencies, and limits on the Federal Reserve's emergency lending authority (Barth, Prabha, & Wihlborg, 2015).

With all these measures in place, one would expect a safer environment in the financial markets and the economy as a whole. However, what is needed to implement these measures is international cooperation. Service leadership demands of leaders to work cooperatively, not only within their organizations but also globally. Owing to the quick mobility of the crisis around the world, its systemic depth, and geographical breadth, political authorities face many challenges in deciding who ought to take responsibility for these events and also in appreciating the significant damage potential such episodes represent (Boin, 2009, pp. 368–9). Owing to its nature, transboundary crisis management requires international coordination and cooperation. In particular, governments and central banks need jointly to improve world standards for prudential supervision and regulation of financial institutions and to monitor and enforce those standards. Cooperation will be vital to ensure a smooth exit from the emergency measures that have been put in place in most economies. Greater cooperation helps achieve a healthier and more stable evolution of the world's financial markets and put in place mechanisms to increase market resilience to shocks. Although progress has been made to improve the supervision of large cross-border institutions, achieving a coherent system of financial supervision in the region and managing cross-borders risks will require a more integrated approach (OECD, 2008).

The financial crisis has highlighted the weaknesses of the current regulatory and policy frameworks and the need to strengthen resilience. It is understandable how governments have responded when the crisis was most acute by refinancing these failed markets and have proposed stronger and stricter regulatory constraints. However, as has been suggested, this attempt to 'solve the problems with the same thinking that created them' does not transform behavior (Thomas, 2009). This is because these attempts largely bypass reflection on ethical possibilities that must be contemplated. Service leadership is needed to deal effectively in the stabilization frameworks that would increase the ability of economies to adjust to shocks.

In summary, the important lesson from this crisis is that when integrity, honesty, empathy, social and moral responsibility, and ethics are lacking, destruction of the economic and moral fiber of society will ensue. It has been noted that 'in the crisis and disaster literature, it is well accepted that failure is not the product of a single, context-free phenomenon. Rather, failure is the product of multiple individual, institutional and societal factors that coalesce in pathological ways' (Hindmoor & McConnell, 2015, p. 66). From a service leadership standpoint, the best approach in times of crisis is to bring the *3Cs* to work together in dealing with a threat.

### 11.2.2 *Fukushima tsunami and nuclear disaster of 2011*

Just as any natural disaster, the March 11, 2011, Great East Japan earthquake and tsunami sparked a humanitarian catastrophe in northeastern Japan and initiated a severe nuclear accident at the Fukushima Daiichi nuclear plant.

Three of the six reactors at the plant sustained severe core damage and released hydrogen and radioactive materials. Explosion of the released hydrogen damaged three reactor buildings and impeded onsite emergency response efforts. The disaster brought with it more than 15,900 deaths and 2,600 missing persons as well as physical infrastructure damages exceeding $200 billion (National Research Council, 2014). It is pointed out that personnel at the Fukushima Daiichi plant responded with courage and resilience, and their actions likely reduced the severity of the accident and the magnitude of offsite radioactive material releases. Several factors, however, prevented plant personnel from achieving greater success – in particular, averting reactor core damage – that contributed to the overall severity of the accident. The National Research Council (2014) highlights the following failures and the lessons that could be learned:

1    Failure of the plant owner (Tokyo Electric Power Company (TEPCO)) and the principal regulator (Nuclear and Industrial Safety Agency) to protect

critical safety equipment at the plant from flooding in spite of mounting evidence that the plant's design basis for tsunamis was inadequate.

Again, this is a pattern similar to that of the financial crisis of 2008 in which the leadership ignored the imminent threat. This suggests that it is not only competence but character and care of the leadership that matter.

2   Multiunit interactions complicated the accident response. Unit operators competed for physical resources, and the attention and services of staff in the onsite emergency response center were diverted.

    This failure suggests that the leadership had not planned properly to provide adequate resources to the units operating in the plant to deal with the threat, and they began to compete with each other for the resources, further aggravating the situation. As part of the 'competence' of service leadership, emphasis is placed on the leader to plan appropriately and consider unexpected threats.

3   Operators and onsite emergency response center staff lacked adequate procedures and training for accidents involving extended loss of all onsite power, particularly procedures and training for managing water levels and pressures in reactors and their containments and hydrogen generated during reactor core degradation. Service leadership emphasizes training in the form of apprenticeship to prepare staff for delivering a service with quality and care. This type of continuous training is aimed at the professional development of employees and has long-term benefits to the organization.

4   Failures to transmit information and instructions in an accurate and timely manner hindered responses to the accident. These failures resulted partly from the loss of communications systems and the challenging operating environments throughout the plant.

    Service leadership emphasizes the importance of communication between all members of the team including the leadership.

5   The lack of clarity of roles and responsibilities within the onsite emergency response center and between the onsite and headquarters emergency response centers may have contributed to response delays.

    Proper planning on the part of the leadership would have been extremely helpful as is suggested in service leadership.

### Lessons learned

This disaster shows how lack of moral leadership can lead to disastrous consequences. Not only were leaders unprepared (implying lack of competence) for a tsunami following a major earthquake, but they also failed to anticipate both the damage inflicted on the nuclear plant as well as the societal costs. The failure to adequately prepare was widespread. The leaders of TEPCO built the reactors on a known fault line and then colluded with government regulators to avoid preparing for the inevitable (IGEL, 2013). Looking at this disaster helps us understand how important the concept of service leadership is. Without *competence*, *character*, and *care* of the leadership and those involved in this disaster, the loss of lives, the environmental damage, and the profound societal and political costs are enormous for the owner company and for Japanese taxpayers: Compensation, decontamination, and dismantling the reactors and radioactive waste storage exceeded 187 billion US dollars (Scheel, 2018). This disaster has brought to the attention of the world community why governmental transparency, public accountability, and being prepared for such emergency are critical.

### 11.2.3 The Ebola pandemic 2013–16

The 2013–16 Ebola pandemic was considered at the time as the largest and longest in recorded history, with more than 28,600 reported cases (WHO, 2015). However, the COVID-19 pandemic (2019–??) has surpassed the infamous outbreak of Ebola, and once again an infectious disease has taken over the world with devasting loss of lives and economic consequences. The Ebola's proximal determinants have been described as dysfunctional health services, a highly mobile and interconnected population, debilitated government institutions, burial practices that involve contact with contagious Ebola-infected corpses, and unsafe and poor-quality provision of care to infected individuals (Chan, 2014). More distal determinants were exploitative colonialism, enabled civil war, resource extraction, and unethical pharmaceutical trials on African people, which have received scant attention (Richardson et al., 2016). Even though there were numerous outbreaks since 1976, the scientific community's understanding of Ebola was limited, particularly concerning the social, political, ecological, and economic forces that promote its spread (Center for Disease Control, 2014).

A study using biosocial analysis that includes the disciplines of economics, anthropology, political science, history, ecology, epidemiology, and physiology (Robinson, 2008) examined the case of the 2013–16 Ebola pandemic to determine the claims of causality (Richardson et al., 2016). This study found numerous factors that contributed to the outbreak.

#### Ecological forces

A research conducted by Bausch and Schwarz (2014) found that ecological forces contributed to the outbreak of Ebola. They described a three-tiered cascade that results in sustained outbreaks: (1) Poverty drives individuals to encroach deeper into forests, making zoonotic transmission more probable; (2) infections are then amplified by a dysfunctional health system; and (3) containment is hampered by poorly resourced governments.

Scientists have long been concerned with the changes in the climate and how its impact is felt around the globe. Climate change may be another ecological factor that contributes to Ebola outbreaks. Alexander and colleagues (2014) suggest that

> increasing climate variability can alter fruiting patterns in West African flora, potentially concentrating reservoir and susceptible host species in areas of increased foraging opportunity. This can lead to increased Ebola transmission in wildlife, which may result in a higher probability of spillover to humans.

#### Economic forces

Another study showed how international agribusiness shaped and took advantage of the 2013–16 Ebola pandemic (Wallace, Gilbert, & Wallace, 2014; Wallace, 2015). The researchers posited that capital-intensive industrial palm oil farms have increased human interaction with frugivorous bats (Pteropodidae), a putative Ebola reservoir, and may explain the association of outbreak peaks at the start of the dry season, when oil palm picking is at its height.

## Cultural forces

Some studies have elaborated on the role of culture in the transmission of the disease and its outbreak. It is certain that the cultural traditions of the people most affected by Ebola, and those charged with responding to it, have shaped the pandemic in significant ways; these traditions have included ways of understanding illness, of seeking care in the absence of a functioning health system, and of funerary practice in the absence of almost anything in the way of assistance for family members (Richardson et al., 2016). They argued that much more can be said about the influence of rapidly changing social institutions and ecological conditions on what are loosely (and inaccurately) termed 'traditional beliefs' and de-historicized the political and economic forces that have promoted the pandemic.

It was believed that the cultures of distinctly transnational institutions (aid agencies) also shaped the Ebola pandemic (Piot, Muyembe, & Edmunds, 2014) by attending mostly to the issue at hand without paying attention, during or after the crisis, to issues such as critical questions on whether the chronic poverty was obscured by international interventions that fetishize epidemiological statistics and 'performance' indicators (Adams, 2013). This view is further supported by Rottenburg (2009) who has earlier posited that statistics, and their exaggerated precision, evoke the power of scientific claims and make it 'difficult to distinguish an emergency [outbreak] from chronic poverty.' In addition, with the input of anthropologists, these statistics tend to reify culture 'as an ensemble of measurable factors with deterministic power over specific aspects of illness.' (Jones, 2011).

## Lessons learned

The Ebola disaster also provides us with important lessons in dealing with a crisis. As stated by Rashid (2011), from early 20th-century smallpox and influenza outbreaks to the 21st century Ebola, transnational relations of inequality continue to be embodied as viral disease in West Africa, resulting in the preventable deaths of hundreds of thousands of individuals. If the global community pays as much attention to the notion of care and empathy for humanity as they do in matters of trade, political dominance, and militarization, the world would be in a better place and everyone would see the benefits of service leadership for humanity through care and empathy.

Leadership does not occur in a vacuum as this global pandemic shows that dependency on approaches that have given rise to these pandemics do not provide solutions. From a service leadership point of view, the convergence of *competence*, *character*, and *care* must be present to be able to appropriately deal with a crisis. The analytical framework must be based on ethics dealing with political, economic, ecological, and cultural issues to be effective in preventing future outbreaks of diseases.

Other researchers have also argued that one must look into algorithms that generate insight into the medical and political dimensions of present and coming health challenges to navigate questions of accountability and ethical 'response-ability' (Haraway, 2007, p. 89; Biehl, 2016). This brings us back to the question of ethical leadership and the imperative of the *3Cs* of service leadership.

In summary, these tragic global events do provide a narrow view of how leadership around the world has responded to them. Some have taken a broader view and have attempted to help those in need and tended to their own needs as well. Others have taken a mistaken view that through competition rather than cooperation and collaboration, they can meet the challenges of the crisis. As it is stated in each of the previously mentioned crises, dependency only on the competency of the service leader may not be as effective as also taking a moral leadership stance that is supported by empathy and care. It is the convergence of the *competence*, *character*, and *care* that leads to better solutions to crises faced by organizations or countries.

## 11.3 Educating students for service leadership to deal with life's crisis

Throughout this text, an emphasis has been placed on *competence*, *character*, and *care* of a leader. Viewed from the perspective of *interpersonal* and *intrapersonal* leadership, moral character, a caring disposition, self-improvement, and self-reflection become critical (Shek & Leung, 2015). Educating oneself for life's crises requires an awareness of self and an individual's disposition in handling crises. In a service economy with dramatic changes, it is imperative then that leadership must be contextualized to fit the current realities (Lang, 2019). Hence, educating oneself on the tenets of service leadership can be an imperative given that the context in this century has changed from a manufacturing environment to one of service.

According to a World Economic Forum report (2015) based on its Survey on the Global Agenda, 86% of 1,767 respondents identified leadership crises as the third most significant challenge facing the world today. Ciampa (2005) also noted that new CEOs failed to perform in their first 18 months because of their inability to go beyond their own competence, or knowledge or experience.

Service leadership reiterates why *competence* or experience alone does not meet the challenges of leadership in today's world. A leader must have the *character* and *care* to supplement competence and experience in delivering quality service, namely, the *3Cs*.

The focus in this text has been that learning involves not just grasping new concepts and acquiring explicit knowledge content but also recognizing in what contexts such learning may be appropriately applied. Chapter 3 discussed various leadership styles and how they were applied in organizational management in which the emphasis was placed on the leader. Service leadership focuses on the totality of an organization in the nexus of leadership, that is, leadership should be exercised by all members of the service habitat.

As the world of work changes, so must leadership approaches. Dramatic shifts are observed in the ecosystem of service where big data analytics, artificial intelligence, and block chain technologies will transform education, manufacturing, financial services, and so on. It is here that ethical and moral leadership, parallel with competencies, is needed to traverse the business environment successfully. It must be understood that the *3Cs* of service leadership should not be applied in a linear, sequential, or separate fashion, as most leadership training tends to be linear, sequential, or separate. This explains why leadership training of the past is not able to respond appropriately when context changes and different events or crises bring with them a multitude of leadership issues to surface. Leaders tend to be encouraged to act with high *competence* alone, without realizing the importance of delivering high levels of all *3Cs*. More recently, there has also been a growing recognition that organizational (Bligh, 2006) and national cultural contexts significantly shape leadership dynamics (Jepson, 2009). In view of increasing cultural diversity in the workplace, the values and identities of leaders and followers in diverse societies significantly affect the possibilities and limits of leadership (Dickson, Castano, Magomaeva, & Hartog, 2012).

With the realities of the 21st century, leadership requires a plethora of thinking that is nonlinear and can solve threats effectively. Service leadership, by its nature, offers a holistic approach when leading an organization and preparing individuals in the group, network, and organization to effectively respond to threats. In the next section, suggestions are offered for faculty members to consider when teaching service leadership courses and how to educate the next generation of leaders.

### Educating students for service leadership

The importance of service leadership and its particulars were discussed in Chapters 1 and 4. Not only can service leadership be applied to the world of work but also in personal lives of students. University education along with their personal experiences will prepare them to meet the standards of *competence* for entry to the world of work. More importantly, *character* and *care*, the other pillars of service leadership, are needed to guide them through their lives in meeting the challenges and threats that come their way. In *The 12 Dimensions of a Service Leader*, Chung and Elfassy (2016) highlight the moral, social, physical, mental, and spiritual dimensions that contribute to the well-being of leaders and their overall disposition in dealing with challenges and threats. From the perspective of service leadership, the self-development of students in using these dimensions will serve as the backdrop for resilience and coping mechanism during a crisis. Other research also shows the link between leadership qualities of students and their well-being. Elements of well-being, such as the spiritual, emotional, mental, and physical, have a positive impact on the ability of students to become strong in character and be resilient (Shek & Leung, 2015; Kia-Keating, Dowdy, Morgan, & Noam, 2011).

A fundamental that should guide instructors when teaching service leadership is to recognize that leadership is the capacity to develop an idea for transformation. This should be based on shared values and rational appraisal of evidence of current practices so that group members can develop and maintain behaviors that support ongoing transformation and betterment. To be sure, educators who teach service leadership principles must themselves show their professional values and commitment to learners. This will allow students to observe in their teachers those characteristics that are essential to learning about service leadership.

*Personal commitment*: Educators must have and be committed toward the intellectual, ethical, personal growth, and well-being of all learners. Dedicated individuals who teach leadership must also practice it in real time. Learners can easily distinguish between those who genuinely show professional commitment compared to those who are simply performing a job. A crucial approach for teaching service leadership is by practicing it in the classroom. As Chung (2012) states, 'the server is the service.'

*Integrity:* An important element of *character* is integrity. The importance of *character* and by extension, integrity, as part of the *3Cs* was discussed in detail. Integrity means thoroughly examining personal and professional attitudes and beliefs and challenging our own hypothesis and skilled practices. Learners need to be informed that systematically examining the links between personal and professional attitudes and beliefs, values, and proficient practices inform and shape the personal and professional development of individuals. This can thereby prepare them to cope with life's challenges and threats.

*Trust and respect:* As in the case of integrity, trust and respect should be emphasized in teaching service leadership. Trust built between the learner and the instructor opens the door for accepting diverse views with rationality. Provision of a safe and secure environment for all learners should be built on the ethos of *care* in service leadership. There should be demonstration of a commitment to motivating and inspiring learners on the concept of service leadership. As in business organizations, educators are encouraged to develop a culture of trust and respect in the classroom so that an appropriate learning environment is developed.

*Social justice:* When speaking of social justice, service leadership emphasizes the importance of personal and social values. Here, the course instructor must inculcate the broad view of social justice that includes recognizing the rights and responsibilities of future as well as current generations and commitment to the principles of democracy and social justice through reasonable, transparent, inclusive, and sustainable practices. Additionally, valuing and respecting social, cultural, and ecological diversity and promoting the principles and practices of local and global citizenship for all learners are essential to teaching service leadership. Finally, engaging the learners in real world issues to enhance learning experiences and outcomes and to encourage learning for life is a necessity.

*Professional commitment:* Classroom instructors should demonstrate their professional commitment to learners through their engagement in all aspects of their professional practice in the community of educators. The learner should be taught and shown commitment to lifelong inquiry. Learning is a lifelong process, and individuals have to commit themselves to it so that they are prepared to meet the challenges of their careers upon graduation and are ready to cope with threats that may come their way.

*Strategic vision:* To show to the learners what is meant by strategic vision, educators must show professional values and commitment to learners, equality of opportunity, ethical practice, democratic values, sustainability, and career-long learning as elements of strategic vision. Classroom educators should guide the creation and the sharing of the strategic vision ethos for the learners. Central to the development and demonstration of this strategic vision is when the educator uses his or her career-long learning as a model of professionalism.

Awareness of the developments that are taking place within the community, such as change in social structures, work patterns, changing family patterns, media, technology, information and communications systems, as well as leisure and politics, have to be known by the educators to influence teaching leadership strategically.

*Interpersonal skills and personal dispositions*: Chapter 5 elaborated on the interpersonal skills of a service leader, which educators must possess to create maximum positive impact on the learner. One is the ability to demonstrate self-awareness and inspire and motivate others. Self-awareness is enhanced through regular inquiry regarding their practice through the processes of reflection and critical thinking. They garner and sustain personal credibility by representing their commitment to career-long professional learning, integrity, and ethical practice, thus increasing a culture of trust and respect. Educators need to analyze and define situations clearly and use wisdom when making any kind of judgment on the learners' work. They need to get engaged in dialogue and promote constructive ways of achieving improvement, displaying an awareness of the ethical use of power and authority in the classroom.

Educators must demonstrate and communicate their deep commitment to the education and well-being of learners in their daily practices. They listen, express their ideas and feelings clearly, engage in professional discussion and productive response, and institute successful organizational communication. They use a variety of communication channels to educate the learner. Their comprehension of the political and social circumstances should provide the learner with a better understanding of the political practices in society, and how the learner should deal with them.

In summary, this chapter highlighted the importance of the *3Cs* in more effectively facing challenges that come from a natural or man-made disaster. The three major global disasters cited in this chapter all point to the need for leadership to recognize that convergence of *competence*, *character*, and *care* must take place for effective and positive leadership.

Educating the future generation of leaders requires a commitment to serve as a role model with values that cherish lifelong learning. The ethos of service leadership not only applies to the world of work but also to the personal lives of students.

## Key points to remember

This chapter discussed the concepts of the *3Cs* of service leadership and its application in times of crisis. Further emphasis was made that service leadership model is multidimensional and that it considers all the different aspects of leadership: Functional, relational, and attributional. Given the nature of crises, it is important to keep the following in mind:

- The modern crisis is highly complex given that it is not confined to local borders; and it quickly becomes entangled with other major problems due to processes such as globalization, deregulation, and developments in communication technologies.
- Leadership in times of crisis is the sum of activities entailing *competence*, *character*, and *care*, that is, the *3Cs*.
- A framework that incorporates the following dimensions along with the *3Cs* of service leadership can serve as a good guideline in times of crisis and how to manage it:

- Early recognition of a crisis.
- Making sense of crisis.
- Making decisions.
- Communicating.
- Implementing.
- Being accountable.
- Learning from the crisis.
- Enhancing resilience.

- The broad dimensions of a global crisis demand more of service leaders to be aware of the larger implication of their decisions.
- Three examples of global crisis (financial crisis of 2008, Fukushima disaster in 2011, and Ebola pandemic, 2013–16) and the COVID-19 pandemic have shed light on the need for the *3Cs* of service leadership.
- It must be understood that *competence, character*, and *care* of service leadership should not be applied in a linear fashion – even as most leadership training tends to be linear, sequential, or separate.
- The realities of the 21st century require a plethora of thinking that is nonlinear and can solve threats effectively. Service leadership, by its nature, offers a holistic approach when leading an organization or a country, thus preparing individuals in the habitat to effectively respond to threats.
- When educating students to the concept of service leadership, the teachers not only teach the important dimensions of leadership, such as moral, social, physical, mental, and spiritual, but also exhibit these dimensions in their own behavior.
- The elements of *character* and *care* of the teachers include a commitment to personal and professional growth, social justice, integrity, trust and respect, strategic vision, and interpersonal skills and disposition.

## Case study

### Adaptive leadership in times of crisis

This case was adapted from *Adaptive Leadership in Times of Crisis* by Khan, S. (2019).

### Background

Amir was the newly appointed Executive Director of Public Service Inc., a faith-based NGO in Washington, DC. The NGO had been around for 20 years and had done pioneering work in training young adults to enter public service careers, inspired by faith and dedication to service. After a series of problems, the organization was facing a host of technical and adaptive challenges and Amir believed he had the solution. He brought a fresh perspective to the organization's issues, having worked in both the public and private sectors. While the Board of Trustees (henceforth called the Board) of the organization thought that the organization faced more 'management' level difficulties, Amir disagreed and thought there needed to be greater 'leadership' in the organization, which meant more change.

Amir was also aware that the Board was responsible for hiring and firing decisions, so the buck stopped with them. The Board was Amir's boss, but he wanted to communicate the challenges as he saw them so the NGO could move toward solutions that properly addressed the problems. Amir believed that with an adaptive leadership style, he could guide Public Service Inc. to chart a new course and emerge triumphant from its challenges.

Public Service Inc. pioneered a model of promoting public service in its community by running an intensive residential program in the nation's capital. The program was very selective in whom it admitted and only brought in the top crop of students. Students received a tuition-free, full-immersion experience in the eight-week residential program and the program was highly regarded initially. However, over the years, due to a series of scandals and mismanagement by the Board, which included wasteful spending, donor confidence eroded, and the organization was now considering charging fees for the program, in addition to making admission to the program less selective.

The mission of Public Service Inc. had always been to inspire and engage young Americans (of their faith-denomination) to enter public service. The organization remained committed to its service-oriented mission, but it was struggling to achieve it. A Board of three young women who lacked experience in the nonprofit sector led the NGO. Their presence on the Board was indicative of the troubles the organization faced; no one else was willing to serve on the Board because of the tumultuous history of the organization, and so these inexperienced staffers were elected to keep the NGO going. As alumni of the Public Service Inc. program, the Board members had a sense of obligation to the organization, but Amir overhead the Board chair saying that her work with the NGO, which was entirely voluntary, took up too much of her time. These Board members had a fragile relationship with one another and also lacked the relevant work experience that might help them appreciate or navigate the broad challenges facing the NGO. The technical challenges facing Public Service Inc. included fundraising issues and budget management problems. In addition, the NGO faced adaptive challenges that involved earning the trust of donors, alumni, and other stakeholders, including the media and general public, among others.

Within the first few weeks of joining the NGO as executive director, Amir had assessed the challenges facing Public Service Inc. and communicated to the Board that he hoped to reshape the organization and draw on his abilities to raise money and energize the donor base. He wanted to bring back donors who had walked away, attract new donors, and manage the reputation of the organization – all of which had suffered due to mismanagement. Amir was confident in his abilities to guide the NGO because of his expertise in managing crises. He had managed a crisis communications campaign for a large real estate client with a billion-dollar portfolio. He had also advised some of the largest and most well-known brands in his previous role as a communications consultant. In addition, Amir also had experience as an entrepreneur running his own consulting firm. Based on his experience, Amir was able to spot a crisis situation with his eyes closed and he was also able to assess potential paths out of a crisis.

When he met with the Board, they advocated that Public Service Inc., and Amir in particular, follow a traditional, tried-and-tested model of management and leadership to manage the NGO's problems. They wanted him to focus on the day-to-day operations. Amir disagreed with them and shared his approach. He believed that he would be able to use an adaptive leadership style at Public Service Inc. to guide the NGO out of its troubles.

Adaptive leadership is a practice and not a theory. Specifically, it is the 'practice of mobilizing people to tackle tough challenges and thrive' (Heifetz, Grashow, & Linsky, 2009, p. 14). Amir believed this style of leadership was required because it would allow for improvisation, learning, and adapting to new situations as needed, rather than simply following models of behavior that were no longer working for the organization. For instance, dealing with a reluctant donor base or addressing many of the questions regarding the Board's legitimacy to run the organization could not be addressed using old and tried methods of establishing credibility; these technical and adaptive challenges needed a more open-ended and collaborative approach, Amir told the Board. He explained that he saw this as an adaptive approach and part of his job to 'lead' the NGO to success and not just 'manage' the challenges facing the organization.

Amir argued with the Board that the context of the operating environment in which Public Service Inc. was functioning was very different from the one that existed when it was founded 20 years ago. This meant that the NGO needed to reexamine each of its stakeholder relationships, the manner in which it conducted its day-to-day business, and the very 'business model' of the organization. Amir explained that simple technical fixes could not fix the deep-rooted structural problems that the organization faced. He noted that this also meant that drastic changes were needed for the organization to succeed.

While the three-member Board was supportive of some of Amir's ideas, they did not agree with all of them. Given their lack of experience, and their lack of confidence stemming from it, the Board had their back up and conveyed that Amir should manage the challenges using methods that followed the organization's traditional policies and practices. Given these dynamics, as well as the gender issues at play, Amir knew he needed to balance his leadership practices with the Board's expectations to avoid coming across as aggressive.

Although Amir attempted to implement some adaptive leadership practices, the Board resisted by putting restrictions on his ability to communicate with donors, media, and others. They also started conducting calls without including him and were not fully transparent in their dealings with him.

The Board may have disagreed with Amir's vision for the turning Public Service Inc. around, but the NGO staffers who worked with him were supportive of his ideas for change and growth. They believed in his assessment that Public Service Inc. needed to be more innovative and collaborative and were happy to accept the responsibilities associated with making the organizational changes Amir proposed. What the staff disagreed with was the Board's resistance. The restrictive atmosphere imposed by the Board quickly began causing friction in the organization, with the three people reporting to Amir threatening to leave. They expressed that they could not function in such a restrictive environment where the Board did not trust the employees.

Amidst this chaos, Amir had received interest from a potential donor. They had agreed to make a $500,000 gift toward the organization, with the condition that the NGO make big changes to how things were done in the organization. The potential donor believed that Public Service Inc. was stuck in its old ways of doing business, including being traditional and wasteful in its expenditures and also not being transparent. They noted that these factors failed to inspire confidence in the organization, contributing to a negative image and making other donors less likely to commit. They believed the key was for Public Service Inc. to change to become more externally focused, media savvy, and forward thinking. Amir and his staff were excited because this donation and its conditions meant Public Service Inc. could focus on shedding its past image and ways of operating. It could rebrand as an organization focused on creating leaders that could deal with the challenges of tomorrow.

## Finding a solution

In presenting the donor proposal to the Board, Amir knew the idea of change would be stressful for them, but he also knew that the uncertainty, stress, and the change were a necessary part of the process for Public Service Inc. to move forward. Amir attempted to mitigate the Board's stress by explaining the positive outcomes that would be associated with the changes. Amir opened by noting that he agreed with the donor and explained that the cash infusion would allow them to radically reshape the organization and ensure their program continued for the foreseeable future. He argued that to be externally focused, media savvy, and forward thinking, the NGO could reach out to stakeholders, including donors, former alumni, supporters, volunteers, and media and engage in more market-oriented activities.

The Board rejected Amir's potential donor proposal without even discussing it with him. Further, they argued that taking part in such market-oriented mechanisms was against the mission of the NGO, which was inspired by service. They noted that Amir should be low key in his approach to align with the NGO's identity and its traditional organizational processes. They also want him to work with the resources they have to carry out programming and try to raise money as they always have. Amir was aware that the Board had the ultimate authority to hire and fire any staff – himself included – but he didn't want to give up on Public Service Inc. What could Amir do to convey the importance of greater marketing and outreach? How could he reconcile his relationship with the Board and help Public Service Inc. succeed? Could he use adaptive leadership to come up with solutions to the complex problems of mission integrity, identity, and organizational change facing Public Service Inc.?

## Questions related to the case

1    What can Amir do to reconcile relations with the Board?
2    How should Amir begin leading his nonprofit organization through this crisis?
3    What parallels do you see in Amir's approach and that suggested by the 3Cs of service leadership?
4    Should Amir accept the Board's demand for being low key and work with the resources they have, or should he implement changes and try to build new sources of funding?

## End of chapter questions

1    Why would the application of the 3Cs of service leadership be more effective than any other forms of leadership in times of crisis?
2    Could the competence of a leader alone solve a crisis effectively? Why or why not?
3    What should be the litmus test of service leadership in a crisis?
4    Does the framework suggested by Boin et al. (2013) show elements of service leadership?
5    What lessons were learned from the financial crisis of 2008?
6    What elements of service leadership were missing in the financial crisis of 2008?
7    What were some important elements of service leadership that were ignored in the Fukushima disaster of 2011?
8    What lessons can be learned from the Ebola pandemic of 2013–16?
9    Do you observe some important service leadership dimensions as New Zealand fought COVID-19?
10    How does learning about service leadership help students cope with crises in their lives?

## References

Adams, V. (2013). Evidence-based global public health: Subjects, profits, erasures. In J. Biehl & A. Petryna (Eds.), *When people come first: Critical studies in global health* (pp. 54–90). Princeton, NJ: Princeton University Press.

Alexander, K., Sanderson, C., Marathe, M., et al. (2014). What factors might have led to the emergence of Ebola in West Africa? *PLOS Medical Journals' Community Blog.* Retrieved from http://blogs.plos.org/speakingofmedicine/2014/11/11/factors-might-led-emergence-ebola-west-africa/

Allison, G. (1971). *Essence of decision: Explaining the Cuban missile crisis.* Boston, MA: Little, Brown.

Argyris, C. (1982). *Reasoning, learning and action: Individual and organizational.* San Francisco, CA: Jossey-Bass.

Bailey, F. (1988). *Humbuggery and manipulation: The art of leadership.* Ithaca, NY: Cornell University Press.

Barth, J., Prabha, A., & Wihlborg, C. (2015). The Dodd-Frank Act: Key features, implementation progress, and financial system impact. *Current Views: The Milken Institute,* 1–31.

Bausch, D., & Schwarz, L. (2014). Outbreak of Ebola virus disease in Guinea: Where ecology meets economy. *PLOS Neglected Tropical Diseases, 8*(7), e3056.

Biehl, J. (2016). Theorizing global health. *Medicine Anthropology Theory, 3*(2), 127–142.

Bligh, M. (2006). Surviving post-merger 'culture clash': Can cultural leadership lessen the casualties? *Leadership, 2*(4), 395–426.

Boin, A. (2009). The new world of crises and crisis management: Implications for policymaking and research. *Review of Policy Research, 26*(4), 367–377.

Boin, A., Kuipers, S., & Overdijk, W. (2013). Leadership in times of crisis: A framework for assessment. *International Review of Public Administration, 18*(1), 79–91.

Boin, A., & 't Hart, P. (2010). Organising for effective emergency management: Lessons from research. *Australian Journal of Public Administration, 69*(4), 357–371.

Center for Disease Control. (2014). *U.S. Centers for disease control and prevention.* U.S. Department of Health and Human Services, Washington, DC. Retrieved November 15, 2020, from https://ballotpedia.org/U.S._Centers_for_Disease_Control_and_Prevention

Chan, M. (2014). Ebola virus disease in west Africa—No early end to the outbreak. *New England Journal of Medicine, 371*(13), 1183–1185.

Chung, P. (2012). *Service reborn: The knowledge, skills, and attitudes of service companies.* New York, NY: Lexingford Publishing.

Chung, P. (2019). *Designed to win: What every business needs to know to go truly global (DHL's 50 Years).* New York, NY: Leaders Press.

Chung, P., & Elfassy, R. (2016). *The 12 dimensions of a service leader: Manage your personal brand for the service age.* New York, NY: Lexingford Publishing.

Ciampa, D. (2005). Almost ready: How leaders move up. *Harvard Business Review, 83,* 46–53.

Coates, J. (2012). *The hour between dog and wolf: Risk-taking, gut feelings and the biology of boom and bust.* London: Fourth Estate.

Comfort, L., Boin, A., & Demchak, C. (Eds.). (2010). *Designing resilience for extreme events.* Pittsburgh: Pittsburgh University Press.

Comfort, L., & Okada, A. (2013). Emergent leadership in extreme events: A knowledge commons for sustainable communities. *International Review of Public Administration, 18*(1), 61–77.

Covey, S. (2012). *The 7 habits of highly effective people.* New York, NY: Simon & Schuster.

Dickson, M., Castano, N., Magomaeva, A., & Hartog, D. (2012). Conceptualizing leadership across cultures. *Journal of World Business, 47,* 483–492.

Duncan, J., Mouly, S., & Nilakant, V. (2001). Discontinuous change in the New Zealand police service: A case study. *Journal of Managerial Psychology, 16,* 6–19.

Edelman, M. (1988). *Constructing the political spectacle.* Chicago, IL: University of Chicago Press.

Fox, J. (2013, November). What we've learned from the financial crisis. *Harvard Business Review.*

Frandsen, F., & Johansen, W. (2011). The study of internal crisis communication: Towards an integrative framework. *Corporate Communications: An International Journal, 16*(4), 347–361.

Furceri, D., & Mourougane, A. (2009). *Financial crises: Past lessons and policy implications* (OECD Economics Department Working Papers No. 668). Paris: OECD Publishing.

George, A. (1980). *Presidential decision making in foreign policy.* Boulder, CO: Westview Press.

Goidel, R., & Miller, A. (2009). News organizations and information during a natural disaster: Lessons from Hurricane Katrina. *Journal of Contingencies and Crisis Management, 17*(4), 266–273.

Greyser, S. (2009). Corporate brand reputation and brand crisis management. *Management Decision, 47*(4), 590–602.

Hamilton, N. (2008). *The financial sector's catastrophic failure of prudence: A time for self-assessment.* A column presented in Minnesota Lawyer on December 15.

Haraway, D. (2007). *When species meet.* Minneapolis: University of Minnesota Press.

Heifetz, R. (1994). *Leadership without easy answers.* Cambridge: Harvard University Press.

Heifetz, R. (2003). *Leadership without easy answers.* Cambridge: Belknap Press.

Heifetz, R., Grashow, A., & Linsky, M. (2009). *The practice of adaptive leadership: Tools and tactics for changing your organization and the world.* Boston, MA: Harvard Business Press.

Hindmoor, A., & McConnell, A. (2013). Why didn't they see it coming? Warning signs, acceptable risks and the global financial crisis. *Political Studies, 61*(3), 543–560.

Hindmoor, A., & McConnell, A. (2015). Who saw it coming? The UK's great financial crisis. *Journal of Public Policy, 35*(1), 63–96.

IGEL. (2013). *Special report: Disaster, leadership and rebuilding.* Knowledge at Wharton, Wharton University, 1–15.

James, E., & Wooten, L. (2005). Leadership as (un)usual: How to display competence in times of crisis. *Organizational Dynamics, 34*(2), 141–152.

James, E., Wooten, L., & Dushek, K. (2011). Crisis management: Informing a new leadership research agenda. *Academy of Management Annals, 5*(1), 455–493.

Jepson, D. (2009). Studying leadership at cross-country level: A critical analysis. *Leadership, 5*(1), 61–80.

Jones, J. (2011). Ebola, emerging: The limitations of culturalist discourses in epidemiology. *Journal of Global Health, 1*(1), 1–6.

Kahneman, D. (2011). *Thinking: Fast and slow.* New York, NY: Penguin.

Khan, S. (2019). Adaptive leadership in times of crisis: A case study. doi:10.4135/9781526464323. Retrieved from *Research Gate* on April 17, 2020.

Kia-Keating, M., Dowdy, E., Morgan, M., & Noam, G. (2011). Protecting and promoting: An integrative conceptual model for healthy development of adolescents. *Journal of Adolescent Health, 48*(3), 220–228.

Kirkpatrick, G. (2009). The corporate governance lessons from the financial crisis. *OECD Journal: Financial Market Trends, 1*, 61–87.

Knights, D. (2016). In denial: The crisis of leadership and ethics in the financial sector. In J. Storey et al. (Eds.), *The Routledge companion to leadership.* Singapore: Routledge.

Lang, J. (2019). Teaching leadership better: A framework or developing contextually-intelligent leadership. *Creative Education, 10*, 443–463.

Leonard, H., & Howitt, A. (2009). *Managing crises responses to large-scale emergencies*. Washington, DC: CQ Press.

National Research Council. (2014). *Lessons learned from the Fukushima nuclear accident for improving safety of U.S. nuclear plants*. Washington, DC: The National Academies Press.

OECD. (2008, November). *Economic surveys: Euro area* (pp. 1–50). Paris: OECD Publication.

Palttala, P., Boano, C., Lund, R., & Vos, M. (2012). Communication gaps in disaster management: Perception by experts from governmental and non-governmental organizations. *Journal of Contingencies and Crisis Management, 20*(1), 2–12.

Penrose, J. (2000). The role of perception in crisis planning. *Public Relations Review, 26*, 155–171.

Piot, P., Muyembe, J., & Edmunds, W. (2014). Ebola in west Africa: From disease outbreak to humanitarian crisis. *Lancet Infectious Diseases, 14*(11), 1034–1035.

Popper, M., & Lipshitz, R. (2000). Organizational learning mechanisms, culture, and feasibility. *Management Learning, 31*, 181–196.

Rashid, I. (2011). Epidemics and resistance in colonial Sierra Leone during the First World War. *Canadian Journal of African Studies, 45*(3), 415–439.

Richardson, E., Barrie, M., Kelly, J., Dibba, Y., Koedoyoma, S., & Farmer, P. (2016). Biosocial approaches to the 2013–2016 Ebola pandemic. *Health and Human Rights Journal, 18*(1), 167–179.

Robinson, J. (2008). *Governance and political economy constraints to World Bank CAS priorities in Sierra Leone*. Washington, DC: World Bank.

Roe, E., & Schulman, P. (2008). *High reliability management: Operating on the edge*. Stanford, CA: Stanford University Press.

Rosenthal, U., Boin, A., & Bos, C. (2001). Shifting images: The reconstructive mode of the Bijlmer plane crash. In U. Rosenthal, R. A. Boin, & L. K. Comfort (Eds.), *From crises to contingencies: A global perspective* (pp. 200–215). Springfield: Charles C. Thomas.

Rottenburg, R. (2009). Social and public experiments and new figurations of science and politics in postcolonial Africa1. *Postcolonial Studies, 12*(4), 423–440.

Scheel, H. (2018). Experiences from the Fukushima disaster. In F. Mihai & A. Grozavu (Eds.), *Environmental risk*. London: InTechOpen.

Shek, D., & Leung, H. (2015). *Promoting service leadership qualities in university students: The case of Hong Kong*. Singapore: Springer.

Sitkin, S. (1996). Learning through failure: The strategy of small losses. In M. D. Cohen & L. S. Sproull (Eds.), *Organizational learning* (pp. 541–578). Thousand Oaks, CA: Sage.

Sulitzeanu-Kenan, R. (2010). Reflection in the shadow of blame: When do politicians appoint commissions of inquiry? *British Journal of Political Science, 40*, 613–634.

Thomas, M. (2009, April 1). *BBC Newsnight*.

Veil, S. (2011). Mindful learning in crisis management. *Journal of Business Communication, 48*(2), 116–147.

Wallace, R. (2015, July 25). Neoliberal Ebola: Palm oil, logging, land grabs, ecological havoc and disease. *Ecologist*.

Wallace, R., Gilbert, M., Wallace, R., et al. (2014). Did Ebola emerge in west Africa by a policy-driven phase change in agroecology? *Environment and Planning A, 46*, 2533–2542.

Wanat, L., & Potkański, T. (2011). Barriers for effective regional leadership in time of crisis. *Intercathedra, 27*(4), 75–79.

Weick, K., & Sutcliffe, K. (2002). *Managing the unexpected.* San Francisco, CA: Jossey-Bass.

WHO. (2015, December 16). *World Health Organization, Ebola situation report.* Geneva: WHO.

World Economic Forum. (2015*). Outlook on the global agenda 2015.* Retrieved from http://www3.weforum.org/docs/GAC14/WEF_GAC14_OutlookGlo balAgenda_Report.Pdf.

# Index

karma 101
Keynes, John Maynard 32

Laozi 102, 110
leaderful practice 44
leadership creativity 49, 51
leadership critical thinking 50, 52
leadership intelligence 49, 51
leadership planning 48, 51
leadership practice 180
leadership theories 40; behavioral theories
    41; contingency theory 42; great man
    theory 41; situational theory 42; trait
    theory 41; transactional theory 43
leadership wisdom 50, 52
Lean manufacturing 119–120, 126
learned helplessness 88
learned optimism 88
learning from a crisis 166
Lewis, Arthur 25, 30
litmus test for leadership 162
Locke, John 105

making decision 164
making sense of a crisis 163
manufacturing mindset 7, 57
marginal productivity of labor 30
Marx, Karl 31
Maslow's motivation theory 3–4
mechanical intelligence 47
mechanistic organizations 131
microenterprises 147–152, 155–158
Mill, John Stewart 104–105, 110
modernity and concepts of ethics 103
moral codes 99–100
morality 6, 58, 100–102, 104, 110
motivators of happiness 91

nirvāna 101
normative ethics 104
Nurkse, Ragnar 25

OECD 26–27, 148, 154
open systems theory 132, 134
opportunism 80–82
opportunist style 45
organic organizations 131–133, 135–136,
    141

perishability 11, 13; see also distinctive
    features of service
PERMA 66–67, 69
personal commitment 7, 175
personal ethics 108–109

phronesis 51
Plato 91, 100–101, 110
positive emotions 67, 89
problematic (ethical conflict) 107
productivity 38–39, 58–59, 90, 93–95
professional commitment 176
Protagoras 100
psychic income 65, 136, 149, 155
psychology of leadership 65–66

rational agent 117
relationship of service economy to
    leadership 32
resilience 8, 133, 167, 170, 178
respect 6, 68
Return on investment (ROI) 73, 75–76, 82
Ricardo, David 20

Schumpeter, Joseph 117, 125
self-actualization 3, 5, 13, 62, 136, 155
self-cultivation 102, 110
self-development 102, 110, 139–140, 155
self-efficacy 120–121
self-leadership 60–61, 63, 68
service: heterogeneity 11, 13;
    inseparability 11, 13, intangibility 76,
    78; perishability 11, 13
service-dominant (S-D) logic 76
service mindset 7, 33, 53, 57, 59, 63, 65
service orientation 32–33
service-recovery cost 58
servitization of manufacturing 25
sincerity 7
situational leadership 42
small, and medium enterprises (SME)
    147–148, 150, 155–156
Smith, Adam 20, 24, 33
social development 23, 58, 125–126
social intelligence 47
social justice 40, 176, 178
social responsibility 40
socio-behavioral skills 31
Socrates 63, 100, 109–110
Sophia 51
strategic vision 176, 178
strategist style of leadership 46
structural changes in economies 30–31
supply chain 119, 126
supply-push 119
systematic change in the workplace 31

Taoist philosopher 102
teleological character 100
teleological ethics 101, 110

Printed in the United States
by Baker & Taylor Publisher Services